Black Elders

EARLY AMERICAN STUDIES

Series editors:
Kathleen M. Brown, Roquinaldo Ferreira,
Emma Hart, and Daniel K. Richter

Exploring neglected aspects of our colonial, revolutionary, and early national history and culture, Early American Studies reinterprets familiar themes and events in fresh ways. Interdisciplinary in character, and with a special emphasis on the period from about 1600 to 1850, the series is published in partnership with the McNeil Center for Early American Studies.

A complete list of books in the series is available from the publisher.

Black Elders

The Meaning of Age in American Slavery and Freedom

Frederick C. Knight

PENN

UNIVERSITY OF PENNSYLVANIA PRESS

PHILADELPHIA

Published by
University of Pennsylvania Press
Philadelphia, Pennsylvania 19104-4112
www.pennpress.org

Printed in the United States of America on acid-free paper
10 9 8 7 6 5 4 3 2 1

Hardcover ISBN: 978-1-5128-2566-4
eBook ISBN: 978-1-5128-2567-1

A cataloging record for this book is available from the Library of Congress.

CONTENTS

Introduction

Word about the day of jubilee spread through the black grapevine. With the federal recognition of freedom on the horizon, African Americans assembled in churches and camp meetings to hear the Emancipation Proclamation. Camp Sexton, just outside of Beaufort, South Carolina, held its own celebration on January 1, 1863. Black women and men gathered with white Union officers and members of the all-black 1st South Carolina Regiment to listen to the reading of the proclamation and to take in remarks from dignitaries in the platform party. The former South Carolina slaveholder W. H. Brisbane, who had emancipated his slaves before the war, read the proclamation. The chaplain presented the colors, which had been donated by Union supporters in New York. With all the scripted pageantry, an unscripted act offstage did the most to charge the atmosphere with significance. After the presentation of the United States flag, a "strong male voice (but rather cracked and elderly)" arose "into which two women's voices blended" and sang "My country, 'tis of thee, sweet land of liberty, of thee I sing." Other black voices joined in, creating a scene so moving that the 1st South Carolina's commander Colonel Thomas Wentworth Higginson recounted that he "never saw anything so electric." His regiment would then deploy to Florida.

Three months later, and after having vanquished a unit of the Confederate Army just south of the Florida-Georgia border, the regiment received orders on April 1, 1863, to decamp from their position in Jacksonville and set up a picket line at Port Royal Ferry, South Carolina. Having experienced a wave of enthusiasm from successfully capturing Confederate territory, the soldiers felt "dejected" by the command. Colonel Higginson described the scene of their departure, a scene of black soldiers waking up early to pack their tents and other supplies and then marching north through Georgia to their new assignment, of their being greeted along the way by black civilians. To buoy their spirits, the black Union soldiers sang "John Brown's Body," "Marching Along," and "When This Cruel War Is Over" as they marched on to their next post. Among the mass of soldiers, one figure stood out to Colonel Higginson. He observed that "at the head of the force there walked, by some self-imposed preeminence, a respectable elderly female, one of the company laundresses, whose vigorous stride we never could quite overtake." Toting a bundle on her head, she pressed on, followed by the drum corps and the rest of the 1st South Carolina.[1]

Two years after the day of jubilee and after Union efforts and a tide of black resistance pushed the Confederacy to the brink of collapse, black leaders in Savannah, Georgia, gathered with Union army officers for an encounter of a different sort. They met face to face with Union Major General William Tecumseh Sherman, who had just led his formidable army units through Georgia to its coast. Followed by African Americans who used the Union's advance to claim their freedom, Sherman asked local black leaders about how to respond to the crisis prompted by those black refugees. The cohort of African American leaders included the 72-year-old Glasgon Taylor. Andrew Neal, aged 61, was also among the number, as was William Bentley, aged 72. Indeed, the age of the twenty representatives, all of whom were men, averaged 50 years old, a number that far exceeded the average life expectancy of black Southerners in the late antebellum period. Their primary spokesman, Garrison Frazier, was 67, a former slave originally from North Carolina. Retired from his vocation as a Baptist minister and with "his health failing," Frazier represented the interests of his community. He represented them well. When Sherman asked about the meaning of freedom, Frazier responded that it "is taking us from under the yoke of bondage, and placing us where we could reap the fruit of our labor." And when Sherman asked how former slaves could become self-sufficient, Frazier replied, "The way we can best take care of ourselves is to have land, and turn it and till it by our own labor—that is, by the labor of the women and children and old men, and we can soon maintain ourselves and have something to spare." Frazier and his peers gave voice to a freedom dream, a vision of forty acres and a mule for former slaves.[2]

In these snapshots of African Americans as they emerged from slavery, contemporaries identified the aged as critical figures in the story of emancipation. Garrison Frazier and his fellow church elders, the "cracked and elderly" lead singer at the reading of the Emancipation Proclamation outside of Beaufort, and the laundress behind whom the 1st South Carolina Regiment marched all held keys that unlocked the prison of enslavement. They, and other black people in old age, are the primary subjects of this book. And, as the interaction between Frazier and Sherman illustrates, their historical experiences evince a broader set of phenomena: the meanings, power dynamics, and social relationships of elders in Africa and its diaspora in North America. Moving across early modern coastal West and West Central Africa, the Middle Passage, colonial slavery, and nineteenth-century African American communities, I examine the various roles of elders in black family, community, and cultural formation. The accounts left behind by Union officers constitute part of a wider array of primary sources that point to the significance of old age in early African American history. The records show quite clearly that elders mattered to African Americans.

From the colonial to the antebellum period and beyond, contemporaries made note of the role and significance of the aged in African American communities. A key feature of that history involved a culture of respect for elders, which enslaved Africans sought to reconstitute soon after their forced arrival in the Americas. The odds were stacked against them given the economic logic of forced labor camps in the Atlantic World, which centered on young people. In the sugar colonies, profits from the cash crop enabled planters to work the enslaved to death and use the surplus to buy new captives.[3] To grow old in enslavement was rare. But even under the forced labor demands, high mortality rates, and short lifespans imposed by the sugar production regime, some of the enslaved survived into old age and sought to forge multigenerational ties, as noted by a contemporary colonial official. In the late seventeenth century, the Frenchman Jean-Baptiste Labat observed in the French Caribbean islands that "All the slaves have a great respect for the old. They never call them by their names without adding 'Father.' Although they are not their parents, they obey and comfort them in all things. They always count the house cook as one of their mothers, and however old she is, they call her mother."[4] Most of the African captives seized in the Atlantic slave trade and transplanted to the Americas were young, but as this record attests, they still carried beliefs and habits that offered respect to elders.

Elders also held a distinct place of respect in slave and free black communities in North America, where the labor conditions of slavery created more time and space for multigenerational relationships to emerge than in the sugar colonies. Being on the periphery of the Atlantic slaving system, colonial North American slave populations increased through higher childbirth and lower mortality rates than in the world of sugar plantation slavery.

Consequently, the aged slave population grew over time, and by the nineteenth century, the aged had become a key presence in slave and free black communities, playing roles as caregivers and protectors. In some respects, elders could become even more important to black families and communities in North America because of racial slavery and the slave trade. With forced labor and migration separating parents from their children, elders cemented kinship and community ties. In this regard, aged slave women played an instrumental role and organized what historian Deborah Gray-White termed "female slave networks," through which they transmitted knowledge to young women about the life cycle and cared for children whose parents worked away in the fields.[5] Older women also served as midwives, nurses, and healers on Southern slave labor camps. In addition, elders shaped the political culture of slave communities. By mediating disputes, they commanded respect from fellow slaves.[6] Furthermore, slavery's survivors remembered slaves who lived exceptionally long lives, experiences of longevity that, in the words of scholar Sari Edelstein, "might be read as a mode of defiance, of bodily refusal to accommodate the economic priorities of plantation culture."[7] In the face of slavery and the political domination to which the enslaved were subject, elders played a prominent role in black kinship relationships, cultural systems, and community development, practices which can be traced to their African cultural roots. As described by historian Sterling Stuckey in his pioneering study of African-based slave cultural traditions, black elders instilled in younger generations a sense of reverence for the ancestors, of the power of story and metaphors to instill spiritual values, and of the moral obligations that bound generations together.[8]

In the most personal of settings, in their households and kinship relationships, African American elders played a significant role in the lives of the young even as the forced labor system of cash crop production segmented African Americans across generational lines. And slavery's survivors recognized the distinct cultural and social meaning of elders. For instance, Frederick Douglass was raised by his grandmother Betsy Bailey and witnessed the respect that the enslaved accorded her.[9] The fugitive Harriet Jacobs received the care of her grandmother Molly Horniblow, a free black woman who enabled Jacobs's escape from slavery, and the fugitive slave autobiographer Charles Ball was nurtured by his grandfather.[10] The former slave Shade Richards of Georgia illustrated the lengths to which such care could go. The child of an African-born father, Richards remembered that "his grandfather came from Africa to buy his son and take him home." Tragically, both his father and grandfather fell ill and died before making their return to Africa, but Richards carried the memory of his grandfather's care well into the twentieth century even in his absence.[11] Being recounted by younger generations, such narratives bear witness to the social and cultural value of the aged to African American families and communities. Focusing on the role of elders in early black America, this book places figures like Betsy Bailey, Molly Horniblow, and Garrison Frazier, as well as their quotidian struggles, their circles of concern, and their web of relationships at its center.

Placing elders at the center of early African American history brings to light the second major theme of this book, what I term the meaning and politics of age. I argue that age, particularly old age, was a point of power, labor mobilization, ideological struggle, transformation, and contestation in American slavery and emancipation. Furthermore, I examine how enslavement in the early modern Diaspora transformed the demographic and social foundations through which eldership and generational relationships operated. Simply put, slave traders and forced labor camp owners and managers in the Americas put their focus on young people. In some ways, the labor of black youth and the separation from kin and between generations *defined* much of the African Diasporic condition in the Americas. This book looks at how these structures operated and how slaves and free blacks in North America contested these conditions and systems of value. Through a politics of age, black people developed competing ideas and practices of aging and eldership, and they drew upon these resources in their struggle to define the meaning of family, community, and freedom.

This argument about the politics of age builds upon scholarship from the fields of cultural and historical studies. The interdisciplinary research efforts of Sari Edelstein and Habiba Ibrahim are especially relevant. Edelstein argues that in slave narratives, African Americans resisted the planter class's aims to devalue the black aged and efforts to deny black people a sense of their own age.[12] In her work, Ibrahim centers black age as a means of rethinking black feminism and black studies, treating age as tool to explain historical change, critique liberalism's claims to the universal, and advance an alternative mode of being human that values different life stages and the relationships between them.[13] The work of a number of U.S. and European historians over the past several decades has also shed light on the historical experiences of old people and how their roles and status have varied, changed over time, and been contingent on other social factors.[14] Furthermore, historians have focused broadly on the meaning and role of the slave life cycle or on distinct phases of it such as motherhood, fatherhood, adulthood, or death.[15] Taking this argument about the historical significance of age further, Corinne Field and Nicholas Syrett make an important assertion in their essay on age as a category of analysis that "by paying attention to when and how age matters in a given context, historians can actually learn much about the workings of the state in constructing particular kinds of citizens, the hybridization of cultures in colonial contexts, the organization of work, the regulation of sexuality, the distribution of authority in kin networks, and people's own understanding of their lives."[16]

My work grounds such historical and theoretical insights about the politics of age in a reading of archival materials on African and African American history from the seventeenth into the nineteenth century. Drawing on such evidence, my work examines how age, particularly old age, shaped social relationships in coastal Africa during the height of the Atlantic slave trade, how it affected slave labor mobilization in the colonial and antebellum South, how slaves and free blacks used age to negotiate kinship relationships and engagement with the state, what role it played in antebellum Northern free black religious organizations and civic life, and how it shaped the Civil War and Reconstruction. Looking at a broad span of time and place, I explore the meaning of age, arguing that a politics of age organized early African American history, a politics that had implications for those who survived into old age and for their relations.

While this project focuses on the historical role of black elders, the idea of the politics of age posits a fluid relationship between old age and power. For example, West and West Central Africans and African Americans drew upon old age and the idea of eldership as social, cultural, and political resources, but that power had its limits, especially in the context of North American slavery. Rather, eldership had the potential to but did not necessarily translate into power. Becoming old did not automatically grant power, authority, or respect, which were determined by a combination of factors. Not sitting in a fixed, transcendent social position, elders had a socially and historically contingent status. At certain moments or in specific situations, all old people could depend on their age alone to expect social entitlements or privilege, but in other cases, status in old age was determined by other factors like race, class, gender, or kin relationships. As black elders moved from one social context to another and as other people encountered them on different stages, the kind of status and social influence that old age conferred could change. Seeing the politics of age as relational, situational, and contextual, I grapple with the varied experiences, meanings, and uses of old age in early African American history and explore the contingent relationship between age, eldership, and social power.[17]

By looking at black elders through the lens of a politics of age—as an embodied experience, as a category of analysis, as a set of resources, as an idea—this project exhumes logics of power and identity in the black experience in early North America. While I consider the biological grounds of age, this book is more concerned with age as a social identity—a complex and intersecting set of labels, behavioral norms, modes of treatment, bodily practices, beliefs, and social groups.[18] This book shows the different ways that black people were classified according to age and how age shaped their treatment and expectations. I also examine how age intersected with their other identities, which could produce quite different experiences for African Americans depending on the combination of their age, gender, and class. Black women performed different types of labor, inhabited different spaces, and carried different symbolic meanings in old age than black men did. Furthermore, young slave women performed labor and experienced sexual violence in ways that differed from slave women elders, who experienced such violence in memory, as witnesses, and as guardians of the young. And young black men had different labor expectations and were generally perceived differently than older black men.[19] Yet, common bonds and responsibilities also bound black people across generations who embodied "Oceanic lifespans" of black age, as Ibrahim puts it.[20] Historical actors in early America considered the age of and the aged among black people, and that seeing led to decisions, relationships, and opportunities that had broader historical consequences. This project on early black America thus sees age, especially old age, as an axis for struggles over labor and material concerns, as ideological resources, and as alternative ways of being human in a world that saw African Americans as instruments.

As such, this book explores a core tension in black history between the pull of African American community formation and the pressures of racial capitalism's forced migration and labor systems, processes that black people in early America experienced differently according to age. The slave trades—both transatlantic and domestic—marked young and old black people differently, shifted young people across space, and disrupted their immediate ties to older community members and kin relations. The scholarly literature on age cohorts in slavery has examined the implications of these forced migrations and attendant labor systems from the perspective of the young by assessing their numbers and experiences in the Middle Passage and by providing in-depth studies of slave childhood.[21] But in capturing the young, enslavement had significant downstream effects for individuals, kinship units, and communities over time and space. What came of the aged who were left behind and how did they pick up the pieces when young people were swept away by Atlantic slavery's forces of commerce, labor, violence, and mortality? What came of young captives who survived into old age? How did the enslaved and free blacks navigate their way through these disruptions and forge new modes of culture and community? In answering such questions, this project demonstrates how within the context of the Atlantic World's forced labor system, old age, eldership, and multigenerational ties among black people developed new meanings in the Diaspora and helped to establish the grounds for African American community formation.[22] It reveals how black elders understood relations of power and the power of relationships, having survived the forced labor, family separations, and physical violence at the heart of slavery in North America. Although they did not have the physical might to break the system, they understood how it worked and sought to stitch together kin and community from among its survivors and advance their collective interests.

While examining black history from the perspective of old age, this book also raises questions about its periodization, disrupting the idea that history operates in discrete time segments that can be embedded in narratives with a distinct beginning, middle, and end, with each unfolding in that time sequence. Historian Ira Berlin's time-space model of slavery in North America takes such an approach. His framework has emphasized how the black experience in slavery varied over time and space, unfolding over five periods—the Charter, Plantation, Revolutionary, Migration, and Freedom generations—and across four major regions—the North, the Chesapeake, the Low Country, and the Mississippi River Valley. Each of these times and places had distinct economic grounds, cash crops, and labor practices, and where different African American generations stood in this matrix of time and space determined other aspects of their social and cultural lives.[23] Looking at early black history from the perspective of aging and old age requires a reconsideration of this model. What did historical generation mean to Garrison Frazier, to the laundress who led the 1st South Carolina Regiment, and to the other elders encountered by the Union Army? Can they be understood only in terms of the late antebellum period and Civil War era's Freedom generation? Or should they be seen as being constituted by multiple generations? How did the matrix of time and space work when black people born at different times and generations inhabited the same space? How did older and younger slaves conceive of space when forcibly separated from family, stretching kin relationships across the South? By focusing on elders and age, this book explores such questions and contends that black people operated in the interstices of time and space, that their experiences, worldviews, and relationships operated within yet also stretched across generational boundaries.

Centering the old in African American history presents a fraught proposition determined by the residue of demeaning, racially charged images that planters and their apologists used to undergird slavery. As scholars of race in America have shown, perhaps no other figures in African American history have been subject to as much public ridicule and contempt as black people in old age. From the early nineteenth century, broad swaths of white Americans used the image of aged black people to reinforce ideas about racial and gender hierarchies. In fact, the image figured into the very birth of U.S. popular culture. One of its originators, the master entertainer P. T. Barnum, centered his first act on Joice Heth, a black woman who he claimed had nursed George Washington and lived to 161 years old. After she died less than a year after his road show began, Barnum held a public autopsy of her in New York City to reveal the inner secrets of Heth's aged body to a mass audience of over a thousand.[24] For white audiences in the antebellum United States, seeing the spectacle of an aged black woman who was supposedly connected to the country's founding was well worth the price of admission, and the portrayal of elderly blacks established a cultural pattern that shaped future generations.

From the antebellum period well into the twentieth century, white Southern elites used icons of aged black people as the public face of slavery to rationalize the institution, deploying images that ultimately served the interests of the planter class. White Southern apologists claimed that Northern capitalists discarded older wage laborers when their productivity tailed off, while Southern planters cared for the black aged in their charge. As part of a larger argument about the paternalistic nature of master-slave relationships, racial ideologues conjured up images of old slaves who lived out their final years under the largess and protection of the planter class. For instance, leading white Southern antebellum propagandist George Fitzhugh insisted that black people did not have the moral or intellectual capacity for independence in old age. "The blacks in America are both positively and relatively weak," Fitzhugh wrote in *Cannibals All*. "Positively so, because they are too improvident to lay up for the exigencies of sickness, of the seasons, or of old age."[25]

Fitzhugh added in his *Sociology of the South*, "What a glorious thing to man is slavery, when want, misfortune, old age, debility and sickness overtake him."[26] Conveniently ignoring how slaveholders depended on the labor of slaves to produce treasures for the exigencies that the master class had in old age, Fitzhugh claimed that white Southern planters offered a benevolent, paternalistic system of care for aged slaves.

The distorted image proliferated in the postbellum period. After the erosion and final collapse of Reconstruction governments, Northern and Southern white moderates and conservatives reconciled their differences through a shared recollection of the Civil War. Joining forces, they fashioned the idea that the war was about men defending their honor, not a war about slavery.[27] Their historical memory of the war as a contest between young, brave, honorable white men stood in sharp relief to their image of the old "Black Mammy." Young white nobility and old black servility became two sides of the same coin. The image of old black people also buttressed the claim of slavery's benevolence, in the olden times, in the good old days of the old South. In this spirit, the United Daughters of the Confederacy built monuments to the Black Mammy, and memorabilia of Mammy and Uncle Mose figures circulated in mass consumer markets.[28] Northern and Southern whites used aged figures, literally, to create harmony between the regions. In parlor rooms North and South, they conjured up in their own minds a harmonious, familial world of the Old South inhabited by contended old black people through visual images on sheet music covers and through songs such as "Mammy's Lullaby," "The Old Home aint what it used to be," and "They Made It Twice As Nice As Paradise."[29] The form treated black elders as objects of derision, sources of entertainment, and laughingstocks in an effort of national reconciliation. For more than a century, white mainstream intellectuals and popular artists incorporated aged black people into the idea of a paternalistic antebellum social order, a narrative that amplified over time and space. Mass-produced images of benign, contented gray-haired black women and men came to represent the slave experience and Southern race relations. And by the means of such portraits, slavery's defenders put up a façade that enabled debt peonage, disfranchisement, the stripping away of black citizenship rights, and Jim Crow to have their way. The image of aged blacks—deemed to be relics from a past, harmonious world—served as a counterpoint to the tensions of contemporary life and reinforced white Americans' self-image as modern subjects. Conjuring up notions of a tranquil era of the past, the one-dimensional image of aged black people masked the long history and ongoing strains of forced labor and violent forms of exclusion that black people young and old experienced.

This project offers an alternative narrative and is organized along chronological, geographical, and thematic lines. The story begins in coastal West and West Central Africa during the years of the Atlantic slave trade, though I do not focus on African influences and cultural retentions in North America, as present and significant as they were to the development of black culture. Chapter 1 pays close attention to the power that African elders wielded and how younger generations contested that power. Drawing on the observations of contemporary European merchants and missionaries who engaged coastal Africans, the chapter argues that power operated along the axis of age in coastal West and West Central Africa. After spelling out the role of elders in early modern West and West Central Africa, the chapter then explores age in the Middle Passage and the political economy of slavery in colonial North America. Chapter 2 extends the discussion of age and the political economy of slavery by focusing on how age shaped labor mobilization on slave labor camps in the antebellum South. The chapter draws on records of Southern slaveholders to provide insight into black age demographic patterns. I also explore how the extreme material conditions of slavery changed the aging process of the enslaved body and how planters used age as a tool to manage their slave labor force.

Chapter 3 examines the place of age, the life cycle, and elders in black families in the antebellum South. Exploring a period defined by family separation, this chapter looks at the experience from the perspective of the aged. It examines how slaves created multigenerational structures of authority, respect, and domestic space despite the limits imposed by the forced labor system. Tracing the role of elders in black kinship relationships, the chapter argues that elders used multigenerational links and their age to wring concessions from the state. I assert that black elders and their family members used a politics of age in petitions to state assemblies, thus claiming rights before the law.

Chapter 4 shifts the focus to the antebellum North and argues that age became the grounds for identity and community formation among free blacks. In addition, the chapter examines day-to-day material struggles that went along with growing up old, black, and poor in the Northern states in the wake of the American Revolution. Within the context of Northern emancipation, I focus on African Americans in Philadelphia to explore the prominent role of aged black women in creating free black communities. The chapter also demonstrates how free African Americans cooperated out of necessity, a shared condition, and a common sense of purpose, while they also had disputes across class, gender, and generational lines.

Chapter 5 examines how age and the aged figured into the era of emancipation during and after the Civil War. It looks at encounters between the Union Army and black elders and how the latter sought to exert authority in the late stages of the war. The chapter also looks at questions of labor, material sustenance, and the politics of age during Reconstruction, arguing that the legacy of generations of forced labor, the domestic slave trade, and war continued to shape postwar multigenerational black relationships. Building on Chapter 4's discussion of black communities in the North, the chapter argues that old age became a driver of black institutions in the postbellum North, focusing on the founding and development of the Home for the Aged and Infirm Colored People in Philadelphia. Not just a home for aged former slaves, the site became a place that encapsulated a range of religious, labor, gender, African Diasporic, and other dynamics.

The book closes with an epilogue that reflects on the ongoing place of elders in twentieth- and twenty-first-century black life, arts, and letters. It draws upon vignettes and samples from memoirs, literature, and the arts to situate elders in African American culture since the late nineteenth century. Far from offering an in-depth treatment of the subject during that period, the epilogue seeks to reinforce the book's argument about the meaning of elders in black history and culture and to analyze how African Americans negotiated old age in different historical contexts. I make the case that age and elders continued to shape black American history and culture well after the period of Reconstruction.

This book demonstrates how elders and the politics of age structured systems of power and authority in African and African American history. Elders influenced the physical spaces they inhabited, and they shaped their working, family, and community lives. Old age served as a constraint and potential, one that took on different contours over time, among different subsets of people, and in different contexts. The book also allows us to see the long-term, downstream social, economic, and demographic effects of class relations, racial and gender hierarchies, and forced labor systems.

Looking at African American history through the lens of age also highlights core values that regulated early African American life. Even though they lived on the margins, black Americans transmitted perennial values across generational lines that included human dignity, collective care, and support. In this regard, *Black Elders* highlights how, even in the midst of internal conflicts and in spite of scarce resources, black people maintained a sense that generations of African Americans were bound by a set of obligations and that people who worked their whole lives and survived into old age could still make valuable social contributions and were entitled to recognition and care.

CHAPTER 1

Coastal Africa and Atlantic Slavery

The Asante Empire emerged in the late seventeenth century and over the following century became the dominant political force in the interior of the Gold Coast. After the Asante moved south to defeat the powerful Denkyira, the Dutch West India Company (WIC) took stock of the new political reality and sought to engage the region's emerging leadership. Based on input from advisors on the Gold Coast, WIC Director General Jan Van Sevenhuysen wrote that the company planned "to send David Van Nyendael (who offered his service thereto) as an ambassador to the very feared Caboceer or Chief of Assjantee." Concerned that the negotiation might go poorly, the company afforded Van Nyendael "with an extensive instruction on how to behave himself, as well as with considerable presents for that Chief and his principal elders, all this in order that the wars may be stopped once for all and the trade may be resumed."[1] Thus did the WIC acknowledge the role of elders as a key to power in Asante. Old age, a doorway to ritual power and communion with the ancestors in Asante, offered a gateway to political and economic power. Not all old people were power brokers, yet gaining access to power required the support, approval, or counsel of elders. Atlantic merchants and missionaries grew to understand this, which they incorporated into their commercial and proselytizing ventures in coastal Africa during the years of the Atlantic slave trade.

Though there was some variability over time and space, elders generally held a revered status in West and West Central Africa during this era. Acquired through lineage, grit, opportunity, or other circumstance, eldership brought honor and deference from others. Senior wives demanded respect from their underlings; elder ritual leaders claimed special access to spiritual power because of their proximity to the ancestors; and older children expected to inherit positions of prestige. Elders surrounded themselves with people and material goods, thus solidifying their status. In this culture of honor, old age and colorful garments carried prestige and elicited social recognition. The slave trade both worked through and altered this dynamic, with European merchants making partners with some elders, facing opposition from others, and creating opportunities for young people to claim commercial and political power.

The historical experience of West and West Central Africans during the years of the slave trade was shaped by, though not reduced to, age. Political identity, class, occupation, lineage, ethnicity, gender, and other social factors constituted their experience, social relations, access to power, and sense of self.[2] But age remained a force, one clearly recognized by Atlantic merchants through their negotiation with elders and their preference for young people in the slave trade. In ways that intersected with their perceptions of gender and ethnicity, merchants assessed the age of African captives as part of the logic of human trafficking and demand for labor in the Americas. They created taxonomies that separated African ethnic groups into distinct body types, which they hoped to sell according to each ethnic "brand's" apparent value to agricultural production in the New World. Merchants on the coast closely inspected the bodies of captives in the Atlantic slave trade, seeing in the external form a window into their productive capacity. Western commercial interests in Africa and the Americas developed price structures for purchase and for sale, and age served as a critical axis to determine a person's price and laboring potential. The value that Atlantic slave traders placed on "strong" bodily constitutions thus pulled young people to the Americas. This chapter explores the tension in the Atlantic World between these two systems—one where eldership had social desirability and clout and another where the labor of young people was paramount for commercial agricultural production at global scales. In the world of Atlantic slavery, age drove social, political, and economic relations.

Bodies

As merchants, sailors, scientists, missionaries, explorers, and others from Europe interacted with African people along the coast, they created ideas and practices about a supposed strong African body. Writers from different time periods and places in Europe conjured up such ideas; the concepts recurred, even in the face of contrary information, suggesting that this ideological process took on a life of its own. Slave traders felt attuned to youthfulness and wanted to buy and sell strong bodies—that is all they saw. For instance, the Brandenburg trader Otto Friedrich von der Groeben remarked about the people he encountered between Cottroe and Cape Lahoe on the "Quaqua Coast" that "They are all as strong as trees."[3] Writing about West Central Africans, the physician Samuel Brun claimed that some children of the Mani Soyo Don Ferdinando were "comparable to giants in strength."[4]

Writers defended their positions with a range of theories, with some claiming that the supposed relative strength of African bodies varied according to region or that agricultural and other kinds of work strengthened the body. They conjectured that African women had vigorous bodies that set them apart as suitable laborers. In reference to Angola in the early seventeenth century, Brun stated, "I have already said that the menfolk in Angola are stronger than in other countries, and the women are not much inferior to them in strength; yet it is to be noted that in the whole of Angola the women must till the soil." He continued that while men hunted, cultivated wine trees, and fished, women "must till the soil with one another, and in this they maintain remarkably good discipline."[5] To such observers, strong, working, disciplined bodies were able slaves in the making.

When writers did not make claims about the invigorating effects of work, they might invoke the gods to explain exceptional black bodies. It was the work of God, they suggested, that built the black body. Concerning people along the Gold Coast, the missionary Wilhelm Müller noted, "They are well fashioned and formed by God their Creator. Both women and men have erect and (in their manner) well-proportioned bodies and elegant parts."[6] The divine sculptor, Müller believed, placed gifts in different body parts. These elegant, divine gifts included "eyes with a large white eyeball, a broad, smooth nose, thick lips, white teeth, small ears and nimble feet and hands."[7] The resulting image was statuesque. Evoking images of the sculpted body, the Brandenburg trader Johann Oettinger described a crew of African canoemen who made it to his vessel off the Gold Coast town of Accra in 1692–1693. He wrote, "The Negroes who paddled it were of splendid physique, apart from their somewhat paltry legs; their bodies looked as if cast in dark, shining bronze (even in colour), especially when they stretched taut the powerful muscles of their chests, backs and arms."[8] From the perspective of agents of the Atlantic World slaving system, people who were elegant, giant, strong, muscular, and nimble were objects of desire and seemed to be made for labor.

Slave traders trafficked principally in young people, whom they perceived to embody desirable physical characteristics. As a logical extension of this line of thinking, some merchants also claimed that Africans lived for a long time. Western merchants, travelers, and missionaries picked up on accounts and told legends about people who lived well past one hundred. Some such African elders had important political or symbolic roles, such as the Mani Soyo of West Central Africa. Accounts about his age varied, with the Dutch trader Pieter van den Broecke suggesting that he was over 140 years old when the Portuguese encountered him.[9] Even older was the father of the ruler of Mbanza Loango. Van den Broecke wrote, "The father of this king is still alive and is said to be 160 years old."[10] Of course, the belief that people in Africa had the potential to live to extremely old ages was not without precedent in Western philosophical and religious traditions. In old age, Abraham and Sarah married and bore their son Isaac. He, Moses, Jacob, Solomon, and Paul became old men. And no one matched Methuselah for longevity. Furthermore, the Greeks had developed askesis, or spiritual exercises, such as diets and contemplative practices, which had the effect on adherents to "live in peace and health to a good old age."[11] With this cultural background, it was no major stretch for traders to claim that people from Africa could similarly live remarkably long lives.

Such stories about old people reinforced Western ideas about the fortitude and strong "constitution" of African bodies, as numerous observers talked about people in Africa who lived long lives. Brun said that in Fort Nassau, "as well at Accara [Accra], I saw people who were 130 years old."[12] WIC agent William Bosman claimed that the king of Whydah had energy that belied his age. He wrote, "The Present King is Aged some Years above fifty, but as vigorous and spritely as a man of five and thirty."[13] Wilhelm Müller observed that in Cape Coast, "in 1669 there died an old soothsaying woman, who could count her living offspring down to the fifth generation." He reported that she "showed herself so merry in dancing and capering at a public dance some days before her end that many Chritians watched in great amazement. It did not even bother her when she had to climb up the high Friederichs-Berg hill, for she managed it as energetically as other young women who accompanied her."[14] Making more general arguments, he concluded that "if one were to search through the Fetu country, one would find many people a hundred or at any rate many years old."[15] He continued that in the Fetu country, people "without exception reach a ripe age and consider it very strange if one of them is overtaken by death while still young."[16] He added that, "One also notices that these heathen people are of a much stronger bodily constitution than we Christians, for most of them always walk and stand without a stick."[17] This notion that Africans had exceedingly strong and able bodies and long lives had very clear implications for slavery and the slave trade, as slave traders saw Africans as durable, with the potential to have labor and profit-making value that would last through the years. In their own way, slavers perceived Africa as a fountain of youth, which traffickers siphoned into the Atlantic.

While many writers claimed that Africans reached exceptionally old ages, some authors implied that the odds were against it. In parallel with ideas about the strong African body, there were claims about Africa's unhealthy environment that made people weak. For instance, Brun stated that Benin was "an unhealthy country, so that the natives often become sick."[18] Looking for reasons to explain sicknesses, a consensus blamed a brew of local land, air, and water for spreading disease. Regarding the West African Coast at Fetu, the climate, in Müller's opinion, lent itself to poor health. He wrote, "Since the Fetu country lies so near the equator and since, in addition, the rainy season . . . brings forth unhealthy, poisonous vapours out of the earth, the air there is intemperate and unhealthy."[19] Brun thought about the Gold Coast that "strange illnesses and disease also prevail there. It is striking that the diseases do not extend further than the gold country. There are all kinds of fever there, not to mention haemorrhages and great headaches, and these are due to the evil, intemperate air." To these conditions, observers added guinea worm, malaria, syphilis, and smallpox to the list of maladies that struck people in Africa.[20] Disease and environment, some Europeans argued, were not the only sources of bodily decay. Immorality was said to be another. Bosman claimed that debauchery cut lives short. "Most of the *Negroes* live healthful Lives," he wrote, "but seldom arrive to a great Age." He followed by arguing that premature and excessive sex left people with gray hair and susceptible to falling mortally ill by the age of fifty.[21]

The desire of merchants for young African bodies had its opposite in aged Africans, who were deemed repulsive. Müller wrote that in old age, "The black skin on their face and all over their body becomes yellowish. The flesh falls away, so that they go around [looking] like masks. Their mouth becomes toothless; the hair on their head and beard grows white, like an almond tree in blossom." Making women the target of scorn, he added that "The old black women, in particular, look very ugly, on account of their long, drooping breasts."[22] Bosman took the insults further, complaining about aged mixed-raced women. He wrote, "The whole Brood, when young, are far from handsome, and when old, are only fit to fright Children to their Beds. If a Painter were obliged to paint Envy, I could [wish] him no better Original to draw after than an old *Mulatto*-Woman. In process of time their Bodies become speckled with white, brown and yellow Spots, like the Tygers, which they also resemble in their barbarous Nature."[23] Thus, European observers looked at Africans from two points of view that stood in tension. In some contexts, they saw them through a lens of contempt, marking their bodies as radically different and unable to withstand Africa's environment. From another perspective, they saw Africans as having potentials and exceptionally strong bodies. Depending on the circumstances or the occasion, Europeans on the coast of West and West Central Africa drew different conclusions about the "nature" of the black body, seeing it as an object of desire or contempt. When it came to the search for labor in the Americas, they leaned toward the former.

The search for young people for forced labor in the Americas and the remarks about robust and sprightly elders worked together, reinforcing the idea that Africans possessed exceptional bodies for labor. The belief that people could live long lives was not new to people in the West, as they had a long tradition of acknowledging the aged. However, the Atlantic slave trade created a new context for the idea of old age, as some like Müller would claim that Africans could be marked as different because of their supposed exceptional longevity. Despite the evidence of short life spans, disease, and injury that Africans faced in Africa, through the Atlantic Crossing, and in the New World, the idea of the African with an inherently strong bodily constitution persisted. It proved to be a convenient fiction, part of a worldview that did not cause but certainly enabled mass enslavement of people from Africa. For slave traders, the belief that Africans had long lifespans and had strong bodies had its limits, however, as old people, as vigorous as their bodies might appear, did not fit the picture of the ideal slave for New World plantations. That ideal remained reserved for young people. However, Western brokers on the African coast did see the significance of elders in other ways, particularly as authorities who shaped African trade and politics. Without question, African elders held considerable authority, governed internal political dynamics, and brokered commercial relations along the Atlantic Coast.

Power

African elders' strength sprang from their knowledge and pivotal positions in social fields. They served as hubs for the flow of information, and they also played central roles in decision making. They exerted influence by exercising spiritual and symbolic power, gained by their closeness to ancestors or control over cultural rituals. Not all old people held such power or esteem, as many lived into old age without acquiring heightened social status. Many would be bound to physical labor and remain unfree through their last years. And even those who did acquire rank could have their standing challenged by other elders or by new generations seeking access to power or resources. Yet, as a principle that defined social hierarchies and power relations, eldership was particularly important in coastal West and West Central Africa during the years of the slave trade.

When Portuguese merchants and missionaries brokered trade and sought converts in West Central Africa, they needed to recognize established local authorities. For example, though their control was by no means absolute, some male elders held substantial political and spiritual power and had access to the labor of women and young people. Central Africans brought the idea of honor and respect for male elders into their encounters with the Portuguese, relating to Iberian traders, royalty, and priests on those terms. This way of organizing social relationships was not completely alien to the Portuguese, who came from hierarchical worlds stratified by gender, age, religion, and rank. Thus, the encounter between the Portuguese and West Central Africans provides a window into the political culture of honoring elders and eldership in the early modern Atlantic World.

Aging and generation became the basis of exercising power in the context of local politics. During the years of the slave trade, West Central Africa was divided into political units centered in towns or Mbanzas, and distinct lineages and elders held positions of local authority. One such elder in Mbanza Loango was Mani Goy. While Mani Goy was blind, was physically weakened, and never held central political authority in the town, his presence still shaped the local political environment through his sons. One of his sons held power, and his sixth son was in line to step in should his older brother die before him. While his father had the spiritual gift of extraordinary longevity, this elder brother reputedly had spiritual power, through which he divined the arrival of the Dutch merchant Pieter van den Broecke.[24] Through these ties of kin, notions about the supernatural, and the politics of succession, West Central Africans vied for influence along generational lines.

The politics of seniority and inheritance played out in relationships between men and women, as male elders increased their power by accumulating wives, who in turn stood in order of authority according to age. For example, the leader of Mbanza Loango in the early seventeenth century was said to have had multiple wives, but it would be through his senior wife that his authority passed. As Brun observed, "If he obtains sons from her, the first of them becomes king over his whole kingdom after his death."[25] If she did not have a son, then his sister's son would receive the inheritance.[26] Through such rules of gender, age, and generation, male elders extended their political authority, and a select number of wives or sisters came to hold a stake in the process of elder politics.

The Portuguese worked through such West Central African elders when they sought to spread their faith. After the Kongolese began receiving Portuguese missionaries in the last decades of the fifteenth century, Portuguese religious emissaries made inroads by offering Catholic instruction, giving baptisms, building churches, and hosting West Central African delegations in Portugal. One of the first people in West Central Africa to convert to Christianity was the Mani Soyo, the fifty-year-old leader of Mbanza Soyo in Kongo. His age, status, understanding of indigenous culture, and connections to local social and political fields put him in an ideal position to spread the faith.[27] When he announced his conversion on April 3, 1491, he used widely understood ideas of political authority to connect with his audience. Drums sounded, ivory trumpets blared, and stringed instruments played, while warriors made a military formation. As people gathered, he proclaimed his Christian faith, was baptized, and took the Christian name of Manuel, the name of the King of Portugal's brother.[28] Manuel, according to missionary accounts, understood his conversion in terms of the threat that aging posed to his soul, since he came to believe that being closer to death meant that he ran the risk of passing before being granted the divine blessing bestowed upon those who entered the Christian fold. Manuel thus sought to live out his old age in penance.[29]

Other West Central African political figures demonstrated the power of old age, even as younger generations vied for political power. For example, Manuel's nephew Afonso shaped Kongolese-Iberian ties from the early sixteenth century until his death around 1542, but even as he assumed power, his elders still played a prominent role in local politics. Upon the arrival of the Portuguese, Afonso's father Joao cultivated a relationship with the newcomers, opening the doors to traders and missionaries. He also sent emissaries to Portugal.[30] Yet even with these overtures, he remained ambivalent about Catholicism, and his sons Afonso and Pango played out this basic tension. While Afonso embraced the new faith, his brother Pango opposed the Portuguese's missionary efforts.[31] The ideological conflict between the brothers simmered beneath the surface and boiled over when their father Joao died, leading to a succession dispute.

The ultimate outcome of the conflict was shaped by the intervention of their family's elders. First, Afonso's mother and Joao's wife played a significant role in determining the result. In the immediate aftermath of Joao's death, she kept it a secret. Understanding the power vacuum that this created and the likely dispute between her sons over succession, she sent emissaries to Afonso to tell him about his father's death. Sensing the ensuing struggle for rulership and receiving his mother's support, Afonso returned home to defend against his brother Pango. For Afonso, the future of the Christian faith in Kongo was at the heart of his struggle with Pango, who rejected the new religion. Some people would claim that angels protected Afonso from ambush.[32] But without the aid and support of his mother, Afonso's political destiny would have unfolded much differently. Second, in the ensuing civil war between forces led by Afonso and Pango, their uncle Manuel played a decisive role. Manuel, or the Mani Soyo, had ardently embraced the Christian faith, hence his natural allegiance lay with Afonso. Manuel helped rally troops, and his role as a pioneering convert added weight to Afonso's cause.[33] But his appeal rested on more than these religious grounds. Rather, he used his own aging body to summon courage and honor from the troops. Asking the forces to bear witness to his old age, he beseeched them, "Behold, my age is now one hundred years, and yet I take arms, being zealous for the religion which I have adopted, and for the homage and honour I owe to my king, and do you, who are in the flower of your age, show timidity and so little fealty to your lawful sovereign."[34] Putting his own body on display, and invoking his seniority, Manuel combined Christian, masculine, and generational principles to shame men to fight instead of shrinking from the obligations expected of them. While pointing forward to a new faith, he remained wedded to prevailing ideas about honor and elders.

For Manuel, outward physical gestures had the power to mobilize people and shift political dynamics. His stance points to a larger set of activities through which elders emanated power. Kongolese elders demonstrated their political and social authority through conspicuous consumption. Their possession of luxury goods from Europe set elders apart. Simultaneous with the spread of Catholicism and literacy, the influx of European material goods reshaped West Central African life. Just as people would go to mass twice daily in open displays of their faith, they also demonstrated their importance through showing off their material wealth.

Figure 1. "Untitled Image (Selling Fiber Textiles)," seventeenth century, *Slavery Images: A Visual Record of the African Slave Trade and Slave Life in the Early African Diaspora.* http://slaveryimages.org/s/slaveryimages/item/2280.

When the Dutch sought to open trade in West Central Africa in the early seventeenth century, they negotiated with men who were practicing Catholics and had already gained access to Portuguese merchants. When they encountered the West Central African Dom Miguel, who was said to be 140 years old, the people and material things around him bespoke his status. Van den Broecke recalled that Miguel was surrounded by a retinue of finely dressed nobles. When Miguel's son read a letter from the Dutch trading agent Wemmer van Barchum, Miguel "sat on a Spanish chair with a red velvet covering and covered with gold tacks. This stool stood on an expensive *alcatiffa*. His clothing was a red damask robe with three wide gold trimmings, a black embroidered hat with gold and pearls, which his subjects had themselves made. On his neck hung a thick gold chain, wrapped three times around his neck. His subjects respect him greatly."[35] Through these public displays of consumption, Miguel garnered his people's honor and recognition, an essential objective of eldership. This historical moment highlights a broader expectation held by West and West Central Africans that elders were entitled to honor.

Honor

The power that elders exercised rested on several premises, not the least of which was the idea of honor. Even with regional variations and changes over time, West and West Central Africans interacted according to honor codes, which on a collective level determined social status, access to resources, and decision-making power. People of honor carried particular social responsibilities, and they also made demands on others for public displays of deference and recognition. The quest for honor could prompt leaders to emerge who helped their subjects meet goals for the common good. But because the stakes usually included a limited range of intangible and tangible goods, it was common for honor to be the basis of conflict, violence, and struggles for power. On a more intimate, intrapersonal level, honor could invoke pride or shame, depending upon whether preconceived conditions were met. Rather than being a fixed social category, honor was a dynamic social and political process that accorded respect and bestowed authority upon individuals.[36]

With their authority, elders set forth norms of conduct for their subordinates and established law and order among their subjects. For example, Miguel of West Central Africa had a reputation for maintaining "very good law and order in his land."[37] Don Francesco Manipango had a similar reputation. He was described as "an old man and of great prudence; and for fifty years he has governed this kingdom without any outbreaks or having once had to be recalled by the king."[38] Other elders defined their standing in spiritual terms. With the arrival of Christian missionaries, some sought to defend their traditional practices while others aligned with the newcomers. Within the context of military conflicts, Manuel inspired young troops by showing them that even an old man like him could stand up and fight for his faith and his political leader. Such was the significance of the honor that derived from his age.

In the encounter between the Portuguese and West Central Africans, each side used ideas about honor wedded to the status of elders to advance their interests. The Portuguese treated an early Kongolese delegation to the Iberian

Peninsula with "honrra, e humanidade," or honor and humanity, which opened the door to Portuguese traders and missionaries into the Kongo.[39] In return, the Portuguese expected the Kongolese to show honor, first to God. King Afonso stood as a clear example. Upon his conversion, he became committed to serve in "honra de Deus," or in God's honor.[40] As important as his conversion was to Portuguese missionary efforts, the Catholic faith could not spread through him alone. The Portuguese King Manuel sent missionary teachers and religious materials such as brocades and silver crosses for Catholic services to the Kongo. Missionaries set up services, teaching about Catholic principles, the arts, and philosophy, and directing religious music. They also aligned with provincial elders, who provided their children with missionary education.[41] And in the early seventeenth century, when the Portuguese had a strong commercial and missionary presence in West Central Africa, the Portuguese forged an alliance with the aged Ferdinando of Soyo to press against the king of Kongo.[42]

In West Central Africa, power operated through the command of elders. Even younger people who sought to exercise political power had to work through older actors. Elders gained their authority through their work as healers or skill in maintaining law and order. The Portuguese worked through elders to gain access to markets or potential converts. And West Central African elders took advantage of these relationships to reaffirm their position atop the social order. In these systems of honor, living people felt a clear obligation to the dead, who in turn could assist the living. To honor the dead, they conducted elaborate funeral rites to guarantee a safe passage for the recently deceased into the ancestral realm.

It was a mark of honor for a person to become old in West Central Africa, where healers developed a set of practices to care for and extend the life of the body. According to one account, the objective of West Central African medicine was on prevention, which was complemented by concepts about the healing powers inherent in substances from nature. Practitioners of herbal medicine prescribed to their clients "herbs, trees, oils, waters, and stones, which Mother Nature has shown the people how to use."[43] Yet, herbal practitioners did more than tend to sick bodies; they emphasized bodily health through moderation and turned to herbs only when necessary.[44] Healers also looked to supernatural forces in treating their charges. Claiming that they had the ability to communicate with spirits to diagnose and treat ill people, they explained that a cure or continued sickness was a function of disharmony with the spirit world.[45] At the heart of their method was a trust between healer and client that developed over time, a value to which elders could lay a special claim.

When compared to West Central Africans, West African elders had similar expectations and sat in a comparable place of honor. Being close to the dead, they had favor among the living. They were repositories of knowledge and had skills in discernment. Consequently, they played a critical role in resolving disputes. While they bound people together, elders also distinguished themselves from their subordinates through social displays of wealth and conspicuous consumption. They also used words to shame younger people about their ignorance and to make them obedient. In important ways, people became stronger socially as they aged, though not in the bodily ways that Western merchants fancied.

Tied to this broader social and cultural context, elders played an important role in the political arena and placed a check on the centralization of power. Normally, the symbolic and political heads in West Africa were aged. At Cape Mount, Bosman met one leader who "was an elderly Man, as appeared by his grey Head and Beard. His Name was *Jan de Cabo Monte*, so called from the Point of that Name."[46] At the Rio Sestre, Bosman encountered a "Silver Haired" man named Peter, "an old Man that looked like their Governour," who invited Bosman to his village for food and drink.[47]

Elders also exercised authority through collective bodies that checked the power of individual leaders. Bosman observed that at Anomabo, "Here is no King, the Government being in the Hands of a Chief Commander, whom they call their *Brasso*, a Word importing Leader. He is a sort of Chief Governour, and has the greatest Power of any in the whole Land, but is somewhat closely restrained by the old Men, who are a sort of National Councellors, not unlike some *European* Parliament, acting perfectly according to their Inclinations, without consulting the *Brasso*."[48] Another contemporary account pointed to the political significance and meaning of the elders on West Africa's Gold Coast. Müller writes, "Although the Fetu people have a king, whom they call *ohin*, the form of government is rather an aristocracy; for the king is not allowed to lay down or regulate anything as a sovereign or absolute monarch in general matters of the country, unless senior personages of the kingdom and the most important [elders] of the people approve it and consent to it."[49]

The wise counsel, physical form, dress, and material effects set elders apart from their subjects. On the Gold Coast in the seventeenth century, "In each little town is a supreme headman, called *henna*, and in addition four caboceers or headmen."[50] They were distinguished by their dress and the stools upon which they sat.[51] An example of such a "henna," or *hene,* was the "old day" Johann Classen of Fetu. Müller wrote about him that when traders from Europe arrive, "he sits down on a stool in the courtyard, dressed and adorned in the best and most splendid manner."[52] Müller continued, "The present King of Fetu, called Aduaffo, is a fat old man, tall in stature. His hair is almost snow-white and he has a large beard hanging down to his chest. . . . Although one finds many people of high status in the Fetu country whose wealth and number of bondsmen exceed those of the king, they yet honour him as a king and hold him in great esteem, principally on account of his great age and powerful *summàn* or *fitiso*." Aduaffo's gray hair and corpulent body demonstrated that he incorporated spiritual power and that he had power and control over others, for his household is said to have included "wives, concubines, and children."[53]

With the expansion of the Atlantic trade, new opportunities arose to exercise power in West Africa. However, people could still adhere to principles of elder authority and inheritance. For example, in the eighteenth century, one *hene* of Kommenda built up considerable wealth, but his younger brother had comparable commercial success, felt entitled to greater honor, and began to covet the *hene*'s position. Seeing this, the *hene* announced to his counselors that, before he died, he would like to pass down his title to his son. The leader of Kommenda also sought to subordinate his brother, who fled to Elmina castle for protection. The brother also attempted to make allies with other coastal leaders. After the "old father" died, his brother set out on a new quest for power. But ultimately, the younger brother failed in his efforts, despite offering gold in exchange for loyalty, because his potential allies adhered to the principles that the old king of Kommenda had followed.[54] The young rival discovered that gold could not buy the status and honor that came with eldership and through lineage.

Ancestors

When West African elders exercised power, they did so in concert with ancestors, seen as an extension of eldership. Through rituals, memory, and acknowledgment, living elders invoked the power and influence of the dead.[55] The succession dispute occasioned by the death of the *hene* of Kommenda demonstrates how descendants carried on the work of deceased elders. Ritualized collective mortuary practices were keys to making a safe passage between the worlds of the living and the dead. For one woman elder in Upper Guinea, proper burial involved a series of steps. First, they placed a cloth over her corpse, brought her into the open, surrounded her, and shaded her body. In the second stage, men distraught with grief ran "about the House of the Deceased, continually and dismally howling" in a public expression of honoring the departed. Then, women "began to lift up their Voices" in such a powerful way that one could not "determine which of the Sexes made the greatest noise."[56] Next, they placed her corpse in a canoe, provisioned it with rice, palm wine, and "all sorts of green Plants," and took the deceased to her hometown. In the final stage, people from her hometown performed her burial, collecting funds for drinks for the last rites and related social gatherings.[57] Such outward gestures of care were not just about the dead but also concerned the living, who outperformed each other in honoring the newly deceased.

In tension with praising the honorable dead, some West African communities castigated the dead who were deemed not worthy of honor, believing that people carried the weight of their actions from the world of the living into the world of the dead. Hence, violating social mores lead to trouble in the afterlife. On the Slave Coast, some believed that "Wicked and Damned" people went to hell, located below the earth, and elders propagated such beliefs and claimed special occult powers that enabled them to access the realm of the dead. For instance, "an old Sorceress" was said to have visited hell, having seen "several of her Acquaintances there, and particularly the last Captain of the Blacks, Predecessor to the present Captain *Carter*, who was there miserably tormented." Her claims to unique knowledge of the fate of people's souls bolstered her moral authority; and though it was said that she came from "some odd corner," her critical remark about a former captain implies that she had some social standing.[58] Her standing reflected a larger recognition of the importance of elders, such that people wanted to become old and invoked the spiritual realm to help them reach a respectable age.

Elders, exercising power within the context of kinship or tributary relationships, did so in part by claiming access to moral and spiritual forces. In short, some people called on spiritual forces to *become* old. Müller claims that women elders in the Fetu country felt that the "old age of theirs brings its inconveniences with it, yet they wish and ask their *summàn, fitiso* . . . that they may be granted a long life."[59] Eldership and the spiritual realm were thus intertwined, as elders invoked the spiritual world for their status and well-being, and the dead continued to inhabit the world of the living and show them how to live. This ideological system reproduced asymmetries of power, with elders possessing mysterious, incontestable, and exclusive knowledge that enabled them to stand over younger people.

Imbuing living elders with spiritual power, the deceased inspired political and military action. Being led by elders into war, young people carried out unresolved conflicts they inherited from previous generations. Elders conjured the ongoing presence of the dead to mobilize people for war, which had grave consequences for the vanquished. An army of thirty thousand Fante soldiers went to war after having been "summoned by the deceased" to attack Elmina and "to make their wives and children their slaves."[60] In such ways, conjuring the spirit of the dead in the context of volatile, divisive, and vengeful political environments moved some people to be honored for achieving great military feats, with their civilian casualties facing a fate of death, social isolation, enslavement, or dishonor.

Spiritual and political notions about elders and ancestors reinforced each other in a tight circular logic and played out in relational and exclusive cultures of honor. It was said that along the Gold Coast in the seventeenth century, "Old age is highly honoured by them. Consequently, no-one is promoted to a rank of honour until he has reached a considerable age." These honored ones defined their status against younger people who were derided as *oba*, or children. Elders would "mock a thirty- or forty-year-old and insult him by calling him an *ubbà* or *mossò*, who is still far too young to assume public office."[61] In cases when they were excluded from positions reserved for male elders, women elders played one up on younger people. During courtship, an adolescent male was expected to shower gifts of alcohol upon older women in the community. If he failed to do so, the women might then "spread the word in the open market and street that he is a *quiteriqui*, a stingy [person], who does no-one any good."[62] Such women elders, closed out of other forms of political activity, used the power of their words to exercise authority, influence young people in the community, and reap social rewards. Old age and long lives were reason enough for elders to exclude young people from seats of political authority that would empower them to offer counsel, regulate the social order, or make decisions about life and death.

Knowledge

Elders exercised power not only through the number of years they lived but also through the amount of knowledge they accumulated. They clung to historical memory including about political conflict. While on the Gold Coast, Brun got wind of a 1618 conflict between the "Abramu" and the "Akanists." Having witnessed or heard about previous conflicts, elders at Fort Nassaw told Brun "that such a battle had not occurred in a hundred years."[63] In the Fetu country on the Gold Coast, elders preserved their knowledge through oral histories and embodied memory. "They have a powerful memory," wrote Müller. "This memory turns out to be accurate, when one talks to them about the arrival of the Dutch at Moree [Mori], the conquest of the castle St. George D'El Mina, the building of this or that fort on the Guinea coast, and of native wars." He added, "Many of the old people are able to give a good account of these stories."[64] Embodying historical and cultural knowledge, elders attracted outsiders and young people searching for information and guidance. Old people would "strengthen their memories by zealously repeating the old stories; for since they often sit around idly all day, they talk to one another of past times. Young people and children listen to such discourse with avid ears, and absorb it in their hearts. In this way the knowledge of the past matters is always propagated."[65] As embodiments of information and knowledge that positioned them to make critical decisions, elders established their place in the social hierarchy.

Through formal and informal modes of training, they learned how to make decisions about the allocation and flow of resources, how relationships should be conducted, and an array of other social and political matters. Elder authority had a coveted status, inspiring people to grow into the role. For instance, in Upper Guinea, Muslim scholars, or "marabouts," traveled widely to collect information about trade, gold resources, the political climate, the natural environment, and other areas of life. Over time, their knowledge added up and became an asset. A marabout named Mahome, "who could not be less in appearance then an hundred years of age," exemplified this idea. His travels covered a large swath of territory, through which he became an expert on the structure of the gold trade, and he informed the British merchant Richard Jobson about local economic and political conditions.[66] Jobson consulted other elders. He learned about the gold trade from "two ancients Mary-buckes," who guided him to safe passage through risky social and environmental terrain. They also possessed more subtle knowledge about interpersonal relationships and honor codes, as signified by the elaborate handshakes they gave upon bidding Jobson farewell.[67] Jobson was but their most recent pupil, as marabouts went about with written texts teaching young people how to read.[68] These men of wisdom inhabited seats of authority that drew others to them and from which they projected their influence.

With power flowing from their knowledge, elders played an essential role in maintaining social order. And having experienced personal trials and witnessed the struggles of others, they used their expertise to resolve internal conflicts. Along the Gold Coast in the seventeenth century, town courts led by a "supreme headman," or *hene*, and several lower-ranking headmen, or *caboceers,* sat in council. Distinguished not only by their knowledge, age, and reputations but also by their dress and the stools upon which they sat, this body of local elder men adjudicated cases.[69] These cases depended heavily upon verbal testimony, with judges being guardians of the word. They had to be particularly attuned to listening, as trials came before "the Ears of those old Gentleman, of which this Assembly or Court is composed."[70] With words being so important, judges required defendants to swear oaths attesting to the veracity of their claims, thus putting their reputations at stake. This method also worked another way, with silences conveying guilt.[71] Discussing a woman elder in Benin, the Dutch writer Olfert Dapper noted her significance, writing, "The King's mother is held in great reverence and has a special court a little outside the town, well and grandly built, where she holds court with many women and girls, and her advice is sought on all the affairs of the land."[72] Thus, court elders wielded considerable authority and sought to guarantee community stability. And they were responsible for enforcing honor codes through the power of the word.

Elders sought to maintain their basic security and, through their knowledge and claims to spiritual and ancestral power, projected an aura of invincibility. Being able to communicate with the ancestors and having faced death, elders held tightly bound and privileged knowledge that attempted to make them impervious to internal challenge. They controlled and oversaw the social order through their knowledge, an asset that put them in a strong position in their relationships with others. Commanding respect by virtue of their knowledge and longevity, they expected young people to be deferential and admonished youth when they stepped out of line. Social ostracism was the price a person paid for disobedience. Because they were such central actors in local social, cultural, and political life, West and West Central African elders played an important role during the years of the Atlantic trade as brokers with merchants from Europe. But while old age played an important role in establishing authority, not all old people had access to such power.

Exclusion

While gerontocrats heavily influenced African social and political relations, their position was defined not only in opposition to young people but also in contrast to old people who did not hold seats of power. For instance, Portuguese missionaries noted on an occasion in the West Central African Coast that its leaders sat waiting in their courts while "numbers of men, women, and children of all ages, as well as old men of eighty years and upwards, pressed forward with every sign of real faith, to ask for the water of holy baptism."[73] During the course of their life cycle, some old people made it to the centers of power, while others like these older converts stood in the margins and tried to push toward the center. Old people who were poor, women, unfree, or in ill health were vulnerable. There were elders, and there were the aged poor.

Some women resided in the circle of power and honor, while others had to defer to male elders. On the Gold Coast, as elsewhere, the oldest wife of a male elder commanded respect from his other wives. "The first wife, who is called *odufù*, is the most important," wrote Müller. "She is honoured above everyone by the husband and concubines. In her daily dress and ornaments she outdoes all other wives, and she has charge over the concubines and domestic servants. The other wives, though free people and of high birth, are considered inferior to this *odufù*; and as a sign of their subordination, they must say '*Acjù*' to the first-chosen wife and obey her orders."[74] Within the context of matrilineal social relations, the *odufù* stood out as a woman of power and a notable exception, with other women providing service or deference to their superiors.

In local political cultures, eldership had a clear politics of exclusion, as elder authority and power could be a largely male domain. Gender divisions of labor shaped the personal trajectories of the aging population, as different occupations had different effects on the bodies of workers. Van den Broecke writes about West Central Africans, "The wives must provide a living for the man by seeding, planting, working the land with hoes, and doing much other, very hard labour. Meanwhile, the man lies idly on his side."[75] In the early seventeenth century in Angola, it was found that some men "take wives wherever and however many they want, but treat them no differently than slaves are treated in Spain and elsewhere; for the wives must till the soil and perform other heavy work."[76] In contrast, men worked by fishing, cultivating wine trees, hunting, and making craft goods.[77] The gender division of labor facilitated the reproduction of male elder authority.

Likewise, the poor kept working as they aged. For instance, in Cape Verde, men wove cloth out of yarn "spun by the old women."[78] Brun noted that in early seventeenth century Angola, "The old people who can no longer walk or see must pump the bellows for the smiths and thus earn their keep."[79] After having been kidnapped and forced to labor for a smith, Olaudah Equiano encountered an aged slave woman who cooked and tended poultry.[80] Clearly, old people could face lives of unending toil, and slavers saw no problem or inherent contradiction in mobilizing the labor of old people or seeing them as pawns. In the rural hinterland, in craft workshops, and on the coast, old slaves continued to work away.

Along the Gold Coast, slaves worked in old age, with some being held by European trading companies. While the Dutch and other slave-trading powers were principally interested in taking slaves for export, they also used slaves to work in coastal trading forts, and some of their slaves grew old. For example, the Dutch WIC agent Jacob Van den Broucke went to Fida (Whydah), where he was able, after negotiating for the right to trade there with the "King and other Chiefs," to buy "122 Ps. slaves both for the replacement of old and deceased slaves on this Coast and for the planting of cotton at various places near the factories which may be appropriate for such an enterprise."[81] In other cases, coastal merchants put old captives up for sale. Brun wrote concerning the trade from the area around Cameroon that "They also have for sale many people, whom they obtain from their enemies by stealing both old and young, and whom they sell for money, or for 3 or 4 *massen* of Spanish wine."[82] Even while they focused on buying the young, Western merchants still found some commercial value in the old.

While they had limited authority, old slaves tried to turn their seniority into political or personal advantage. In Elmina, the slave Bossoe borrowed gold from a Fante man named Tennufoeba. Bossoe, a Dutch WIC castle slave, claimed that he had "consumed the said amount during the famine of some years ago, and that he, being an old gray man, is unable to contribute anything" and could not pay off the debt. Tennufoeba sought to take possession of Bossoe from the Dutch for defaulting on the loan. The Dutch saw Bossoe not as a notable elder but rather as a "macron slave," and they also feared that holding onto Bossoe might lead residents to attack the Dutch to settle this dispute and other scores. Ultimately, the company felt that "this old and disabled slave was not worth the risk" of protecting and released Bossoe over to Tennufoeba.[83] This episode clearly illustrates how old people who were unfree had limited claims as elders and how the practice of honoring elders broke down under these class conditions. It also demonstrates the underlying logic of the Atlantic slave trade's goal of trafficking in young people.

For some, the journey from birth to death brought greater social respect. But such an ascent was by no means guaranteed. To the elderly woman that Olaudah Equiano encountered, as well as to "macron slaves," Bossoe, and countless others, aging carried no such prestige. Many worked well into old age, tending livestock, spinning yarn, helping smiths, or engaging in various other tasks. Over time, a clear gap widened between free and unfree old people. As Bossoe discovered in the negotiations between Tennufoeba and the Dutch WIC, being old did not necessarily bring honor, protection, or sympathy. Rather, he faced indebtedness and its attendant vulnerability. He clearly stood in a precarious position; however, even the most well placed could see their authority tested. And traders from Europe took this into account.

Challengers

Throughout West and West Central Africa in the years of the slave trade, elders practiced strategies of exclusion and tried to place limits on the centralization of power into a single person's hands. Holding an honored status, they used their knowledge, social connections, and claims about the spiritual world to exercise power. Age also made a difference in determining the relative status of young people, even those from the same family. In an ongoing, circular form, the most privileged of elders held their position because they were first born.

In Kongo at the turn of the seventeenth century, it was commonplace for power to be passed to the eldest son. Even powerful elites had to comply. Concerning the province of Pemba, Duarte Lopes wrote, "The governor is Don Antonio Manipemba, second son of the late King Alvarez, and brother of the reigning sovereign. So much was Don Antonio beloved by his father that he assigned this governorship to him, not knowing what better to give, unless it were the royal kingdom itself, which he had desired to do, for he was more after his own heart than the eldest son; but this was not permitted according to the royal law, and could not have been permitted."[84] Along the Gold Coast, the eldest children received gifts because of their relative age. For example, the aged local leader Jan de Cabo Monte had sixteen children—twelve sons and four daughters. But of them, his eldest son and eldest daughter gained control over eight homes.[85] By creating patrimonies, male elders offered their eldest children reason to support the social order. However, this process had its limits. Old age served as a marker of status but could also limit the social roles of the aged, particularly in war. Faced with the prospect of succession, elders debated who would inherit positions of authority. Furthermore, young people challenged their elders and made claims to power. The Atlantic slave trade exacerbated these underlying intergenerational tensions, as some young people saw in the trade opportunities for political, military, or economic advancement.[86] The power of elders, while an important organizing force in West and West Central Africa, could be as ephemeral as their bodies.

On a material level, being an elder involved transformation of the body, one with different physical capabilities and one not usually prepared for war. While some worked in material production well into old age, others had a reduced physical capacity. For example, Mani Goy, the father of Mbanza Loango's leader, was said to be very old and had become weakened over the course of his life. At the time of Pieter van den Broecke's visit to West Central Africa, the patriarch Mani Goy was blind and "had so little strength that he could not lift the weight of a Dutch lb off of the table."[87] In the context of war, old people felt an acute disadvantage. Though elders sent young people to battle, the theater of war was usually no place for the aged. It was said that on the Gold Coast, "everyone who can fight must go to war. The old people and women, however, stay at home."[88]

While kinship, local interests, ethnicity, and empire drove African political conflicts, they also played out through age difference. Standing atop the social hierarchy, elders mobilized young people in war as a defense mechanism or to claim people, land, or trade with force of arms. Yet, deploying young people in the military could have unforeseeable consequences. Young soldiers developed their own objectives that did not always follow the dictates of their elders. In November 1739, the Dutch commercial agent Verschueren wrote with concern about the conflict between the "Elminase" and "Fantynen" on the Gold Coast, a dispute that took a generational turn. He reported that the Dutch "have made great presents to the Fantynen in order to quiet them down. We are not so much worried that the Elminase will be beaten by the Fantynen, but rather that the Old Men will no longer be able to stop the Young Men from attacking *us*."[89] To Verschueren, the conflict that first seemed to be between competing ethnic groups exposed more significant cleavages along generational lines, which elders had a limited ability to control because they did not wield the weapons.

As with war, elders sought to control trade but could not monopolize commercial power despite their efforts to maintain it. Some commercial ties between European traders and African elders were by their very nature impermanent and contingent because they depended upon personal connections that were severed at death. But even when elders had developed strategies to set up replacements in their networks, the stresses and uncertainty of war could disrupt their plans. Such was the case on the Gold Coast at the turn of the eighteenth century. Dutch merchants had developed a thriving gold export trade through their connections with elders on the Gold Coast. The Dutch agent Willem de la Palma noted in an October 10, 1703, letter that the Dutch "had the honour of being Chief Merchant here at Elmina, in the year 1690–91, when in just two extracts more than 500 marks of gold used to go to our coffers." He feared, however, that trade would not recover after recent heavy rains and warfare disrupted economic relations. De la Palma predicted a commercial decline "because most of the old or deceased ones (traders) have now been replaced by young ones who have no experience in trade."[90] The death and supersession of elders created new uncertainties, which created opportunities for young people.

While elders held a great deal of power in West and West Central Africa, their positions did not go uncontested. They controlled property and position, and they conjured a sense of spiritual power through claims to ancestral connections. But cracks developed. Mortality had its say, and every elder perished. Though they established systems of inheritance, succession was not always a smooth process. After war, young people sought access to privileges like trade on the Atlantic Coast, which had previously been controlled by elders. The complaints and concerns of European merchants about young merchants lay bare how the relative position of some elders shifted as the slave trade expanded.

Power, and more importantly people, slipped through the hands of the aged with the expansion of Atlantic commerce. The case of an "old woman named Esuon" who lost her children through the trade illustrates this larger point and shows the generational breaks wrought by the Atlantic slave trade. While most captives of the traffic had been prisoners of war, Esuon's children entered through family debt and panyarring. To buy trade goods from European merchants, some Africans went into debt and used their children as pawns, which placed them at risk of being collected as final "payment" for debts and then shipped across the Atlantic. Some pawns faced kidnapping or panyarring. The African agent of the English slave trade Tom Awishee from Anomabo had apparently panyarred Esuon's children, put them on an English ship, and gave orders "never to set those slaves free." Esuon made a pained appeal to the Dutch, who received word that the English held her children near the Slave Coast town of Jakin. The Dutch agent recounted how Esuon came pleading to them under "hot tears about the loss of her children, begging us to arrange with our Governor, Mr. Hertogh, for their release, offering us money to buy them free."[91] Awishee rejected her appeal.

Situating her in a larger context, Esuon's grief and helplessness indicate the significance and limits of African elders and agency during the slave trade. Even with her ties to the Dutch, she lost her children to competing English slavers. And her experience illustrates a larger point about the transformation of social relationships in Africa during the years of the slave trade, as the authority and degree of honor held by the aged transformed in the face of market forces and claims by the young, wealthy, and ambitious. Consequently, many an old person in Africa like Esuon would lose their loved ones. And young people, who constituted most captives in the slave trade, found themselves without the daily connection, advice, counsel, and authority of their elders. This separation had profound implications for their experience in the Diaspora.

Contracts

In coastal West and West Central Africa, the aged held significant social, political, and religious power and influence, to which young people could aspire. Once the young entered the world of Atlantic slavery, their prospects dramatically diminished. From the point of purchase on the coast, through the Atlantic crossing aboard slave ships, to landing in the Americas, Western slave-trading merchants and planters tried to reduce African captives to their physical productive capacity. With demands in the Americas for forced labor, slave traders set their eyes on young people, perceived to be the strongest of the strong and with valuable constitutions. Age was a critical factor in the world of Atlantic slavery, and the leg from coastal West and West Central Africa to the Caribbean islands played this out.

Slave-trading merchants developed terminologies and shorthand to speak about young people, referring to them in some cases as "Pieza de India," equivalent to an able-bodied slave between the ages of fifteen and thirty-five. The *pieza* became a fundamental value for commercial exchange, intimately linking the lives of young enslaved Africans to Atlantic commerce.[92] For his trading expedition to Ardra on the Slave Coast, Martin Witte of the Dutch WIC had instruction to buy slaves and "pay special attention to their quality, so that they are all *Pieza de India* of such a constitution, age and sex as stipulated in the contracts between the Company and the proxies of Don Juan Barroso y Poso."[93] In the early eighteenth century, the South Sea Company set the value of a *pieza* at a 16-year-old or older male or 12- or 13-year-old or older female. Unlike its 1713 contract, their 1717 agreement allowed traders to buy children under ten. The company valued boys younger than sixteen and girls younger than twelve at two-thirds of a *pieza*. The company also deemed "children under 6 Years Old" to be worth one-half or one-third of a *pieza*.[94]

This *pieza* system connected to commercial preferences and prices, which investors set based upon age, gender, and other factors. Though the currencies and specific cut-offs varied over time and place in the slave trade, traders maintained a link between age and price. The ship *Dragon* set the price of men at "forty to forty eight copper bars per head," women at 28 to 36 bars, boys from 20 to 40 bars, and girls from 17 to 30, with the exact price being determined by "their age and constitution."[95] Setting the cost of humans trafficked to Santiago in Cape Verde, the Royal African Company priced 6- to 10-year-old children at £10 while adults from 12 to 40 years old cost £18.[96] The prices reflected demand on Atlantic World slave labor camps and their expectations of production. The calculation of slave traders and plantation owners was to catch a person in the market at the right time in their life cycle and with the right "constitution" for maximum exchange value or material production. The market, accounting methods, and management practices reflect the significant weight British slaving merchants placed on age.

While merchants generally preferred males to females in the trade, its hazards ensnared girls and young women, whose age and value were determined in part by their overall physical appearance or the quality of their breasts. Complaining about the relatively high prices for slaves on the Slave Coast, one slave trader wrote in October of 1733 that "The female slaves are invariably bought for 3½ oz. here, but this is because no other women than young ones with firm breasts are sold here, and these are naturally more expensive than the old ones."[97] The Prussian sailor Otto Friedrich von der Groeben remarked that local African traders at the mouth of the Rio Sueyro de Costa "offered us cheaply two of their children, little five-year-old girls. . . .

The captain bought one, because she was beautiful, for three muskets and a *cabes* of glass beads."[98]

Merchants developed elaborate, and at times invasive, physical examinations to determine the age and value of captives. Potential buyers wanted to make sure that they were getting young people and tried to detect any signs of aging. One trader looked for African captives who were "black and handsome."[99] The appearance of gray hairs, unfirm breasts, or "ugliness" could thwart a sale, as some traders rejected older slaves. Groeben wrote, "When we wanted to set sail, a Negro came on board with two of his wives, both forty years old, to judge by their appearance, and wanted to sell them for twenty bars of iron. But they were ugly old devils, they did not suit our requirements."[100] To sort out the young from the old, one captain had the ship's surgeon conduct physical exams on slaves, "making them jump, stretch out their arms swiftly, looking into their mouths to judge of their age." Because some African coastal traders tried to conceal the age of slaves by shaving them to hide any gray hair and by polishing them with palm oil, slave ship surgeons could be left with few signs to detect old and thus undesirable captives. As the British captain wrote, "'Tis no easy matter to know an old one from a middle-age one, but by the teeths decay."[101] Some traders went as far as to lick the chins of captives to determine their age by how much facial hair they had.[102] For agents of the Atlantic slave trade, the ideal slave was young, and brokers paid considerable attention to the physical form of African captives, looking for young, virile, and strong bodies.

At times, ship captains embarked on their slaving voyages with very specific instructions about what ages to get. In the 1670s, the ship *Arthur* arrived on the West African Coast. On March 6, 1677, the captain Robert Doegood noted in his journal that he bought three males and one female. But he was even more precise. He wrote that they "appeare very good negroes nott forgettinge your hon'rs orders that none exceed the age of fourteen neither under the age of twelve yeeres as heatherto had Been minded and accordingly B'ot." Twelve to fourteen was the optimal age range for this slaving voyage, and by procuring "very good negroes" in this narrow age range, the captain showed his acumen and trustworthiness to investors.[103]

In most cases, captains had more general orders and contracts about what ages to get. A 1721 letter from Daniel Wescomb to Francis Lynn directed Lynn to buy two thousand people from the Slave Coast towns of Whydah and Jacquin and one thousand from Angola. The orders went on to say that "2/3 of these [should] be Men and Women, and 1/3 Boys and Girls not under

10 years old." The command also delimited the age of the men and women they sought—between 16 and 25 years old.[104] When the Royal African Company entered a contract in 1713 to buy 4,800 people from Africa for the South Sea Company, the latter indicated their age and gender preference. Two-thirds needed to be males. The contract then specified that "none of the said 4800 Negroes shall be under the Age of Ten Years, and that nine parts in Ten of the said 4800 Negroes so to be furnished shall be of the Age of Sixteen Years at Least and None of them shall Exceed the Age of 40 years."[105] Captain William Barry received instructions to "buy none but what's healthy and strong and of a Convenient Age—none to exceed the years of 25 or under 10 if posible."[106] Furthermore, Captain Robert Davers had a contract to bring sixty captives between 14 and 30 and thirty children from 10 to 14 to Barbados.[107] At the heart of British slave-trading contracts were prospects for young people bound for the West Indies.

In managing their human cargo, slave ship captains often divided men and women along the lines of sex, and they also enforced divisions according to age. James Barbot observed that slave ships kept men secure in the holds and women "between decks." They didn't divide children along gender lines; the ships held young people "in the steeridge." But they were not spared the slave-ship conditions such as its "intolerable stench."[108] Captives also ate separately, with men taking their food under heavy armed guard, women eating near the crew who maintained watch, and boys and girls eating apart from older subjects.[109] In terms of how ship captains kept them in space, the captives onboard slave ships lived in quarters separated by both gender and age.

Ultimately, in the Atlantic slave market, the idea of age was a blunt instrument to assign economic value that provided scant details about the actual identities or ages of enslaved subjects. In their logbooks and for accounting purposes, captains counted men and women and boys and girls in aggregate. For instance, the account book of the seventeenth century ship *Sarah Bonaventure* tallied rough categories of "Men Slaves," "Women," "Boyes," and "Gerles" as so many muskets, iron bars, or cloths.[110] The accounts of the *Swallow* and the *Arminian Merchant* similarly lumped together all men, women, boys, and girls into units.[111] Writing from Jamaica, John Merewether wrote that "we want Girls" to send to the Cuba market.[112]

The goal then for European merchants was to buy people at a prime age and with "lusty" bodies for American slave markets. This was part of a larger Atlantic commercial strategy of depending upon the labor of young people to drive the economy. Ships required "lusty" white bodies to run them and "lusty" black bodies to carry across the Atlantic. Speaking about himself and his crew, Captain Black informed the Guinea Company during a bout of disease sweeping through the crew on his ship that he was "at present very well and lusty and I hope with In a short tyme to see all the rest up againe and lusty."[113] Promoting the prospects of the slave trade on the Alampo, or Slave Coast, whose captives had a reputation for being "the worst and most washy of any that are brought to the West-Indies," one agent rebutted that by saying that "they seem as well limb'd and lusty as any other negroes."[114] In the mid-seventeenth century, the British Guinea Company gave instructions to James Pope to "buy for us 15 or 20 young Lusty Negers of about 15 yeares of age."[115] Upping the ante, the company then ordered him to "buy as many good lusty negers as shee can well cary."[116] Furthermore, Captain Samuel Kemptone loaded his ship with supplies to purchase "300 Lusty and Sound Negroes."[117] Such traders envisioned a system that would extract energy from "lusty" people, deemed to be at their optimal working age and of the highest commercial value.

Using instructions from ship owners or trading companies, Atlantic slave-trading captains needed to keep only vague records of the age of enslaved Africans. And looking forward to New World slave markets, captains saw no need to keep precise records about individuals, whose purpose as commodities and short life expectancies made specific knowledge about their age or other individual identifiers irrelevant to prospective buyers. From the perspective of human traffickers, the most important reason to account for the "age" of enslaved Africans was their purchase price, potential sales price, and productive potential. To agents in the Atlantic trade, age established eligibility thresholds for purchase and signified commercial value, which operated in relation to trade goods or constituted the *pieza*. In this context, the bodies of Africans moved around that Atlantic basin as commodities and currencies whose values were pegged to their place in their life cycles.

Macrons

While some merchants specifically indicated their search for the ideal, "lusty" slave, the trade could fail to live up to those demands. Periodically, traders complained that some slaves were too young, too old, or not quite lusty enough for the market. William Hardringe and Nicholas Prideaux of the Royal African Company recognized that one cargo of African captives from West Africa's Gold and Slave Coast "were very Young, but wanting victualls, were Reduced to Greate Poverty."[118] Having sailed from Whydah and the Gold Coast to Martinique, Edwyn Stede and Stephen Gascoigne complained to the Royal African Company about one shipment of slaves that "abt 1/3d part of those he did bring were very small most of them noe better then sucking Children," deemed to fetch low prices in the slave market.[119] Similarly, two agents of the company bemoaned that many of their slaves were "Leane and Sickly" and that 1/3 of the slaves aboard the ship sailed from Angola by Captain Nurse were boys and girls.[120] Captains carried young children to the Americas despite contractual restrictions, leading to grumbling when they landed in the Americas. Writing from Nevis, Henry Carpenter and Robert Helms informed the Royal African Company that forty children younger than 8 years old arrived on the ship *George and Betty* despite what was in the ship captain's charter.[121] While traders targeted "lusty" slaves, the reality of the trade proved to be more complicated.

With a preference in the New World market for young people, captains had a general disdain for the old. Traders, as we have seen above, labeled old slaves as *macrons*. One Dutch agent stated, "These are such as are above five and thirty years old, or are maimed in the arms, legs, hands, or feet, have lost a tooth, are grey-haired or have films over their eyes."[122] Some *macrons* arrived in the Americas on board slave ships. For example, some "weake, old, and very sickly" captives from Ardra on the Slave Coast landed in Barbados aboard the ship *Arthur* in the 1670s.[123] The presence of aged slaves forced negotiations over prices. In the mid-seventeenth century, Pedro Diez Truxxilla trafficked sixty-two slaves, but for accounting purposes the number was recorded at sixty "on account of the old and young which are among said negroes."[124] Another Dutch colonial figure priced slaves between ages 8 and 30 at two hundred reals, but disclosed that "old and deformed ones, must be disposed of at a special and lower price."[125] Among the captives sold in Montserrat and St. Christopher's were "an old Man and old Woman of little worth and another old Woman which was much bruised and dyed there."[126]

Ultimately, slave traders devalued *macrons* because of their projected productive capacity. On one ship, the old landed in such bad condition that they couldn't climb over the side of the ship on their own power. What concerned slave-trading agents, ultimately, was whether the Royal African Company should bear the cost for those "not of the right Age" or if the captain should take financial responsibility for purchasing old slaves.[127] In these ways, captains, merchants, and planters figured the ages of slaves in their commercial strategies and negotiations, which translated into their ideas of personhood.

In the seventeenth century, Captain Gallop manned the ship *Thomas and Francis*, which carried on board "29 Negroes and halfe or 30 Negroes."[128] From the point of purchase, through the Atlantic crossing, to the point of sale, the traffic in Africans placed a premium on people of the right age.

In the world of Atlantic commerce, Western merchants and planters came to the markets looking to buy young black bodies. The immediate capacity and future potential of young people drove enterprising Caribbean planters to the slave market. Their desire for sugar, indigo, and other commodities depended on it. At the same time, they wanted and gained the right to possess these young people and the fruits of their labor forever. The sugar plantation world of the Caribbean maintained this relatively young demographic shape over a stretch of time. Planters bought young people in the slave market, worked them to early deaths on highly profitable sugar plantations, and used the profits to invest in more young people. But a different story unfolded in North America.

The Prime

As planters in North America tapped into this market, their system of labor mobilization took a different form over time. Its slave population reproduced and grew older. But at the outset of colonial settlements or the establishment of new estates, it was primarily young people that prospectors or planters pursued. As in other parts of the Atlantic World, North American colonial elites specified their desire for young people. Working on behalf of Director General Peter Stuyvesant of the Dutch WIC, Vice Director Matthias Beck selected "negroes for your honor, two boys and a girl" for shipment from Curaçao to New Netherlands. Beck also notified the company that he would "be sending a young negro girl for Mr. Augustinus Heermans according to his request."[129] In addition, the Virginian William Byrd craved young people, and he used his connections in the broader Atlantic market to fulfill his desire. In 1685, Byrd worked with his agent to acquire on account "4 Negro's, 2 Men 2 Women not to exceed 25 years Old & to bee likeley."[130] A year and a half later, he reported that they "proved well," but was disappointed that "two of them had contracted small pox."[131]And the British naturalist Mark Catesby spelled out his desire for a young person to support his scientific work. Suffering from heat, fatigue, and illness during his research on the natural environment of South Carolina, he planned "to buy a Negro Boy which I cannot be without."[132]

South Carolina's Henry Laurens played a more prominent role in the traffic in young captives. For example, they figured into his calculations of the rice economy's balance of trade. Laurens informed Peter Woodhouse in a 1755 letter that the market was saturated with a range of goods and that "The only Article can be brought here to any Advantage are very prime young Negro Men from the Gold or Windward Coast or Gambia."[133] The plan was to buy young people to grow rice and in turn buy more young people. His correspondence closely mirrored the writings of slave-ship captains, with the terms "likely," "prime," and "young" suffusing his letters, and he tended toward young, male bodies. Laurens wrote to Thomas Hinde about market conditions in South Carolina that "some prime Men sold as high as £330 per head."[134] He later informed Robert and John Thompson that over the course of three months the price fetched for "prime Men" had fallen to £240.[135] He reported how some Carolina planters were willing to pay "very extraordinary prices" for them. He also indicated that the market demanded the highest price for "fine men."[136] Using this very broad brush to paint a picture of the slave traffic, he often portrayed the "prime fine man" as the ideal slave.

Laurens refined this picture by defining other features of and by excluding some people from the category of "prime." He and other South Carolina elites preferred captives from certain regions of Africa. He advertised in the *South Carolina Gazette* in 1756 the sale of a "cargo of prime ANGOLA Men and Women SLAVES, Chiefly young People and healthy."[137] Laurens wrote the merchant Richard Oswald that "very prime Gambia Men" had the highest commercial value of all enslaved people in the market.[138] And he informed another set of merchants about the sale of a "Cargo of Gambias" who were "grown People & most of them prime slaves."[139]

For Laurens and other colonial masters in the market, youthful bodies brought along beauty and health. Facing competition in the South Carolina market, he lamented after a major sale of "a most butifull Cargo of the Sort chiefly young People from 15 to 20" that the market had a dearth of desirable slaves.[140] The market, he wrote in another letter, preferred "young robust People.[141] With this work being done on the front end of the market, buyers could pick up the *South Carolina Gazette* and read advertisements that Laurens placed for "Likely young GAMBIA NEGROES" or "Likely Healthy Young NEGROES."[142]

Colonial officials like Laurens factored age into a wider set of variables they used to calculate the costs and desirability of the enslaved. They considered ethnicity, gender, "health," "robustness," or "likeliness" along with age to

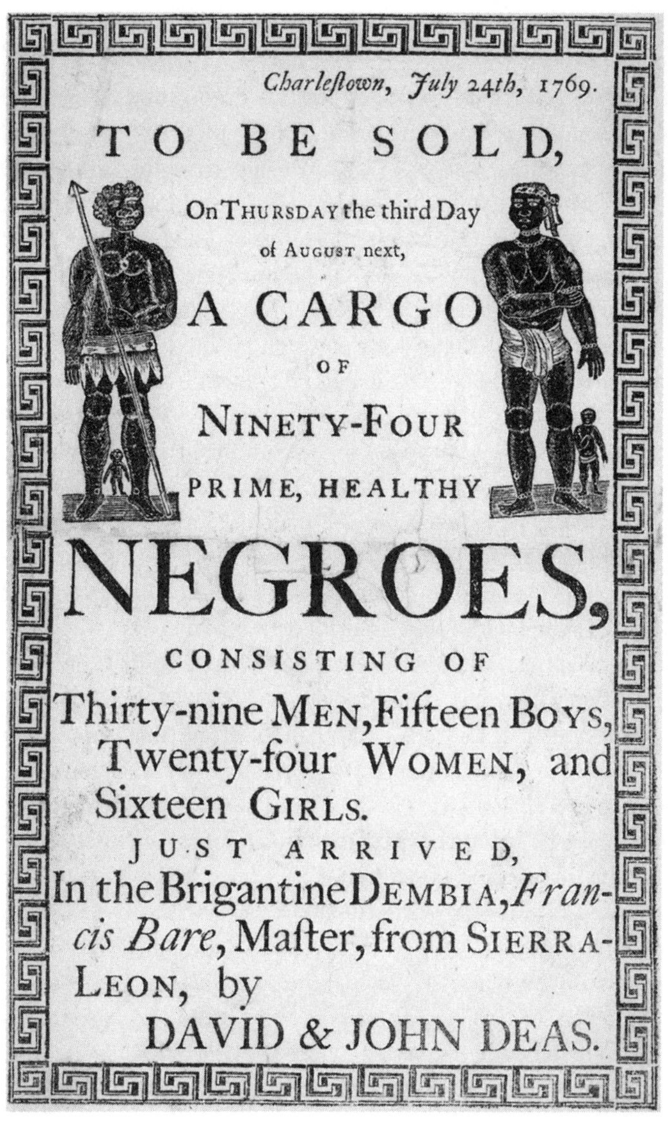

Figure 2. South Carolina Slave Advertisement, 1769, David & John Deas (Firm), "Charlestown, July 24th, 1769. To be sold, on Thursday the third day of August next, a cargo of ninety-four prime, healthy Negroes . . . Just arrived, in the brigantine Dembia, Francis Bare, master, from Sierra-Leone, by David & John Deas," 1769. Courtesy of the American Antiquarian Society. https://catalog.mwa.org/vwebv/holdingsInfo?bibId=317021.

set market prices. While they preferred young people, they concluded that not all young people were alike. They set different "prime" age ranges, which varied based on gender, ethnic identification, timing, and other factors. For instance, Laurens informed James Smith that selling a "Parcell of Callabar Boys & Girls from the Age of 13 to 18" would yield the most profit.[143] He refined his position the following year in a letter to John and William Halliday, which warned them that colonial planters avoided enslaved people from Calabar older than 16 or 17.[144] Around the same time, he set a different range for captives from Gambia and along gender lines. Like traffickers on the West African Coast, he wrote that the market sought "males from 14 to 20 or 25" and "females from 14 to 20 if Possible none of them have fallen breasts."[145]

In the eyes of merchants and planters, young objects of their desire stood in stark contrast to those whose old age diminished their value. Laurens wrote Richard Oswald about a group of twenty newly arrived captives that included some who were "very Grey." He added that five of them were "very near their end," so he advised against sending them to auction.[146] Such was the problem of old age that merchants saw it as a disease. Laurens wrote that one group of slaves could not be sold at auction because they had "the worst infirmity of all others," that being "old Age."[147] As a result, some old slaves stayed in the market for a much longer period than their younger counterparts.[148] In one case, Laurens had buyer's remorse that among one set of human cargo there were "two or three of them so old that they won't bring with us much more than their Passages," and in such instances, he sent them to auction where he couldn't expect them to go for much.[149] He also pointed, in at least one instance, to prospects of resistance as a reason to avoid buying older slaves. Laurens reported that the ship *Africa* had disembarked a cargo of young captives between the ages of 15 and 20, which sold quickly, not only because there was little competition in the market. He also pointed to the preference for this age group over older people because they "are not accustom'd to destroy themselves like those who are older."[150] With the goal of putting labor directly into indigo and rice production, South Carolina slave traders saw the aged as having limited or no value to the plantation economy.

These beliefs about age played out on North American forced labor camps. Entering the slave market, lowcountry colonial planter Peter Manigault looked to purchase "men," "women," "boys," and "girls." While he and his agents often used these unspecific age categories, they in some cases drew age distinctions. As part of their business model, they looked for recent African arrivals, "New Negroes" who came across the saltwater of the Atlantic to develop their plantations. Out of one cargo of African captives, his estate bought "25 Men 15 Women & 15 Boys."[151] In another instance, Manigault wrote that he had purchased "12 Men 12 Women 11 boys, & 8 Girls New Negroes."[152] In other cases, he was less specific in his descriptions, using the term "able Hands" or "fine Slaves.[153] Yet even with this imprecise terminology, his correspondence indicates that he accounted for age.

Though planters held ideal types of slaves in mind, the reality of managing labor conflicted with these ideas. Manigault informed his manager Ralph Izard that he wanted to use his slaves to open a new set of fields at the Camp plantation, and he cautioned that "it will be very hard upon old Negroes to be moved such a Distance from all their Friends."[154] For his Santee River property, he saw the advantage of combining a labor force of a "few seasoned Negros," plus a set of enslaved people "bought of Matthews," and "20 New Negroes" that he sought to buy.[155] In addition, he complained about one estate that put up forty-five enslaved people for sale but only two were most desirable. He added that among the rest were "about 24 Working Hands, the Rest are old & young." Using age as a proxy for the working capacity of the enslaved, he drew a distinction between "Negroes that cant work" and "Working Hands"[156] He also criticized the price fetched by the planter Dutarque, who got high sums for slaves deemed "by no means an extraordinary Parcel, one half of them being either too old, or too young to work."[157] Manigault's correspondence shows how planters used age to appraise their own and each other's property in people. For them, age was significant because it roughly translated into economic potential.

The day-to-day management of colonial North American plantations meant accounting for productivity in the present and taking stock of their human assets, which led planters to track the number of young and old slaves. For example, the Virginian Edmund Jordan, born in 1707, began to accumulate young labor before he turned 30. Between 1736 and 1755, he gained the possession of eight newborn enslaved people. His son Robert, born in 1731, started even younger, possessing nine newborns between 1751 and 1777.[158] And as they accumulated and accounted for their property in people, planters lumped them into broad categories of young and old, "whole," "half," and "third" shares. One colonial planter noted that he owned "8 shares," with the adults "Matt, Isaac, Breechy, Easter, Kate, And Beck & Zady" probably accounting for full "shares" and the children "John and Gabriel Boys, Lucy a Girl" amounting to one-third "shares." In addition, he "hired old Negro Jean and added to the above gang as a half Sharer, which makes up the who 8 1/2 shares."[159] The accounting of age that shaped the contours of the Atlantic slave trade—with the very young and old counted as less than a whole person—continued into the colonial North American context.

Encoding these economic strategies, colonial legislatures enacted laws on race and age to establish the boundaries of slavery and freedom in colonial Virginia. While the Chesapeake colonies defined slavery as a chattel, racialized, heritable, and lifelong condition, they continually updated their codes because of the presence and potential growth of a free black population. In Virginia's reaction to the interracial Bacon's rebellion of 1676, the colony enacted laws regulating free blacks in 1791 that made black skin a barrier to freedom, and they also made old age one as well. They specifically sought to prevent former slaves from becoming dependent on the state or "chargeable." The law claimed that "great inconveniences may happen to this country by the setting of negroes and mulattoes free . . . or being grown old bringing a charge upon the country." Consequently, they required slaveholders to pay for the removal of free blacks from the colony within six months of their emancipation, avoiding the potential costs of support for the black aged.[160] Pennsylvanians had similar concerns and required colonial slaveowners to give provisions to former slaves after emancipation, fearing that they might "be driven by necessity to wicked actions, or . . . may fall a charge to anybody."[161] For planters like Robert Carter, the code influenced his approach to labor management. He wrote about his slaves to his London agent, "Nine of the negroes . . . are so much past their labor that they are a rather a charge than anything else. Their levy and clothes come to more than they make."[162] Without recourse for support from the colonial government, Carter saw his aged slaves as charges and economic liabilities.

Concerns about the age of slaves shaped other aspects of colonial law. When assemblies mandated that slaveowners provide a count of their slave labor force, they set age limits on who should be counted. For example, New Jersey's system of counting slaves hinged on age. In 1712–1713, as part of the law on punishing slaves for capital offenses, the colony required constables to collect and deliver to the county courts a list of all "negro, Indian, and mulatto slaves" each May and June. The lists had to include all slaves between the ages of 15 and 49 except for those who were "disabled or incapable of performing their master or mistress' service." The colony, seeing slaves as potential subjects of capital punishment, accounted for the living in case a slave was executed by the state; this, they reasoned, would prevent owners from removing alleged offenders from the colony. Under the law, an executed slave could be valued up to £20 for a woman and up to £30 for a man, the value being determined by the assessed value of comparable slaves in the state. The system of punishment—of execution and compensation—exposed the value that colonial elites placed on the prime slave.[163] Through such means, colonial legislatures encoded race, gender, and age simultaneously into their slave laws.

Signs

Colonial planters wanted permanent control over young black labor, but the experience of slaves who lived beyond their "prime" years defied those expectations. Enslaved Africans came from worlds that honored long life, elders, and ancestors. In the Atlantic slave trade, merchants hid gray hairs of aged captives to boost their market value. But in the colonies, the reality and signs of old age would reappear. Despite the harshness of forced labor camps that cut lives short, slaves in colonial North America fought to survive into old age. Runaway slave advertisements reflected their presence and reveal a wider struggle over the black aged in colonial North America.

Fugitive slave advertisements marked individuals by identifying their origins, occupations, color, name, dress, family relationships, gender, and other traits including references to age. Planters identified elder runaways by pointing to signs of old age that fell within several broad categories; they recognized aged slaves through their numbers of years, characteristics like gray hairs, embodied physical traumas, and scars from work, disease, or punishment. However, not all indications were clearly visible. Planters also pointed to inner traits of "sensible" old slaves. In addition, they identified slaves through family histories, migration pathways, and social relationships. Being old, from this vantage point, was not simply a physical attribute but also had social and personality dimensions, qualities planters used to surveil and lord over their property. Inspecting them from head to toe, in their histories, and in their connections, planters identified aged runaways through a complex set of signs.

In a world where most slaves were young, older slaves stood out and could be identified by something as quotidian as their hair. Quamony, probably from the West African Gold Coast and enslaved in Richmond, Virginia, could be spotted because "his head and beard [were] almost white."[164] Pompey, from Angola, had "hair very grey and his face wrinkled."[165] Charles of Virginia, "about 50 years of age," was "a little grey."[166] And Spencer of Virginia had a beard that had turned white.[167] In the day-to-day world of North

American colonial forced labor camps, men like Quamony, Charles, Pompey, and Spencer had gray or graying hair, embodying features of the aging process and making them identifiable upon escape.

In the slave markets of the Atlantic, traders inspected the teeth of captives to estimate the age of enslaved Africans and to look for evidence of decay. After years of work on slave labor camps, some would show that sign of growing old. The 45-year-old Caesar of Maryland was "well made, [would] hold his head very high," and he also "lost some of his fore teeth."[168] Joe from Maryland, of about the same age, had "lost some his upper fore teeth."[169] The 50-year-old carpenter and cooper Curry Tuxent had "lost most of his upper fore teeth."[170] Planters thus distinguished between the old and the young, "robust," and "likely," whose vitality and laboring potential could be known in part through the state of their teeth.

In the context of the forced labor system geared toward maximum extraction of work to produce commodities for export, the bodies of enslaved Africans churned like a machine. Consequently, they carried wear and tear as they aged, dealing with aching joints and limbs. Some carried scars from disease. Sambo of Ashepoo, South Carolina, an "elderly Fellow," had deep scars from smallpox.[171] So did the 47-year-old Jacob who ran away from his owner in Dorchester County, Maryland.[172] And the "sensible old Negro" Hector of South Carolina could be identified by pox marks.[173] The aged carried other kinds of marks from birth, work, injury, or conflict. The "stout elderly Angola fellow" Dick had a "scar a little above the wrist of his left arm."[174] And Buck, though "stout made" also walked "with his right foot much pointed out."[175] Over the course of the life cycle, the enslaved picked up and carried around these wounds, making them identifiable by colonial authorities.

The signs of old age extended into their joints and effected their gait, which led slave catchers to identify some as "lame." The 40-year-old "knock-kneed" Peter suffered from rheumatism, "which appears by lumps and knots upon his Hands and Wrists.[176] The Georgia fugitive Chloe was "lame in her right hand."[177] Others walked "lame." Fifty-year old Ben, though "a lusty well made fellow," had suffered a broken leg, causing it to be shorter than the other and for "him to halt very much in his walk."[178] Observers noted that Jim had a foot injury that made him "walk lame," that the "lusty" 58-year-old Sampson "goes very lame," and that Cupid, though "lame," still fled from a South Carolina plantation on Wando Neck.[179] Ned of Virginia and John of Georgia also ran away, even though they "stooped" when they walked.[180] Even with frames that had been bent by the weight of their experience and had been considered "lame," aged slaves made their way out of the boundaries of colonial slavery in North America. They carried around less visible markers as well. The aged Quash was "blind in one eye," and so was a 50-year-old who was considered to be "an old man" and had also "lost the great toe of his right foot."[181] The gray-haired Jenny had "lost the sight of her right eye."[182] And the 46-year-old Pompey was described as "dull of hearing."[183] When and how slaves made their escape without eyesight, body parts, or hearing is unclear in the advertisements.

When they ran away, the aged were identified not only by their bodies; advertisements also revealed the relationships they developed over the course of the life cycle. For instance, some of the aged ran away in search of kin. After the "tall, black, elderly" Cain of Virginia was separated from his wife who belonged to a different owner, he possibly fled to her in North Carolina.[184] When Gabriel ran away, he probably went in search of his free black wife Betty Baines.[185] Carolina ran to reunite with his wife Kate, and Bob sought out his wife. Mary went out in search of her three sons London, Bob, and Bristol.[186] In other instances, aged slaves ran away with their kin. Sue ran off with her daughter, Sam absconded with his 20-year-old son George and three others, and Crita took flight with her daughter Hannah and an 11-year-old boy, Harry.[187] And in at least one instance, multiple generations made an escape together. Old Rose, an Ebo, escaped with her country-born husband Cato; her children Celia, Dick, and Sue; her 6-year-old granddaughter Elsey, and Kate from Angola, Sciopio, Town Sue, and Will.[188] Over the course of the life cycle, their personal connections became more complex, shaping their movements, strategies, and objectives, with family ties being the end or means of escape.

Those aged slaves had gone through multiple phases—coming of age, bearing children, marrying. Yet the slave market and planter mobility threatened those internal, community-based experiences and markers of time. Each sale or movement of a plantation brought a social rupture and temporal marker, placing on the enslaved a new label that planters used in their system of control. For example, after their sale, Quaco, Fortune, and Maria fled from their new owners, who used their knowledge of their past owners to try to track them down.[189] Luce experienced even more disruptions. "An elderly Negro Woman," Luce had passed into William Brown's ownership from Richard Mason and Robert Young, and before him she "had many other masters."[190] Her separation replayed the experience of generations who had preceded her in the Atlantic crossing. The gray hair or stooped bodies of aged slaves meant they had become ever more likely to have experienced or witnessed the trouble of enslavement at its core.

Being an African captive or descendant on a colonial North American slave labor camp had multiple meanings. Being removed from the land in Africa also meant removal from ties to kin and elders. The enslaved drew upon their ancestral memory, survival skills, and sheer will to reconstitute intergenerational ties in the colonial era. After they established a modicum of family stability by the late eighteenth century, the disruptive forces of the cotton revolution and the domestic slave trade placed new demands on black labor, dealing yet another blow to black intergenerational relationships.

CHAPTER 2

Management, Labor, and Life Cycles

In old age, Isaac Jefferson spoke a lot about work. When his story was recorded in the middle of the nineteenth century, Jefferson was enslaved on the late Thomas Jefferson's Monticello estate. His mother, he recounted, was a pastry cook, washerwoman, and children's nurse. She trained the young Isaac in the world of work, sending him out for wood that he toted back to her for her laundry fire, and he eventually became a blacksmith. About 70 years old when his story was recorded in 1847, the aged Isaac Jefferson started out his personal narrative by centering it in work.[1] Jefferson clearly understood that work, property, and production stood at the heart of the slaveholding enterprise, and he reminded his audience of the role he and other slaves played in the Southern economy. Colonial and antebellum slaveholders were driven by property values and productivity, using quantitative and qualitative measures and an overwhelming use or threat of violence to organize black labor. And through their economic lens, they saw people as abstractions. For example, the slave traders Betts and Gregory in Richmond, Virginia, understood black people as numbers by pricing "Extra Men" at $1,600 in the slave market, "No. 1" men at $1,550, and "Second Rate or Ordinary" men at $1,500, while "Extra Girls" went for $1,450, "No. 1" girls were marked at $1,400, "Second Rate or Ordinary" girls went for $1,350, and "boys 4 feet high" were priced at $1,300.[2] Similarly, the Virginia planter Charles Friend focused on the general laboring capacity of the enslaved and thought of them in abstract terms. While his list of sick slaves includes individuals by name, Friend's work log also speaks of the enslaved as merely "hands." He records "making Tobacco Hill with all hands save 4 plough men," and he jotted down "all hands setting tobacco."[3] As Isaac Jefferson and other slaves clearly understood, their day-to-day lives and life cycles were bound by such ideologies and plantation management strategies.

In their profit seeking, planters sought out the ideal, young laboring black body. Yet, over time and in different contexts, the idea of the "prime" slave bumped up against the aging process. And while the bodies of the enslaved aged and changed over time, those changes did not come about naturally. Rather, the forced labor system changed black bodies in particular ways. Slaves died young, got injured, battled chronic disease, or lived beyond their "prime" years. Yet the search for the prime slave continued through the antebellum period.[4] It shaped plantation management schemes, the domestic slave trade, and the demography of slave plantations. Even with the idea of the young slave in mind, slaveholders did not give up on extracting labor from the old, who continued to add incrementally smaller yet significant inputs to the plantation economy. At the same time, if they survived, slaves carried the remnants of each illness, each work injury, each period of deprivation on their life's journey. As planters and merchants accumulated wealth from slave labor, the enslaved accumulated wounds in their bodies. Seeing the slave population grow old, slaveholders tried to adapt, creating a management system that sought to maximize labor output from the enslaved regardless of their age. Building on the previous chapter, this chapter examines aging and the life cycle of slaves in the antebellum South. It analyzes the nexus between slave labor and the life cycle and examines how the aged operated in the larger system of forced labor in the antebellum period. In the day-to-day operations of antebellum plantations, age constituted a key organizing principle.

"About"

Though the caption to Mary Brice's photo describes her as middle aged, a closer examination raises questions about that description. The hint of gray hair at her temples, the lines on her forehead, and the shadows under her eyes suggest otherwise. Her portrait indicates the methodological challenges posed by plantation recordkeeping and the archive in the analysis of age in the black experience. The planter class, depending as they did on slave labor, left behind voluminous records about their human property, listing them for tax purposes and accounting for the wealth they planned to maintain and pass on to their heirs. However, as extensive as the records are, slave lists offer just a snapshot of a few moments in time. As plantation census records, they often lacked precision, were inconsistent, were based on guesswork, or clearly distorted the age of the enslaved, an issue that was particularly so for the aged.

Figure 3. "Mary Brice (or Bryce) of Point of Honor, Lynchburg, Virginia, half-length portrait, seated, of middle-aged African American enslaved woman," c. 1853. Courtesy of the Library of Congress.

When it came to keeping account of slave elders, slaveholders and plantation overseers often recorded their ages with amorphous terminology, regularly using the shorthand of "old" to document their age. Virginia's Bolling Haxall kept records from 1856 into the Civil War of his slave population; some he sold off, at least one ran away to the Union Army, and another grew old. Among the slaves that Haxall listed was "old Bob," who lived his last years on the estate, likely dying before the war ended.[5] The 1850 and 1858 slave lists of the Manigault estate in Georgia did not identify the age of slaves, except for two children and Fortune, Abraham, Hannah, Daniel, Mariah, and Clery, who were marked as "old."[6] Virginia's Binns family estate listed Amy Amonds as "the old cook" next to her valuation.[7] The Scott family in Virginia kept records of the "ages of Negroes" in their account book, listing the year and in many cases day of birth of most of the slaves on their plantation. However, they listed Lizzie without a birth year but rather as a "very old woman" who died in January 1859.[8]

The numerical pattern of slave ages, even on a single estate's records, raises questions about their degree of accuracy. On an 1860 inventory of James Scott's slave population, all the people older than 33 had ages listed as a factor of five—Patsy, 40; Edmund, 45; David, 50; Caesar, 55; Humphrey, 60, Jacob, 65, Booker, 70; and Sylvas, 100, while the younger population had much more variability.[9] The Gooch family of Virginia, used a combination of exactness and guesswork in recording the names and ages of their slaves. They wrote that the 12-year-olds Emanuel and Solomon were born in January and on Easter of 1827, respectively. The 10-year-old Horace was born in January 1829, and the infant George was born on March 7, 1839, the month of the census. In contrast, that census listed Turner as being "about 32," Sarah as "about 39," and "Old Eve_guess - 74." An undated census taken years before guessed that Old Eve was "about 62," and stated more definitively that Sarah was 30 and Turner was 25.[10]

Perhaps the information on the 1839 census was a simple error. But perhaps the estate had an interest in distorting the ages of Sarah and Turner, making them appear younger than they were while not concerning themselves with Old Eve because they did not have as much of an interest in her labor and market value and no need to manipulate her age. Maybe they perceived Old Eve as older than she was in 1839 because of the toll that forced labor had upon her. Perhaps Old Eve gave an older age in 1839 to gain respect. In any event, in the records, she "aged" faster than the younger Sarah and Turner.

The uncertainty about age applied to free blacks as well. When Southampton County enforced the code to register its free black population, their ages often came in as estimates. The free black woman Zeller Jones was "about 34 years old," Nat Whitehead was "abt 48 years old," Judith Whitehead was "about 60 years old," and William Blow was "abt 63 years old."[11] Even with these systems of record keeping and surveillance, some information about exact ages of African Americans slipped through the cracks.

Documenting different phases of the slave life cycle, plantation records accounted for slave births, seeing with each newborn the potential for more labor, profit, and wealth but also leaving behind eerie accounts of infant mortality. For example, the Bolling estate's detailed "Register of the births of Slaves" gives the exact date and place of birth of slave children on their Virginia plantation, as when Aggy gave birth to her third child, Isaac, on March 14, 1832; he died in October of that year. [12] Other plantations recorded the birth of children who did not make it through infancy. For example, Ann on Virginia's Dickinson plantation lost her 2-week-old child Annie, and Martha's 7-month-old passed away.[13] On the Richard Eppes estate in Virginia, Sally Lewis's pregnancy did not make it to term. Eppes wrote in his diary that she became prostrate, suffering pain in her womb and hemorrhaging blood before having a miscarriage.[14] In making note of slave births and pregnancies, the records also demonstrate how the life cycle of slave women was marked by mourning.[15]

The knowledge that planters had about the age of black people had its counterpart in the knowledge practices of the enslaved, even as both ascribed different symbolic meaning to age. For example, one former slave recounted in a 1949 interview, "My name is Fountain Hughes. I was born in Charlottesville, Virginia. My grandfather belonged to Thomas Jefferson. My grandfather was 115 years old when he died. And now I am 101-year[s]-old." By pronouncing his old age from the beginning, he signified its value—both he and his grandfather were claimed to be centenarians, defying the brutal conditions of slavery that he described in other parts of the interview. On the other hand, Frederick Douglass, mirroring the written records described above, opens his *Narrative* with a disclaimer that he did not know the exact year of his birth because of the oppressive nature of the plantation order. He wrote, "I have no accurate knowledge of my age, never having seen any authentic record containing it. . . . The white children could tell their ages. I could not tell why I ought to be deprived of the same privilege. I was not allowed to make any inquiries of my master concerning it. He deemed all such inquiries on the part of a slave improper and impertinent, and evidence of a restless spirit." Access to knowledge about age thus became a point of struggle between slaves and slaveholders, with slaveholders withholding information from slaves amounting to "age theft."[16]

As much as planters counted slaves for profit and to comply with the law, those motivations did not guarantee complete accuracy, so the records they left behind are imperfect accounts of slave ages. In some cases, owners and managers noted the exact date of slave births, viewing them as prospects for financial growth. But at other times, the records used generic labels like "old," rounded ages to a factor of five, or gave approximations by saying black people were "about" an estimated age. But as imperfect as the records are, they can be read in ways that reveal the logics of age and its economic value on Southern plantations.

Census

Planters became informal census takers, taking snapshots of slave populations and capturing their names and ages. As limited as they are, the records can yield insights into how plantations organized life along the lines of age. Slaveholders or their managers kept records of slave names and ages for the purpose of management, taxation, or transferring their human property upon death, marriage, or sale. And the records they left behind demonstrate the demographic shape of slave populations in specific locales. Given how commonplace the records about slave age were, age clearly figured into the economic strategies of the planter class as they sought to maximize property values and productivity. The demographic shape and relative economic value associated with the life cycle of the enslaved reveal several things about slavery as an economic system. They show the search for and value of the "prime" slave and the relative prices of other slaves against the price of those deemed "prime." Based on the chattel principle that every slave had a price, plantation owner by plantation owner did the calculating work of ascribing a financial age value to the enslaved.[17]

The price of the enslaved followed an arc depending on where they stood in the life course. For instance, in 1817, slave prices on Virginia's Pollard estate rose from $50 in infancy up to $400 for slaves in their twenties and thirties. And while the prices followed an overall pattern, they could vary substantially. Slaves in their twenties had a range of prices, from $100 to $400, a range that cannot be fully explained by the different value of men and women. By the time slaves reached the age of 40, the physical toll of forced labor, their future laboring prospects, and the expectations of the market meant to the planter class that older slaves had lived past their prime. Slaves who were 50 or older were valued at $50 or less, nearing the end of their property value to the Pollard family. Their records demonstrated planter perceptions and the varied paths of slave labor over the life cycle.[18]

The market value of cohorts of slaves did not move uniformly over their life course, but generally, age and property value bore a strong relationship when looking across plantations. On the 1837 Ambler plantation, the value of the enslaved began at $75 for 2-year-old Davy, peaked at $950 for the 25-year-old Brice, and dropped to $125 for the 60-year-old Venus.[19] On the Burwell estate, the value of slaves peaked at 20 years old, and from that point forward, their price went on a steady decline until the age of 50, when they returned to the price they had shortly after birth.[20] The prices indicate planter optimism about the laboring prospects and capacity of slaves during their

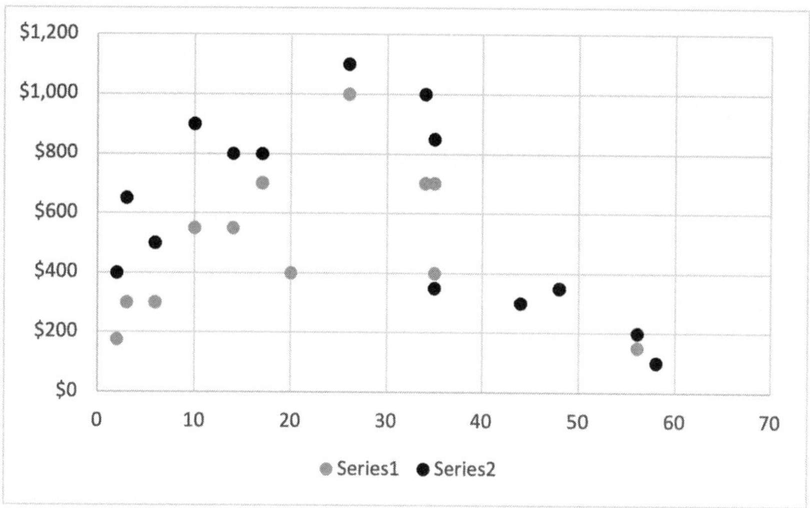

Graph 1. Slave Values, Dickinson Family Estate, 1855 (Gray) and 1859 (Black)
Source: Inventory of Negro Slaves upon Berry Plains, Plantation Account Book, Dickinson Family Papers, Virginia Historical Society.

younger years. The prices of slaves went up relatively in sync with each other until they hit their "prime." Even on the eve of the Civil War, planters maintained this hopefulness, such as on the Dickinson family estate where the value of their slaves followed a similar arc in both 1855 and 1859.[21] However, fissures became much more apparent after the age of 20, and the values of the enslaved became more varied. On the Branch family estate, as on the Pollard, Dickinson, Ambler, and Burwell plantations, the estimated financial value of slaves of the same age varied considerably after they reached the age of 20.[22] Planters thus turned their perceptions of difference in gender, skill, and physical ability into numerical values on their slave lists.

The underlying logic that tied age to price was a calculation of what slaves could get in the market and a projection about their future labor productivity. Some made the connection between age and productivity explicitly numerical. The Corbin and Dampierre rice estates listed the names, ages, and "rates" or "field rates" of each slave on their plantations.[23] As with price, the rate of labor expected of slaves varied according to age, with the rate increasing until the age of 20 and then leveling or falling off from that point. Yet, in comparison to the shape of slave prices, the labor rate—the amount of labor power and productivity planters expected from the enslaved in the present—was represented

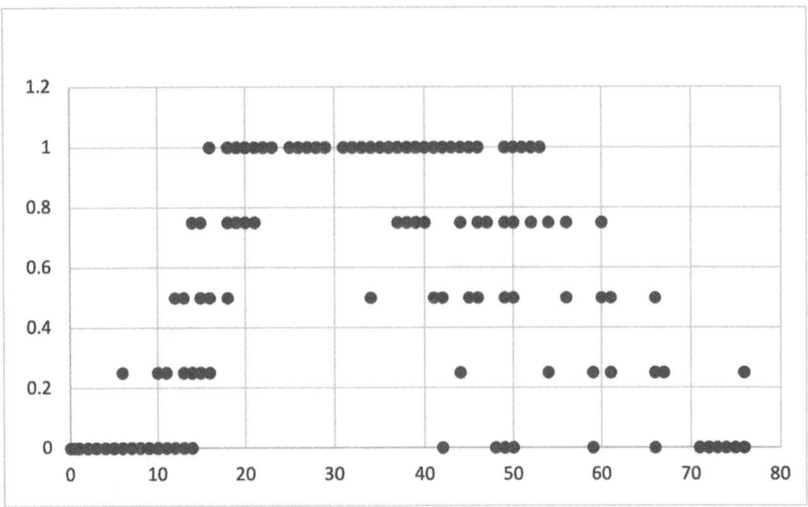

Graph 2. Corbin Estate Labor Rate, 1861
Source: Hopeton Plantation Slave List, March 22, 1861, Francis Porteus Corbin Papers, 1662–1885, David M. Rubenstein Rare Book & Manuscript Library, Duke University.

more as a plateau than as a humped curve. This tells the story that an enslaved person, even though they might not be worth as much in the market, could still have the same labor demands as those in their late teens and twenties. Daily in 1859, 1860, and 1861, they would be expected to work the soil, harvest the crops, and do all manner of other taxing physical labor as they grew old.

As was the case in the colonial era, the quest for young labor did not automatically translate into reality. For planters' bottom line, they preferred a captive labor force between the ages of 16 and 40, but the experience on their plantations did not match that ideal. The age demographic trends varied over time on specific estates as well as from one forced labor camp to the next. The Virginia Pollard estate possessed relatively few slaves in their twenties and thirties and had a large population of child labor—presumably for this plantation to function, they would have forced slaves in their teens into the fields.[24] That was also the case on the Branch family estate, where the bulk of slaves were 20 or younger.[25] Given the shape of these populations, very young people would most likely be pushed into work.

The demographic shape of plantations tells another story of the life cycle of slavery—childbirth and infant mortality rates. On the Toler and Burwell estates, there was a significant drop in the size of the age groups of slaves from ages birth to 5 to ages 6 to 10.[26] At least two forces can explain this difference: the birthrate on the plantations increased over time or infant and early childhood mortality rates became episodically high. In contrast to this demographic shape, some planters faced a relative dearth of labor in their twenties and thirties, possibly a function of the persistence of earlier patterns of infant mortality or birth rates. The impact of the domestic slave trade that targeted labor in this age group can also explain a dip in the slave population in their twenties and thirties on these Virginia plantations. In the case of the Eppes estate, they faced a labor shortage of slaves who were between the ages of 25 and 30. Similar patterns played out on the Ambler and Dupuy estates, where slaves in their twenties and thirties were outnumbered by younger or older age cohorts.[27] The Gooch estate of Virginia had relatively few older slaves, but still a substantial proportion of their slave population was 15 or younger, a pattern that persisted over time.[28] The life cycle of slaves in North America thus was anything but smooth.

Mortality rates, epidemics, changes in fertility, work hazards, and the slave trade created a jagged and treacherous life course, which was reflected in the demographic contours of specific plantations. The Tayloe family properties reflected such variability of cohort sizes with an age structure that resulted from the domestic slave trade. On their Mount Airy plantation in Virginia, there was a significant drop off from the 16-to-20 age range to the twenties. In comparison, their plantation on the Alabama frontier had more slaves in their twenties, a pattern that indicates the shift of "prime" slaves to the cotton frontier in what was becoming the black belt of Alabama.[29]

The slaveholding frontiers had a special interest in mobilizing young labor, as indicated in the early years of the Corbin estate in Georgia. In 1806, the Corbin estate recorded the first names and ages of its more than six hundred slaves. Over half of the population was bunched in the age range from 16 to 30, and the estate had a substantial population of enslaved people younger than 6. Likely, this plantation fed off young labor entering Georgia in the last years of the legal slave trade.[30] With the bulk of their labor force between the ages of 16 and 30, the Tayloe plantation in Alabama and the early years of the Corbin estate were primed for production.

But over time, these demographic structures transformed. In comparison to the 1806 figures, the percentage of the Corbin estate's slave population between 16 and 30 on the eve of the Civil War had been cut in half to 25 percent. In addition, about one-third of the population was younger than 16,

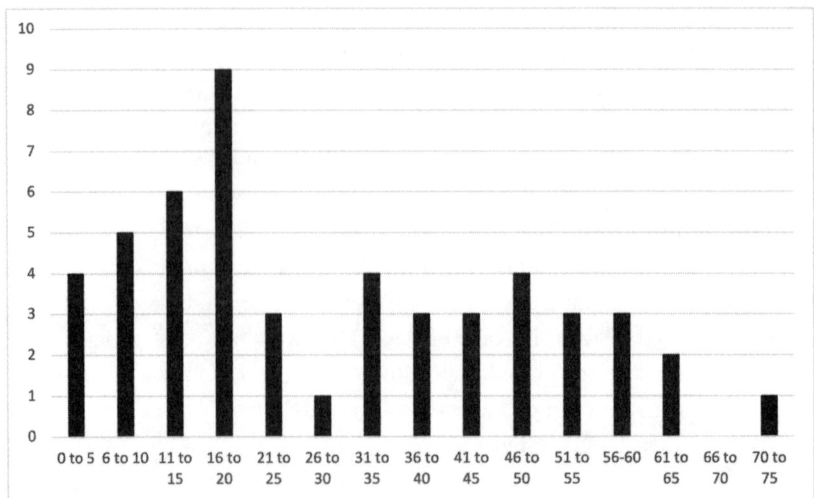

Graph 3. Tayloe Family Estate Account of Slave Ages at Mount Airy, 1838
Source: Mount Airy Estate Slave Inventory 1838, Tayloe Family Papers, Virginia Historical Society.

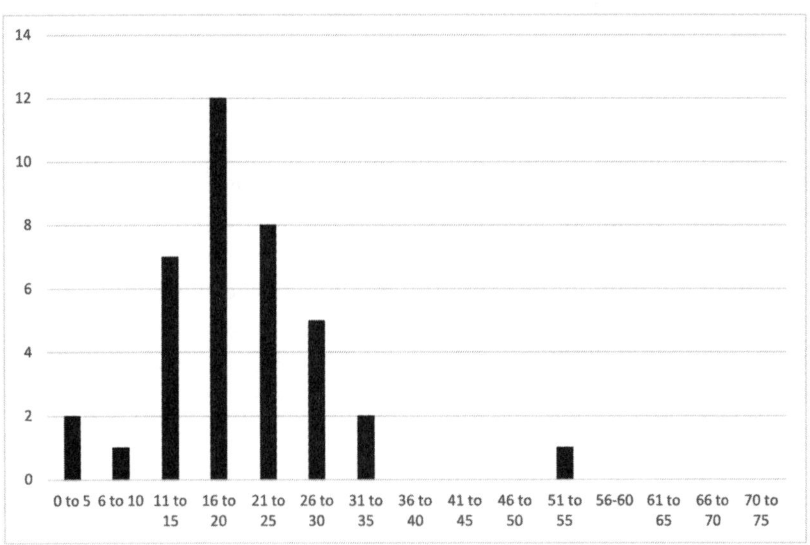

Graph 4. Tayloe Family Estate Alabama Slave List, 1835–37
Source: Account of Ages (1838), Alabama Estate Slave List, Inventories, Tayloe Family Papers, Virginia Historical Society.

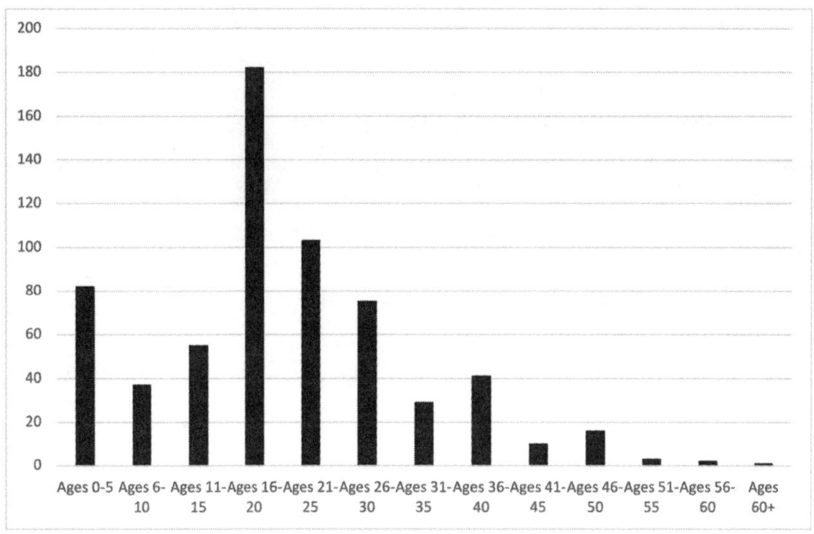

Graph 5. Corbin Estate Slave Census, 1806
Source: Account of Ages (1806), St. Simon Slave List, Francis Porteus Corbin Papers, David M. Rubenstein Rare Book & Manuscript Library, Duke University.

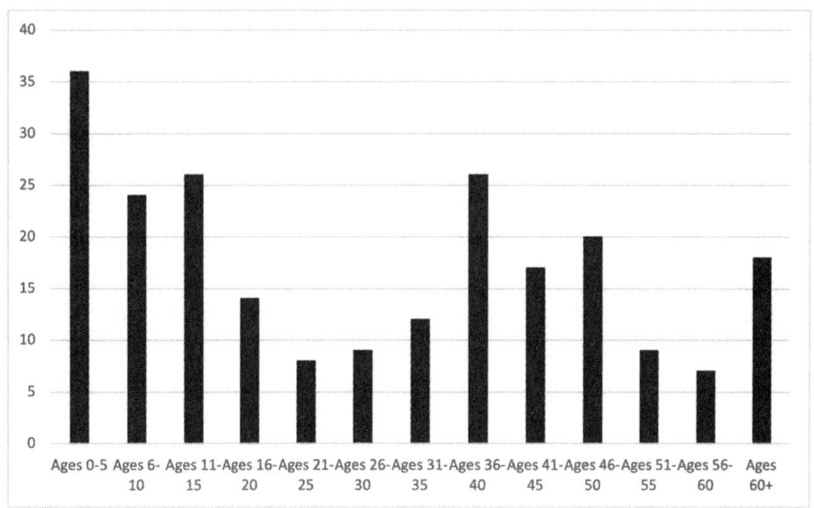

Graph 6. Corbin Estate Slave List, 1861
Source: Account of Ages (1861), Hopeton Plantation Slave List, March 22, 1861, Francis Porteus Corbin Papers, David M. Rubenstein Rare Book & Manuscript Library, Duke University.

and the percentage of the population older than 40 grew by four times to 20 percent; similar patterns can be seen on the Dampierre estate.[31]

Slaveholders built their fortunes on black labor and had a penchant for young people. If they had their druthers, they would maintain a labor force between 16 and 40, as indicated in their prices and the expected "rate" of production. But plantation records show substantial departures from that norm, as various age patterns emerged over time and across plantations. Despite the adverse conditions of forced labor, slaves would have children or live beyond the ideal years for agricultural labor. Simply, some slaves grew old. And while planters did not have the same expectations about what they could extract from the aged, they still worked and were accounted for by the planter class.

Liabilities

Aged slaves constituted a small fraction of the million black captives forced to move across state lines through the domestic slave trade after the War for Independence. As discussed above, plantation expansion was built off the work of young people, who cleared and cultivated the cotton frontier. They felled old trees, developed the land, and cultivated cash crops. Slaveholding frontiers separated older slaves from the young, and the latter had to rebuild their lives from their memories and the resources of the new environments they faced. But within this overall flow of young people into the frontier, some aged slaves got forced onto new plantations through the internal slave trade.[32]

Most planters did not expect to get much if any cash by selling the aged. In contrast to the more liquid asset of young people, the elderly did not generally command much in the market. Nor did they heavily figure into the wealth that planters bequeathed to their white progeny. Planter inventories reflected as much. The estate of the late General D. L. Clinch appraised the slaves that he passed down to his children at prices that ranged from $0 to $1,800, with an "Old Betsy" estimated at $50.[33] The Peter Evans estate listed "Old Abraham and wife Fanny" together at $0 on one inventory and on another as "Abraham 60 $150" and "Fanny 58 $50." As the Evans family passed along human property from one generation to the next, they clearly saw the aged as superfluous. In his deed of gift to his daughter and son-in-law, Evans gave them Loui and five of her offspring, using young slaves to cement his family bond and reinforce himself as the patriarch of the family.[34] The slaveholder Francis

Dickens put the opinion about the worth of their aged slaves more bluntly, writing that "Betty is the old woman" and "not worth one cop[p]er."[35]

While merchants and planters generally bought and sold young people in the slave market, it ensnared some old slaves in its commercial web. The head of the Thomas family of Augusta, Georgia, inherited their slaves but also entered the market to build its labor force, buying "an old woman by the name of Patience," who was "the first servant he has ever bought," for $100.[36] In other cases, planters bundled older slaves into larger packages for sale. James Smith offered to sell John Swann "an elderly wench, a good field hand and good plantation nurse & spinner," along with her 17-year-old daughter for $550 deliverable within a year. Smith also tried to discard a 26-year-old man and a woman, two girls aged 5 and 7, along with "an old fellow the father—a half hand" for $1100 cash.[37] They ended up closing the deal, with Smith using the aged male slave as an additional bargaining chip. Smith complained about his transaction with Swann that "tho the offer for the sale of ten Negroes is lower than their value I will accept the $900 for the four & will send the old fellow also."[38] The planter James Hamilton worked through his agent James Patterson to spend $2,450 for "twelve certain negroes," which included "Will an old Man, Nanny his Wife, and Will their Son."[39] And in Bibb County, Georgia, on the eve of the Civil War, the 65-year-old James and his wife Fanny got sold shortly after New Year's Day. Harriet Jacobs recalled a similar episode in coastal North Carolina, writing, "I knew an old woman, who for seventy years faithfully served her master. She had become almost helpless, from hard labor and disease. Her owners moved to Alabama, and the old black woman was left to be sold to any body who would give twenty dollars for her." Thus, Jacobs reflected, "New Year's day comes laden with peculiar sorrows."[40]

Other elders got pushed into the slave market. On the antebellum estate of Martha Wales, most of the seventy-two slaves were younger than 40 years old, but they lived along with Rachel, deemed "old and valueless," Kate, 65, Essex, 65, and Ben, 60. Rachel had at least one kin member present, the 12-year-old "George (grandson of Rachel)." The death of Wales in 1849 occasioned the breaking up of the slave community as a committee liquidated the estate. Essex got sold for $110, Kate got shipped off in a bulk sale with other slaves, and the estate fetched $260 for the 60-year-old Ben. The young George yielded $365, and his grandmother Rachel brought in $15 in an auction in Roanoke. There is no telling from the records what came of them and whether they stayed together, but the variability in the sales records suggests that the auction moved them apart.[41]

In the market for hire, as in the market for sale, planters used aged slaves to make a bit of cash on the margins. While most slave hires were young, including children, whom owners leased to neighbors, some slaveholders tried to put elderly slaves into the hiring market.[42] The George family hired its young slaves for as much as $175 and hired "Billy (old)" for $70, the elderly Ned for $26, and the aged Hannah for $20.[43] The slaveholder Thomas Walton rented his slaves right after Christmas, getting $69 for his most expensive hire, $8 for "Frederick a small boy," and $6 for the child William. Walton hired some in family units, like Agnes and her three children; Tom, his wife, and their five children; and Sucky and her two children. Walton also hired the aged Judy to "the lowest bidder" Asa Dupuy, who hired her along with Agnes and her children. Other slaves were scattered about to different renters.[44] Though speculators, planters, and renters preferred young people, aged slaves still circulated in antebellum Southern markets. In many cases bundled with young slaves in package deals, black elders were among the millions of African Americans who were forcibly moved around the South during the antebellum era.

Danger

Over the course of their life cycles, slaves faced chronic uncertainty about whether they would be sold, hired out, or separated from family members through forced migration or premature death. Adding to the individual and collective strain of movement and separation, the enslaved also carried the weight of day-to-day work of material production. Through quotidian work in the fields, workshops, households, docks, and waterways of the South, slave labor was the engine that drove the Southern economy. The kind of work they performed differed across sectors and along gender lines, and it also varied across age cohorts, which was reflected in antebellum plantation records. When slaveholders established slave market values, sales prices, labor "rates," and hiring-out practices, they indicated their strategy of pushing work onto the shoulders of the young and extracting labor from old people on the margins. And those records also indicate the impact of forced labor, which picked away not only on slave families and communities through the slave trade but also picked away at the individual flesh of slaves as they aged.

The antebellum forced labor system constantly exposed the enslaved to physical danger, and it showed on their bodies. On the North Carolina Glenn estate, 23-year-old Sam had "lost 2 fingers," 40-year-old Jada suffered from consumption (tuberculosis), and 27-year-old Aggy had "1 arm stiff." Brunswick, 25, and Jerry, 48, were "crippled," the 27-year-old Isabel was "subject to fits," and Daniel, 23, was said to be "deformed." As they aged, they carried the physical memory of forced labor in their bodies.[45] The slave population also bore the brunt of epidemics that swept through the region. The Virginian slavery booster and planter Edmund Ruffin recounted in 1837 that "Hands and children have suffered very much from colds—in fact cold has been quite an epidemic." He added that a cold spell in November 1851 was accompanied by "quite an epidemic amongst the hands."[46] Plantation sick lists also tell the tale of the exposure of slaves to disease and injury under the forced labor system. On the Virginia Friend plantation, slaves were held out from labor for having suffered from asthma, chills, cold, pleurisy, fever, pain in the side, pain in the back, and cramps during pregnancy. One was "injured by a fall" and another was "stung by hornets." In two cases, the disease from which slaves suffered was "misery."[47] The slave Ned Oldham of Virginia also took a hit from forced labor. He was "reported to have fallen down" in the "hay house last night and injured his back, having struck the reaper."[48]

At times, neither rain nor cold stopped the wheels of the system from turning. Cotton, rice, wheat, or cotton fields had to be worked, and regardless of conditions slaves had to do it. The Dickinson family estate was one such hive of activity. The manager of the corn and wheat plantation recounted one summer day with "rain off & on all day continue to cut wheat—corn is looking well, cloudy and cold a very destructive hail storm passed through the forrest, heard it laid 8 inches deep on the ground."[49] Slaves on Edmund Ruffin's estate faced similar demands. In January 1851, the enslaved plowed and manured the fields, dug ditches, built a chimney for a new quarter, and hoed old fields. And on the last day of the month, when the temperature hit 8 °F, Ruffin forced some slaves to haul ice. Given these conditions, he made the surprising observation about the physical health of the enslaved that "Hands and children very free from sickness." But that wouldn't last, as he reported the following month that "Hands and negro children have suffered much from sever colds—apparently an epidemic—I had it myself." Slaves carried similar workloads in the winter of 1856. In the cold of December, slaves hauled crops and planted fields of corn. Ruffin remarked that it snowed on the twenty-first of December and that two days later it was an "awfully cold day—Heavy wind from N. all day—Thermr all day about 18°—could do no work but haul and cart wood and grub in the woods." And a day later, on

December 24, he recorded his slaves "hauling ice—2½ in to 3 in thick" and added that it was "freezing all day."[50]

Other dangerous conditions lurked, which planters noted because it impacted their bottom line. Though the cause was not identified, Daniel Johnson did not live up to the expectations of his owner. He was listed on an inventory as an "imbecile physically in his arms and sent to farm."[51] As on the Middle Passage, the "flux" on antebellum plantations could take its toll on the enslaved. Overton Harris of Virginia wrote his brother that "among the Negroes, we lost Charlotte's youngest child with either flux or worms."[52] When it came to injuries and disease, the concern of planters was largely about the laboring potential of the enslaved, as we see in the sale of a slave named Bins by the Virginia estate of Richard Eppes. Eppes reported in his diary that he fetched $1,490 for Bins through the Richmond auction house of Dickson and Hill. Eppes added that "The loss of two joints on the four finger of his left hand injured his sale though altogether it was a high price for him."[53] To Eppes and other slaveholders, the injuries to the enslaved had their impact on their profits, which could also be "injured."

With forced labor organized along the lines of age, working conditions had different effects on the young and the old. For example, on a wheat, corn, and cotton estate on the outskirts of Atlanta, Georgia, slaves plowed, manured, and broke stubble in the fields; hoed cotton; cultivated corn, wheat, cotton, and peas; hauled coal wood; split rails; slaughtered and salted hogs; fixed fences; ginned and spun cotton; cleared brush; and husked corn. But a patch of inclement weather exposed the vulnerability of the estate's aged slaves. The owner reported that "all the others nearly well old women excepted."[54] Trying to extract as much work as possible out of slaves, plantation managers accounted for the age of slaves to keep the engine churning year-round.

Workers

Even though they faced such dire working conditions, some slaves still survived into old age and continued to work. On the Branch family estate, the 50-year-old Nancy ginned cotton, 54-year-old Isaac built slave cabins with the 19-year-old Hudson, and the 65-year-old Dublin built a fence alongside the 25-year-old Rosetta and 31-year-old Maria.[55] And while some of the enslaved worked alongside young people, plantations tended to create divisions of labor along the lines of age. Field work dominated the lives of slaves from their teens through their forties. But if they survived into their fifties and beyond, slaves generally moved closer to the plantation household, the slave quarters, and other domestic spaces. The aged still provided meaningful labor, caring for young people, serving as midwives, or cooking, cleaning, or tending to other domestic chores. Some still worked in the fields. Though not directly contributing to cash crop production, their work still contributed to the operation of plantations because of their auxiliary and complementary functions. Even into old age, the forced labor of slaves kept the system in motion.[56]

Among factors including skill and gender, age became the basis of organizing slave labor, as evidenced in plantation records. For instance, Tener, 65, on the Branch family plantation, was listed as a "milker."[57] The manager of the Corbin estate made specific references to age and aged slaves in the labor force. Of the ninety-two slaves on his plantation in 1833, sixty-seven were counted as "capable of working in the field," sixty of whom he listed as "field hands." This did not count seven children, "who will be at work in two years—Nelly and Rachel sooner," with Nelly working in the household before being sent to the fields. Among those counted as "field hands" were a blacksmith, an engineer, a cooper, and "Ben, who has not worked since the amputation of his thumb." Job worked in the house because his "defect of sight prevents his working out." Others worked in the yard, drove cattle, cultivated the garden, or worked as carpenters. In previous years, the aged had performed and witnessed similar work, and continued to work, albeit closer to the household. Among the labor force that the manager listed as working outside the fields and yard were two "cooks—old women," one old woman who worked in the hospital, and one "children's old woman."[58] One aged black nurse worked nearly to her death. In accounting for the health of the slave labor force, the Corbin estate manager noted that the old woman "Diana, the children's nurse has died. Her strength has been gradually failing for years, and she went off very suddenly. She has been one of the most valuable and faithful negroes on the plantation."[59] In her final years, as a children's nurse, she worked to care for the next generation. Like Diana, other black women elders provided care to the rest of the community, labor that was recognized by the planter class. For example, Old Louisa was respected for her healing knowledge. Richard Eppes noted in his diary that "Old Louisa our midwife sent over two bottles of her medicine to little Joshua today," and the planter gave her $5 "for her attendance on Elise when confined."[60]

Travelers making it through the South depended on occasion on the labor of aged black women. One group passing through South Carolina noted on separate occasions of being "entertained" by two different aged black women.[61] These women likely worked as cooks, as did the "old cook" Becky in the Branch family household.[62] Alexander Dick, traveling through Washington, D.C., identified one aged black woman as a washer woman and depended on another during his travels near Camden, South Carolina. With rains making roads impassable on his travels on New Year's Eve of 1808, his party searched for lodging at one inn, which could not accommodate them. They then "came to a paltry shop—the owner was from home—but an old Negress who was left in charge of the House gave us what we wanted for our horses & also fried Fowl & also Hoecake and milk for ourselves for which we were very thankful."[63]

Even as they grew old and moved out of work in the fields, the aged could be sought out for their labor and figure as laboring subjects in the imagination of Southern elites. Martha Dabney was one such elite, who described herself as "feeble" and was confined to her chamber during the winter. While bed-ridden, she spent her time corresponding with family, reading the Bible, and reflecting on the state of her soul. "I try to pray that my Heavenly Father may touch me to look through the mist of time to the glory of eternity." Yet while still inhabiting the earthly realm, she sought the physical comfort of the slave Levenia. Though she was considered by her owner to be "of little use being old and feeble," Dabney wrote, "I want her to stay in my Chamber and wait on me, she shall be well taken care of as long as she lives." Making her plea to be gifted Levenia, Dabney added that her husband "would never buy an old negro—I don't suppose she would sell for anything." Martha thus aimed to use both her own and Levenia's old age in this slaveholding transaction.[64]

Through years of work and connection to the land, aged slaves acquired knowledge of environmental and economic history. One such figure was Old Cato. At 92 years of age, he described changes to the local environment to his owner Richard Eppes. Cato recalled that what in 1860 were wheat fields had previously been covered with pine trees. He added that field "no. 6 was cultivated down to the edge of the creek and was very good land." He added that another piece of land was "never cultivated being left for rail timber." He observed other changes, including the history of one creek that "had filled up a good deal" and carried "large vessels when he was young . . . to take off flour to Branchester mill and [be] shipped to New York." Cato also recounted "that the tide overflowed now portions of the swamp that formerly were dry owing to the creek filling up."[65]

The plantation enterprise extracted as much labor as possible from the enslaved even as they grew old. Plantation account books that assigned low or no numerical financial value to the aged concealed the ways that slave labor estates continued to work African Americans in old age. Though not central to the antebellum South's emphasis on cash crop production, the labor of the black aged added to the region's economy in ways that numbers alone obscured. While old age changed the form, it did not keep the aged enslaved out of the labor force.

Relief

When slaveholders managed their labor forces in the fields, workshops, or households or pushed them into the market, they accounted for age. They also factored age into the equation when cementing family relationships or negotiating with the state. As family heads, they used slaves to secure relationships with their children, thereby reinforcing their place at the top of the social hierarchy and securing wealth and power for the next generations who were on the path to inherit slaveholding status.[66] It became a self-reinforcing system that created intergenerational wealth. For instance, the Virginia planter Smith Shepherd bequeathed slaves to his wife Hannah, and he also promised his son John Shepherd "one Negro Luke also two hundred Pounds in cash to him and his heirs forever." To his daughter, he gave "Sue, Mary, and Affrica."[67] Will by will, younger slaveholders inherited the assets of previous generations, gaining the rights to the labor of enslaved black Southerners.

As they entered old age or sought to manage aged slaves, slaveholders pursued different options to plan their estates. For instance, free black slaveholder Sally Fain proposed one option. In her 1841 will, Fain divided the bulk of her property between her former husband and her daughter Amy and her children. She also ordered the estate to use her assets to take care of her "two old slaves Dick and Sally." Fain added that she wanted Sally to live with her family. But this approach was limited in scope because Fain outlasted Dick and Sally. When she updated her will, she only included her landed property, giving no mention of her two slaves.[68] In contrast, William and Elizabeth Pickens petitioned the North Carolina state assembly for the right upon their death to emancipate their two slaves Jack and May. William stated that they were essential to his care, "particularly of late in his old age," making the case that their role in his care as an aged person entitled them to freedom. While the state rejected the petition, their case highlights how in old age the Pickens family used their slaves for care.[69]

Slaveholders used slaves for other kinds of elder support. When the planter Izard Bacon proposed to free his slaves, he required that a portion of their wages be used to support the aged. When he wrote in his will that he sought to emancipate his slaves upon his death, he was limited by the state's requirement for a special bill to be passed by the assembly if they were to be entitled to stay in the state. Realizing both the external limits imposed on him by the commonwealth and the social and political significance of elder care, he wrote in his testament, "It is my will and desire that respecting my slaves and their increase, that they shall be emancipated, as soon as a law can be obtained giving them leave to remain in the state, and in the mean time, that they shall be disposed of in the way most consistent with their happiness, and so the proceeds of their labour shall go to the support of the aged, infirm, and unfortunate." Ruling on the case, Judge William Hening enabled Bacon's slaves to select their employer, work for wages, and put their earnings in a trust to pay for their removal from the state. Hening's decree also added, in keeping with Bacon's will, that "the proceeds of their labour shall go to the support of the aged, infirm, and unfortunate." After three years, the freed men and women earned enough to make the move out of state, with most moving to Pennsylvania. Bacon's will allowed for the payment of $250 to Nath. O. Crenshaw to care for the aged Dick, perhaps making him vulnerable given his separation from the rest of the community of former slaves.[70]

In unusual cases, slaveholders made provisions for the aged in their wills. John Warwick of Amherst County, Virginia, used his will to emancipate his slaves and support their move to a free state, preferably Indiana. He set aside land and money for Frederick and his family, noting that 48-year-old Frederick was "very infirm and his family a helpless one." Warwick also set aside property for Caleph, 70, and the 50-year-old John, noting that they "from age and infirmity, will be unable to support themselves in a Free State."[71] The Fife family of Virginia set up a more elaborate system, using their land to establish an annuity for old slaves. Their estate used the net proceeds from renting its property, after tax and management fees, to cover food, clothing, and burial expenses of the aged slaves James, Bob, Rose, Lucy, and Jack. For example, the estate was charged for "cloth to make Jack a great coat," one bushel of "corn for Lucy having made none," "4 pair shoes," "4 pair stockings," and "a coffin & burying Bob." And the "1/2 gallon brandy" charged to the estate was possibly meant for surviving slaves and community elders to pour libations for James, the first of the five to die.[72]

In other cases, slaveholders used the old age of slaves to wring concessions from the state. While they tried to compel aged slaves to work, they were limited in some cases and sought relief from county governments, which became arenas to debate slave elder care. For instance, Caroline Sharman of Lancaster County, Virginia, requested a tax exemption for her "superannuated negro man named Jacob, who is, by reason of his age and infirmities, unable to render her any or very little service; by no means equivalent to his support." Seeing the aged Jacob as a financial liability, she asked the county to strike his name off the tax list.[73] Elizabeth Ruckle and her husband Samuel also sought relief. After the death of her first husband, Elizabeth took control over her dower slaves, most of whom were younger than 9 and unable to work. Also included among her dower slaves were "two old negroes." Elizabeth married Samuel Ruckle, with whom she had a child. They complained that the expense of raising the young slave population to maturity and caring for elderly slaves placed a financial strain on the family, and their child bore the brunt of it while having no future right to own her slaves. They thus asked for an amendment to Virginia's "unjust and unequal" law to give Elizabeth greater leeway in managing and passing along her property. The age of her slaves and her son, she reasoned, needed to be considered in the rules governing her dowry.[74]

The executors of Isham Tatum's estate also sought special consideration before the law because of the presence of aged slaves. Tatum included in his will a provision that, upon his death, his slaves Jim, Jeptha, Thaddeus, and Timothy would be free "whenever the youngest of them should become 21 years of age." After Isham Tatum died in 1850, his executor Nathaniel Tatum filed a request that brought attention to an aged man among the estate's slaves. Nathaniel insisted that "one of the said negroes is superannuated and worthless unable to leave the state or maintain himself." Without the resources to pay for the aged slave's exile as required by law, Nathaniel asked the state for permission to sell all the remaining slaves, contrary to Isham's will. The "worthless" aged man served as an excuse for Nathaniel Tatum to sell young and old and cash out the estate. The age of slaves served as the grounds for such intergenerational struggles within the planter class.[75]

The case of Thomas Brooks of Virginia also reveals how the propertied elite took their grievances about the black aged to the state. Brooks demanded relief from Jefferson County for supporting the 80-year-old free black Jim, who had belonged to Jack Hope. Jim lived on Brooks's land and had become "an incumberence on my hands, destitute of food, raiment, and shelter; other than furnished by me without remuneration." He added that Jim was attached to "a negro woman (named Viney) occupying the same House between fifty or sixty years of age formerly belonging to the estate of Col. Diggs for which I beg that the court will appoint a *master*, or . . . to be sold for her support." Brooks demanded that Jim "be supported at the expense of the county" or by his former owners. Otherwise, Brooks threatened, he would "reject [Jim] from the house he now occupies, as well as from my premises in which case he must either perish or obtain his support by pilfering being a man over eighty years of age and unable to support himself by manual labor."[76]

In going to the courts, slaveholders, their heirs, and the public relied on the idea that black elders had outlived their economic utility. The ways that planters pinned a low financial value on aged slaves in their diaries and account books had their counterparts in their legal records. While legal documentation and processes created bonds between generations of slaveholders, they also reveal the pressures of slavery and provide evidence of the ways that African Americans built multigenerational relationships. But whether to claim exemption from taxes, waivers from rules concerning property rights, or other support from the state, white Southerners conceived of aged African Americans as liabilities in the face of the law.

Death

As much as the plantation system tried to extract from the enslaved, death inevitably intervened. In their management and census procedures, slaveholders accounted for slave deaths in different ways—with the word "dead," with dates, through detailed descriptions, with lists of those who died, or, simply, by crossing out names from slave lists. Through a stroke of the pen, they documented slave deaths. They also provide a window into the arc of slave life cycles and what black elders witnessed.

In the margins of their papers and record books, planters noted the loss of their human property. For example, an 1860 list of slaves owned by James A. Scott accounted for the names and ages of the enslaved, and as time wore on, he crossed some off the list. Among those who died were the 6-year-old Truman, 17-year-old Minirva, 50-year-old Sylva, and 100-year-old Sylva. They were all crossed out with the notation "dead" inscribed next to their name.[77] Death on Garrett Scott's plantation got recorded differently. The plantation census put an x next to or over the name of those who died or got sold. For example, May, 6; Lucy, 2; Phillippa, 1; Mary Alice, 2; and Allen, 2, had their names marked with an x and did not make it into adolescence; while Lizzie, a "Very old woman," saw all of them die and would live until the eve of the Civil War, passing in January 1859.[78] The George family's list of deaths provides a grim picture of child mortality and the deaths of the aged. It noted the death of Patty's 8-month-old child, Abner's son Abb, Lucky's child John, Sarah's child Indiana, and Margret's unnamed child.[79]

Markers of birth and death stood side by side in the records, as planters noted the fluctuations in their assets in people. In the margins of an agricultural manual, one planter noted slave deaths, including the passing of Virgil, the death of Amanda at 48, and the death of "Old Albert," who "died between 3 and 4 O'clock on Thursday morning the 3rd of April 1856."[80] The Jerdone family listed the birthdates of slaves and added the date of death in the margins. For example, Lilly was born on July 21, 1760, and died October 6, 1779, while Ally was born on August 8, 1761, and died in November 1781.[81] A century later, the daily records of black mortality continued. African Americans around Charlottesville, Virginia, had deaths within their community recorded in the Christ Episcopal Church record book, which noted that Sally Sargent passed at 11 months, Lewis Dunlop died at 2, Julia died at 2½, and Rosalia died at 6 months.[82] Their family members were left behind to grieve lives cut down at such a young age.

Death came in waves, such as during the cholera epidemic that swept through Richmond in 1849, claiming young and old, black and white. The board of health reported that during one period of that year 191 black people succumbed to cholera, and the city responded to the public health crisis with a racial policy of separate cemeteries, interring many of the African American dead in Shockoe Bottom Burial Ground. Among them were the 55-year-old free black woman Polly and the 68-year-old Lewis.[83] Cholera also hit rural areas, taking slaves to their graves. The Corbin plantation manager Edward Rawle reported "that Litty was dead and Old Bacchus. I have now to add the names of Old Toby, John, two children Elizabeth and Maria, Luke, and last and best, Anna, daughter of old Betsy."[84] Later, the cooper Tom died from the disease.[85] While epidemics brought about mass death across the color line, slaves were particularly vulnerable to their impact.

From a wide range of causes, slaves died one by one, some soon after birth, others while at the apex of their life, and still others while old. On the Branch family estate, child Parelle died at 19 months, and Berry, son of

Rosetta, made it only to 2 years old.[86] On Edmund Ruffin's plantation, Milly, about 36, suffered a "sudden and distressing death." He wrote that she was "about the most hearty healthy and valuable woman on the place, returned from work about dusk, in fine spirits and health; was seated foundling her children, and was heard suddenly to cry out 'Oh! My head' (the first indication of disease) and within 1½ hours was a corpse." Ruffin lamented the loss, noting that "she has for years back been one of my main wheat shuckers."[87] Losing her labor was his ultimate concern.

Planters noted that other slaves made it to old age, and their descendants continued with the demands of forced labor after they passed. There was "Aunt Polly (old servant)," who in December 1856 "died of old age—20 years ago she had 51 descendants in this state besides others in S. West."[88] Considered "moral and industrious to those around him," another slave named Jack was a respected elder. He was stricken by an illness that left him weak, dehydrated, and under a doctor's care. He tried to get out of bed and fell only to be discovered unconscious; he died soon thereafter, away from his loved ones. Jack's owner wrote about Jack that "I regret that he did not see his family before death," reflecting his isolation and defenselessness in old age.[89]

The stories of Polly and Jack dying while separated from family members replayed itself countless times, whether family members were separated on the same plantation or through sale. The machine kept running amid the dead and dying. Planters kept track of their human assets through plantation lists, which can be turned into bar graphs that represent the demographic shape of local slave populations according to age. They reveal the cold, calculating labor management methods of slaveholders. The jagged lines of the graphs reveal the volatility of the experience of enslavement, which shaped a distinct lifecycle for African Americans. The numbers mean that black people lost neighbors, friends, kin, children, or grandchildren to death or sale. Amid these day-to-day shocks, black Southerners struggled to survive into old age and maintain multigenerational relationships.

CHAPTER 3

The "Law of Respect to Elders"

The work demands on Southern plantations superseded everything else, shaping not only African American life cycles but also the dynamics of black family relationships. The childhood experience of Frederick Douglass lays this bare. In all three of his autobiographies, Douglass describes how the forced labor system separated him from his mother, who was captive on a separate part of his owner's estate and who managed to break away only four or five times throughout his entire childhood to see him, visits that happened in the dead of night. Given the pressures on this mother-son relationship, Douglass's grandmother Betsy Bailey served as a surrogate parent to him. At a point when she no longer went into the fields to cultivate export crops, Bailey kept working by raising her grandson. She and her husband Isaac turned their household into a nursery for the young Douglass, and they established the social and moral foundation for his later development.[1]

Douglass's childhood experience points to the place of the aged and multigenerational relationships among the enslaved. Given the revered place of elders in African and African Diasporic cultures, the disruptive impact of the domestic slave trade on black families, and the jagged age structures of slave populations, African Americans in the antebellum period navigated the world by forging relationships that spanned multiple generations. And those relationships demanded work. In their younger years, slaves worked primarily in fields and workshops. If they made it to old age, the work continued but took a different form; elders shifted to domestic and kinship labor that reproduced ties of family and community, as Betsy and Isaac Bailey's labor attests. To protect the fragile ties they forged across generations, black Southerners maintained spaces for those connections in their households, and their practices of multigenerational power and kinship extended into engagements with and defiance of the state.

Following the example of Frederick Douglass and Betsy Bailey, this chapter focuses on the tension between economic and state forces and the place of elders in black family relationships in the antebellum South. Elders played key roles in preserving African American families, which could also make them potent symbols and agents. To Douglass, for example, the treatment of his grandmother signified slavery's moral failure and demonstrated the problem of the planter class's unchecked power. From Douglass's vantage point, his grandmother deserved respect. In numerous other instances, slaves and free blacks, the young and the old used the idea of respect for elders to hold families together or challenge a system that had the power to tear them apart. With a focus on black multigenerational kinship strategies, this chapter highlights the obstacles that slaves surmounted to become elders and examines their place in antebellum Southern black families. African Americans used individual, familial, and collective knowledge and ideas about the old to exert social and political power. Standing on the boundary between the dead and the living, black elders, their families, and their communities turned the position of old age into a political resource.

Loss

Becoming a slave elder meant being baptized, again and again, in the waters of impermanence. Witnessing, experiencing, or struggling against loss and forced movement, elders had an intimate knowledge of the slaveholding system. Picking up on those lessons, figures like Douglass gave voice to the experiences of slave elders. Their experiences can also be unearthed from plantation records when looked at against the grain of their intent. Though written from the perspective of the plantation managerial class, slave lists and plantation ledgers—the ledgers of racial capitalism—tell stories in the margins about the routine experience of death, change, migration, and loss that slaves witnessed as they came of age and became elders.[2]

When looked at across spans of time, through their interstices, and with a focus on individual slave subjects and their web of relationships, slave lists reveal the perilous journey of becoming a slave elder. For example, Federick came of age on the Dupuy estate in Virginia. Born on July 25, 1810, he saw people come and go. His owner bought Henry, Frances, Eliza, Lucy, Prudence, Horace, Agness, William, Richard, Sam Hines, 51-year-old Liddey, and 62-year-old Lew. As he grew older, the newborn also entered Federick's life.

Eliza gave birth to Amelia, Caty, Sam, Diley, Tom, and Wesley, and she also gave birth to triplets—Susan, Lizzy, and Nannie—who all died young. Likely in honor of the infant she lost, Eliza named her next daughter Susan. Frances bore Whitfield, George, and Preston. In addition, Federick saw people including Nancy, Lucy, and Sally disappear through sale. And he saw young people die before he did. Along with Eliza's triplets, Frances's son George and Prudence's namesake and her daughter Ritter died at early ages. Federick's life as a slave had been marked by instability and flux, and he survived it all, living through the Civil War.[3]

Plantation records demonstrate how the baptism in loss started early and continued if a slave made it to old age. Still of childbearing age, Kitty experienced enough grief to have a perspective akin to that of someone much older than she was. Between 1822 and 1838, she bore nine children, and she lost six of them to sale or death. Her first three children, William Lee, Elizabeth, and May, all survived and lived out their younger years with their mother on Virginia's Billups estate. But her next three children, Harry, George Washington, and Dudley, got sold away. Carrying this experience of loss, Kitty had three more children—Miles, Samuel C. Tompson, and Nancy—all of whom died before Kitty.[4] Left with only the three eldest of her nine children, Kitty had seen enough of slavery's impact as she came of age. The loss of young people dealt an emotional blow to the community of slaves. For example, on another estate, the enslaved clearly expressed their grief when the slave Albert's life ended too soon. He "was killed by the falling of a limb, while cutting wood in the forest." In a "slowly moving procession," slaves followed his coffin as a cart carried his remains to the slave graveyard, where the mourning reached a crescendo. An observer wrote, "Their weird singing, and their unrestrained grief at the grave could be heard from quite a distance."[5]

The experiences of other slaves, as reflected in plantation slave lists, demonstrate how living a long life was against the odds and what those who reached old age witnessed over their life course. For example, Old Eve had her losses to the slave trade. In the margins of one slave list, her owner wrote "sell Juliet & child & Milley & put two boys in their places Sell Will & replace him with likely tractable boy for the house." The threat of separation thus hung over Old Eve and the 11-year-old Milley, 21-year-old Juliet, and 30-year-old William.[6] While a later 1839 list indicates that Milley was spared the auction block and stayed on the estate with Old Eve, Juliet and William were gone.[7] Sarah on the George family estate had a comparable experience. Listed simply as "old" in the inventory, she passed on Christmas Eve of 1854

Figure 4. "Funeral Procession, Virginia, 1880," *Slavery Images: A Visual Record of the African Slave Trade and Slave Life in the Early African Diaspora.* http://www.slaveryimages.org/s/slaveryimages/item/1848.

but not before outliving a host of other people. In growing old, she had seen her own elders die. Old Man David, Old Ned, Old Hannah, and Old Tom died before Sarah. She also saw young people cut down. She knew about the death of Polly's 8-month-old child, and perhaps she went to the funeral of the child for whom Gus Jarvis made "a small coffin." Then there was Moses, who rumor had it "was whipped to death by Carter Turner." She heard rumblings about Lucy, who was accused of poisoning her son John to death. By the time she died in the decade before the Civil War, Sarah had seen her share of death.[8]

Slave elders on other plantations across time and space had similar tales to tell. On the Jerdone family estate in colonial Albemarle County, Virginia, Old Sarah lived with her husband Will, a carpenter, and other elders, including Old George. Sarah and Will saw Moll die, leaving behind two children, orphans who had elders such as Old Sarah, Will, and others in the community to care for them.[9] On the antebellum Florida Branch family estate, Tener survived into their seventies. When the Civil War came so did a wave of deaths of slaves on both sides of the age spectrum. Old Winney died two days after Christmas, in 1861, and the 72-year-old Dublin passed in 1863. But perhaps it was the child mortality on the estate that hit Tener the hardest. Between January 1859 and October 1861, seven of the twelve newborns died soon after birth on the Live Oak property, while Tener continued to live into old age. For instance, Caroline's son would live to "about 10 days old"; Tener could be there for Caroline after her infant's life, as fragile as it was, came to an end.[10] Another elder named Sam on the Thomas estate in Georgia had his own experience of vulnerability and intergenerational ruptures as he made it to old age. The elder Sam had his freedom granted to him by his mistress only to remain enslaved because a slave trader took "charge of his paper (free papers) and never returned them to him." He also remembered "the separation of his daughter from him and her separation from her children."[11]

The life course of slaves in the antebellum South was marked by sales, death, instability, and movement, creating strain that compounded as they became old. In the case of Peter of Virginia, his longevity meant that he outlived not only the young but also his peers. Listed as being 56 on William Beverly's 1834 slave list, he lived alongside the 57-year-old Abby, 53-year-old Ursula, and 46-year-old Cornelius. But sixteen years later, he was the only one to have survived among his cohort.[12] He not only saw his peers succumb but also witnessed the death of people much younger than he was. The children Rachel, General, Stuart, and Liverpool died before reaching their second birthday, and Barnaby died around the age of 53. With people dying around him as he lived past 80 and dying in 1861, Peter's mere survival set him apart from the rest of the community. And, into old age, he knew the names of those who died before him.[13]

While the experience of slave elderhood generally occurred in a collective context, the demands of forced labor and the loss of children, family members, and friends could lead to social isolation. That was likely the case with Peter. The domestic slave Jinny suffered a similar fate. After she performed domestic chores and nursed white children during the height of her physical ability, Jinny's health went into decline over her last twenty-five years. She later developed "disease of the heart and Reumatism," from which she mounted a recovery. But later in life, her health took a blow that took her to the grave in a matter of six months. Given her separation from the rest of the community, the wheels of the plantation kept churning, and the rest of the slave population went into the wheat fields while Jinny was interred.[14]

Slaves struggled against such isolation in old age and sought social recognition from family and the broader community. The elder Fanny had a different fate than Jinny during her last rites. The Cohoon family of Virginia bought Fanny and her two oldest children, Henry and Mary, from the Whitlock estate between 1816 and 1818. Living to be 68 years old, Fanny had her own elders and almost surely knew Old Martha, Old Rose, and Old Parrish, who were listed as living to be 100 years old. Fanny must have also known Old Rachel and Lizz, who made it to 90, and Milly, Peg, Celia, and Bristol who lived past 60. So, connections to the aged were routine to her. Having lived a long life, Fanny received some of the attention that a well-respected elder would expect after her own death. A note in the Cohoon account book said, "Fanny died 7th April 1857 at half after 11 Oclock . . . in her 68th year of age; she was a good and faithful servant, leaving many children and grand children to mourn her loss." Fanny and her spouse Jacob had at least eight children, some of whom would be there to grieve together. Henry and Mary, Charles and Rachel, Margaret and Matilda could be there to bury their mother. But others could not. Jefferson who likely died before his mother, and Lucy, who had been sold, would be absent from their mother's gravesite.[15]

Such was the respect for recently departed elders that black people tried to maintain last rites even during the Richmond cholera epidemic when survivors and the city faced the grim task of burying the dead. During the epidemic, the city's overseers of the poor had the charge of interring the destitute including slaves and free blacks. As the city's board of health determined, "Persons who die in the streets and such others as have no friends, or families, to defray the expenses of burial, are, by law, to be buried by the overseers of the poor."[16] But in other cases, black family members took care of the dead. For example, the family of 50-year-old Polly Scott moved into action to care for her dead body. The records note that "Polly Scott free and Pauper . . . claimed by her children and buried without the city."[17]

While death and loss cut across antebellum Southern society, slaves and free blacks experienced it in particular ways determined by the system of racial slavery and laws regulating free blacks. Many slave newborns never survived infancy. The gears of forced labor ground many young people to death, while millions got treated as pawns in the domestic slave trade. For slaves who survived and were held captive in the older eastern slaveholding states or grew old in the new slaving frontiers of the Cotton Kingdom, they saw people come and go. In the context of this social and demographic instability, elders served as a stabilizing force for family units and slave communities, and their experience, years of labor, knowledge, and insight became the grounds of respect within black families and communities.

Respect

Bound by understandings about the proper role of people at different stages of the life cycle and grounded in African cultural foundations, black Southern practices of eldership took on new dimensions in response to the pressures of the colonial and antebellum plantation elite. While slaveholders valued young people for their labor productivity on cash crops, the slave community expected the young to honor their elders. South Carolina's Taylor family offers evidence of such practices. Among the estate's slave elders were Poll, Sampson, Quaminoe, Bob, Primous, Robin, Prince, Phillis, Joan, and Tom, all marked as "old" in the estate's 1771 slave list at their Warrhall property. The list also pointed out that two young slaves, "Ned and hannabell yett @ Goose Creek, To tend old Toney, thair Father."[18]

Marked by tenderness, the bonds of care between elders and the young worked the other way around, such as when Old Toney lost his son Ned. Thomas Smith described Ned in a letter to absentee owner Peter Taylor, saying that Ned was "allways tender and allways spoke as if something ailed his throat." With a set of ailments deemed to be incurable, Ned died in 1773. The loss took a toll on Toney. The letter continued that Ned "was Toney's favorite Son, and the old man droops much since his loss."[19] As Toney, Ned, and Hannabell's experience illustrates, elders and juniors had social and moral obligations that carried a physical and emotional cost. And while they often clashed with the logics of plantation domination and the slave market, Southern black families and communities were willing to perform such emotional labor and sought to build ties across generations.[20]

Through parental commands, young people learned their place in family hierarchies and cultures of intergenerational deference and respect. Harriet Jacobs explores these dynamics in her autobiography. For example, she describes how her brother William learned the importance of deference when he followed the command of his mistress rather than that of his father, who reprimanded William with the words, "'You are my child . . . and when I call you, you should come to me immediately, if you have to pass through fire and water."[21] Such cultures of belonging and deference spanned multiple generations in the Jacobs family and became particularly important when her family members died or got sold away. Jacobs's mother died when she was 6 and her father died when she was 13, so her grandmother Molly Horniblow stepped in as a surrogate parent. With the support of her grandmother, Jacobs coped with her parents' deaths, resisted the sexual violence of her owner, negotiated motherhood, and ultimately escaped from slavery. As an elder, Horniblow used the power of words and shame to exert moral pressure against Jacobs's owner. Confronting him directly, Horniblow "told him pretty plainly what she thought of his character." Horniblow's status as a free woman of color and grandparent shielded Jacobs from some of the most extreme forms of slavery's violence; but Horniblow's power had its limits. After all, while she eventually bought her own freedom, "none of her children escaped the auction block."[22]

Slaves who stayed alive, got spared from the domestic slave trade, and grew to old age developed attachments to space and households, which became temporary refuges for young people. This was certainly the case for Douglass and Jacobs. It was also true for Charles Ball. Losing his mother through the domestic slave trade and his father who ran away on the eve of being sold, Ball turned to his grandfather for support. Ball described the emotional impact of his grandfather Old Ben, remembering that "He manifested towards me all the fondness which a person so advanced in life could expect to feel for a child." At the age of 80, Old Ben no longer lived or worked in the slave community but rather lived in a "small cabin of his own" and cultivated a small plot of land for subsistence. As with Molly Horniblow, Old Ben did not have the power to protect his descendants from sale, and Ball got shipped away to Georgia and South Carolina. But the influence of his grandfather endured. On his forced trek down South, Ball remembered his wife and children. And he writes, "I also thought of my grandfather, and of the long nights I had passed with him, listening to his narratives of the scenes through which he passed in Africa."[23] In a highly volatile world of death, hard labor, and human trafficking, black grandparents provided stability through their presence in memory and the flesh.

Grandparents did not stand alone as elder authority figures; rather, slaves used capacious, flexible concepts and practices about kin relations to establish and reproduce the authority of elders. Through acts of public recognition, verbal gestures, or granting titles, slaves in North America reinforced eldership. Having observed the African American community in Washington, D.C., in the early nineteenth century, Alexander Dick wrote, "It is amusing to observe the politeness which the Negroes observe among themselves and the common titles of respect they use to one another—'Yes sir' dito 'ma'am.'"[24] The practices of verbal deference continued well into the nineteenth century, practices that Frederick Douglass observed when he came of age. Explaining the term "uncle" that slaves used to refer to slave artisans, Douglass states, "These mechanics were called 'uncles' by all the younger slaves, not because they really sustained that relationship to any, but according to plantation etiquette, as a mark of respect, due from the younger to the older slaves."[25] Along with such verbal acts, young people also offered physical gestures to show deference to elders. Douglass observed that "A young slave must approach the company of the older with hat in hand, and woe betide him, if he fails to acknowledge a favor, of any sort, with the accustomed '*tankee'ee,*' &c."[26] To Douglass, respect to elders was essential to slave culture, and he concluded about slaves that "There is not to be found among any people a more rigid enforcement of the law of respect to elders than is maintained among them. I set this down as partly constitutional with the colored race and partly conventional." He added, "There is no better material in the world for making a gentleman than is furnished in the African."[27]

Though Douglass praised "the law of respect to elders," he also pointed out its limits. Specifically, he critiqued slave elders who used corporal punishment to discipline slave youths. For instance, the slave doctor and counselor Uncle Isaac had respect in and beyond the slave quarters, but he also used violence to gain compliance, wielding his "hickory switch" on Douglass and other young people as they learned the Lord's Prayer. When instructing them on their devotionals, Uncle Isaac paused to correct them "and bang would come the switch on some poor boy's undevotional head."[28] Aunt Katy had a similar temperament and resorted to beating and starving Douglass to impose her will.[29] In comparison to his relationship with his grandparents Betsy and Isaac Bailey, his ties to Uncle Isaac and Aunt Katy showed the underside of eldership and exposed the vulnerability of youths who were caught between extremes of behavior by elders. To Douglass, respect for elders came with the expectation that they would use their power to protect rather than hurt the vulnerable.

With authority they established through time, practice, and conduct, slave elders cultivated a moral force that enabled them to mediate family and community disputes. Such was the case with Jenny Oldham. Born just two years after the Constitutional Convention, Jenny Oldham lived through the antebellum period and became enmeshed in multigenerational family networks on the Eppes plantation in Virginia. She bore at least four children—George Oldham (born 1804), Sally Lewis (born 1815), Lucky Page (born 1817), and Mary Jane Morris (born 1821). Jenny Oldham then became a grandmother when Lucky Page gave birth to Eliza Page (1838). Jenny's daughter Sally Lewis gave birth to at least four children—William Thompson (born 1840), Nancy Thompson (born 1842), Ansy Thompson (born 1850), and Ada Lewis (born 1858). And Jenny's daughter Mary Jane Morris had at least one child, George Morris (born 1843). In an unstable slave population marked by mortality and sales, Jenny Oldham and her peers Matthew Slaughter (born 1781), Hannah Slaughter (born 1786), and Judy Harris (born 1787), were relative constants, surviving, being spared the auction block, and remaining on the estate over the course of the tumultuous antebellum period.[30] Through biological and social ties, enslaved women elders like Jenny Oldham held multiple generations of family together. They needed her when the slave Ned struck his wife Fanny, a conflict that escalated and later was defused. After the plantation owner Richard Eppes had the parties punished "according to our Laws," he sent for Jenny and another slave woman "to secure the separation of the parties engaged in the fracas."[31] He also ordered Oldham to take care of a child who had been entangled in the conflict and to "do the cooking for the farm hands." She had the authority and respect needed to extinguish the flames of domestic violence. To the highly volatile conflict, the aged Jenny brought a cool head.

As African Americans sought to build multigenerational community, elders exerted their authority when they could. But the domestic slave trade presented a formidable obstacle, scattering slaves across the deep South and creating physical distance between the young and old. Yet spatial separation and the passing of time did not destroy multigenerational memory and bonds of kin. African Americans wanted to reconnect and be remembered across generations, they wanted respect—to be brought together or be seen again. For instance, Paul had been separated from his relatives and reached out to them and his friends on his former plantation. He wrote Lucy Marks of Albemarle County:

> Dear madam I take this opportunity to inform you that I am well and I hope that you are in the same . . . and I will be much oblig to you if you wil Will write to me by the first opportunity and to send me word how issabella and all the rest of the family becky X suzy desired to be

> remembered her father and all the family Easter Desire to be remembere to Dan brother an sister and all the family nancy desired to be remembered to cosin suzy I remain your most affectionate
>
> Uncle Paul[32]

As he makes plain in his letter, Paul remembered his family and wished to be remembered, as his long-term kinship relationships transcended space and time.

The work of maintaining relationships across generations and space could put African Americans in the difficult position of having to communicate through the planter class. And they appealed to old age in doing so. For instance, the aged slave Charles sought to reconnect with family members across space, and his old age informed his request. Born with the name of Stephen Greenhill in Virginia, Charles got sent to the deep South and was eventually purchased by David Callahan of Campbell County, Alabama, an owner to whom he "belonged for 25 years or upward." Now up in years, Charles sought to reconnect with his brother Jacob through his owner William Greenhill. The distance and time meant that Charles may have been "obliterated" from Greenhill's memory and that neither Charles nor his brother could know whether the other was alive. He wrote Greenhill about his "brother Jacob if he is yet alive perhaps may suppose that I am no more." Charles added, "Thanks be to all superintending power I am yet numbered with the living and in the enjoyment of health and strength perhaps superior to most of my age." Raising another point about his old age, Charles continued, "It would be extremely consoling to me to hear from you and to hear from my Brother and his welfare would liberate and strengthen me in my declining years." Having gotten word through slave information networks that they might be relocating to Alabama, Charles asked them to call upon him, given that, he said, "You will pass near where I live as a I live in a mile of the road you must travel if come through Campbell."[33]

In the face of forced labor and the domestic slave trade, black Southerners struggled to maintain family and community ties across generations. Elders like Betsy Bailey, Molly Horniblow, and Jenny Oldham managed to lead families across generations in discrete locales. The experiences of Federick on the Dupuy plantation and Peter on the Beverley plantation reflect how enslavement splintered black multigenerational relationships. And figures like Charles of Alabama and Paul of Virginia attest to how, even amid loss that came through movement, the bonds between elders and younger generations spanned time and space. Elders used their memory; they remembered; they wanted to be remembered. And they drew upon the memory and knowledge of plantation life that they accumulated over their long lives to restore bonds of kin. Others used the state, as slaves and free blacks turned to the courts and state assemblies to maintain multigenerational bonds.

Character

The respect that black elders commanded did not end within the boundaries of African American families and communities. Their influence also extended to state governments, which became sites of contestation where elders used their old age and social ties to attempt to exert power. While African Americans across the age spectrum made individual and collective appeals to the state, elders cast their arguments in ways that defined and highlighted their old age. Furthermore, black elders turned their knowledge of plantation economic affairs and property relationships into a political resource to extract concessions. Using their personal experiences of longevity to make their legal challenges, the sum of their ad hoc actions added up to a larger argument for the extension of political entitlements to the black aged.

Beginning in the late seventeenth century, Southern colonies and states passed a string of expulsion laws that banished free blacks upon emancipation. Many simply ignored the law and stayed.[34] Other slaves and free blacks filed petitions to state assemblies or filed suit in the courts for exemptions, and they made a range of arguments to make their cases to stay.[35] Old age became one of the grounds for appeal, and their arguments show the complex understanding that enslaved and free blacks had about aged personhood. At the point of old age, elders carried a long experience of subjugation, and their identities were shaped by the structures of race, forced labor, gender, and family. Elders understood this complexity, using their aged, racialized, and gendered bodies, nativity, family relationships, sense of time and death, and other means to act as political subjects and extract resources from the state. In most instances, they sought time, wanting to be left alone and allowed to remain in the place they had come to know as home.[36] Case by case, elders gave voice to how state policy, forced labor, and the slave trade placed strains of uncertainty and separation on black individuals, families, and communities. Case by case, black elders turned old age into political power, seeking to mobilize it to preserve their ties to family and land.

The appeals made by black elders for freedom or residency often required broad-based white support, a system of patronage that was shaped by related concerns that the state had about maintaining the aged and the poor. As reflected in legal codes and practices dating back to the colonial era, Southern lawmakers feared that the elderly poor would become "chargeable" wards of the state.[37] To avoid the costs of supporting chargeable aged slaves abandoned by their owners, the state regulated slave manumission and placed restrictions on freeing the aged. For example, Virginia's 1782 manumission law allowed slaveholders to emancipate their slaves on the condition that "Slaves being above the age of forty-five years, or being males under the age of twenty-one, or females under the age of eighteen years, shall respectively be supported and maintained by the person so liberating them, or by his or her estate."[38] Black and white petitioners looked for workarounds and sought exemptions. Their pleas offer a glimpse into the life course of black elders and demonstrate the complex relationships and identities that they developed over their long lives.

Petitions for black elders were often backed or written by white supporters, which was not always a key to success. For instance, a petition for Ned was presented to the North Carolina General Assembly in 1836 based on a provision in his master Benjamin Davidson's will that Ned should be free if he was able to "give bond and security for his good behavior." Informing the state that he "was getting advanced in years," Ned recalled how he spent his early years as a slave of Davidson, who died around 1826 and left his widow behind. For the next six years, he "provided for her comfort," and after her death around 1832, he hired out his time. When Ned and his advocates made the case for his emancipation, he pointed to his years of labor and to Davidson's will, an appeal that the assembly decided "against."[39]

The petition of the aged Frederick James met with a neutral response, even though he had the support of white patrons. As with Ned, James provides a brief biography that attested to his sacrifices, grounding his appeal to the North Carolina General Assembly in the idea of labor and service. But for James, it was through the military. James put his body on the line during the American Revolution, and when he became old, with a broken body, he sought the "full privileges of a free man." Born to free parents, he served in the revolutionary army and left the war a scarred man. During the armed conflict, the British captured him and held him as a prisoner of war. Once discharged from prison and the military, and "after having thus devoted the prime and best days of his life" to war, his body had become "impaired and broken." His petition continued that despite having sacrificed the "prime" of his life in the war, he never received compensation or a pension from the nation's treasury. By the time he filed his petition in 1816, three decades had passed since his military service, and he eked out a living for his family by selling refreshments in Bertie County. He was not accorded the respect of a veteran, an elder, or a property owner, and people stole his refreshments and would also "spurn at and abuse him." Being subject to abuse by strangers and neglected by the government, "he ask[ed] with submission can this be a just policy as it respects him." James answered his rhetorical question, saying that "His feelings tell him it is not and he prays, your Honorable Body to change it."[40] He wanted to enjoy the fruits of his labor and to have the right to testify in court against those who stole from him. As he was deemed an exception to what they perceived to be a necessary and just rule, "which excludes the evidence of persons of his color from being received against white persons," a group of white citizens backed James, being "perfectly satisfied that the privilege prayed for him would not be abused in his hands."[41] Referring to his age, physical condition, service, and work, he pulled in white patrons to support his case, one that led the assembly to indefinitely postpone its decision. As the cases of Ned and Frederick James indicate, white backing did not necessarily dictate what legislatures would decide.

Though they could not determine the outcome of cases, white patrons backed black elders by referring to their work histories and prospects in old age. The length of black elders' labor, for whites, created the conditions for exemptions. For instance, the free black Richard Morris of Wheeling, Virginia, lived into old age, and his white neighbors centered his standing as a worker in their 1848 petition on his behalf. At the time of their support, he was around 56 years old. With Morris having been a "resident of said city for about thirteen years past," the petitioners felt confident about giving an estimation of his character. Having placed Morris under constant surveillance, they characterized him as being "honest, faithful, laborious, respectful and orderly in his deportment." Adding his seasoned age into the equation, they reported that Morris was a "worthy and inoffensive old man."[42] Over his thirteen years under their watch, he walked a constant tight rope to maintain his standing in the community.

Daniel gained a comparable reputation. Born around 1790, he lived the first six decades of his life as a slave. His owner filed a petition in 1850 in Montgomery County, North Carolina, asking to emancipate Daniel, telling the assembly that he "is advanced in life." The petition added that Daniel's long and "faithful" service was enough for him to "be at liberty" and that Daniel's father, "an old colerd man" named Danel Shed had been emancipated around 1810, lived in the county, and "supported a good honest character."[43] Evinced by the longstanding performance of father and son, the petition sought to convince the assembly that Daniel represented an exceptional case. James Dunn rested his petition upon similar grounds. Born a slave, Dunn acquired his freedom through self-purchase, and he then bought and freed his mother and wife. Becoming old, he sought permission to buy and emancipate his son Lewis, whose character was said to have matched his father's. Dunn and his advocates sought to turn his longevity and his behavior to the family's advantage, seeing the credibility he accumulated through his years of reputable conduct as something that could be passed onto the next generation.[44] Having held them under a long period of intense scrutiny, the long list of white signatories to petitions vouched for black elders they deemed to be "faithful."

Serving as character references, white petitioners deemed long stretches of "good" behavior as the grounds to call for an enslaved person's release. When Buffaloe Sam's owner Osborn Jeffreys filed a petition in the North Carolina General Assembly in 1798 asking for the right to set him free, the record argued that Sam had earned his freedom because he "by his honest industry raised and paid to his master forty-five pounds Virginia currency as a consideration for his freedom."[45] The owners of Betty filed a petition requesting to emancipate her on the grounds of her work history, but they added additional factors. Filing their petition in 1855, Caroline Winslow and Malinda Carmon claimed that Betty's "meritorious and praiseworthy service" entitled her to freedom. They also brought to the assembly's attention that Betty had given birth to seventeen children, asserting that her longstanding service and role in reproducing the slave population made her a worthy candidate for emancipation.[46] The petition submitted for Dolly gave a much different portrait. Changing hands between multiple owners, Dolly had belonged to Phillip Raiford and Larkin Newby before being purchased by Dr. Hiram Robinson of Fayetteville, North Carolina. There was no reference in the record to her black family ties; what mattered to the local white citizens was her work habits. She was "a good Honest industrious woman," who was skilled as a nurse and "a good cook and honest and upright."[47]

Similarly, white citizens of Fayetteville, North Carolina, characterized the slave Lewis Williams as an exemplar. A group of whites saw him as "a man of good moral character; peacable and quiet, and very much respected in the community where he resides."[48] In the case of the slave Fanny Hickman of Georgia, her long marriage to her white husband Paschal Hickman became the grounds for her freedom. She paid her dues through a marriage that lasted "more than thirty years." They had seven children together—John, Grove, Henry, William, Hetty, Eliza, and Frank. Because of her lengthy marriage and family life with Paschal, the state passed a law recognizing the freedom of Fanny and her children that placed them on "the same legal footing that free persons of color" enjoy.[49] Thus, white patrons hit on multiple registers when filing their petitions and affidavits of support, with recognition about the industriousness and "faithfulness" of black elders being key reasons to extend entitlements to them.

The records, though intended for an audience of legislators and refracted through the lens of white citizens, provide a glimpse into the long individual and collective struggles of black elders and how they made arguments ensconced in age differences. For example, Blackwell McAlester of Brunswick County, North Carolina, made claims about rights to freedom that were not available to young people, a difference that he recognized and sought to circumvent. McAlester gained his freedom through "meritorious service." Though free, he still had slaves in his family, with a grandson whom he wanted to purchase and set free. Realizing the power of old age, he argued that his grandson "is too young to have rendered meritorious service, and he is therefore advised cannot be set free by the county court of Brunswick." But invoking his eldership, McAlester asked the assembly "to grant an old man the freedom of his grand child by a law emancipating him by the name of Joseph Blackwell."[50] Using his position as a grandfather and the support of his allies, he successfully advanced his case, with the committee of emancipation being "of an opinion from representation that the prayer of the petitioner ought to be granted."[51]

The power of the legislature and white citizens to determine the fate of the aged put the aged in a precarious position and subjected them to the narratives of others, as growing old meant that they had spent a long time walking a tightrope. While black elders tried to craft their own stories, they could be overshadowed by white fears and anxieties that accumulated over time. The case of Lucy Boaman reveals how the support of white patrons was not always clear-cut and could be clouded by conflicting opinions. In some ways, Boaman seemed to present a straightforward case of how being old could offer some relief from the state. A group of white residents filed a petition on her behalf, pronouncing her as having "always borne an excellent character."[52]

In addition, Richard May remarked that she was a woman of "uncommon character" and that she and her owner John Winn were "on the best of terms" before he died. Besides, he reasoned, her old age made expulsion a problem.[53] The petition stated, "The said Lucy is so far advanced in life, that a removal from the Commonwealth . . . is impractable."[54] Boaman also tried to control her own narrative and claimed her freedom based on her owner's will, which stated upon his and his wife's passing that Boaman would be free. She appealed based on her old age, stating that she "was about sixty years of age, in delicate health, and wishing to remain here the remainder of her life." Concerned that she might not get the freedom to which she had been entitled, she asked that at a minimum she be able to choose her owner if she were to be sold.[55] According to the records, she was "between 55 and 60 years of age and is infirm" and thus pled that expelling her from the Commonwealth would bring an abrupt end to herlife, "which in any event must be but short."[56]

But other deponents painted a different picture. While Boaman had support from most of the estate, another member of the estate crafted a counter narrative. In her affidavit, Charlotte Winn suspected foul play. Boaman had demanded her freedom, Winn argued, and poisoned her owner John Winn and her mistress Priscilla Winn to get it.[57] For two years, this legal drama played out with Boaman's status in limbo until the assembly ultimately rejected her petition.[58] Her case demonstrates the precarious standing of aged black petitioners, who often depended on local references and whose longevity could expose them to competing narratives about their personal histories and character.

The case of Amy Grason also reveals how white character references were insufficient to persuade the state to act on behalf of the black aged. According to the court of Loudoun County, Virginia, Amy Grason had overstayed her welcome after being emancipated around 1825. County authorities indicted and convicted her for violating the state law requiring her to either leave or ask for permission to stay in the commonwealth. Having been through that legal ordeal, she sought relief from the legislature. She counted on her former owner Presley Cordell to vouch for her character. Having owned her for twenty years, Cordell "emancipated her for good conduct and meritorious service." Grason lived in the county since her infancy, but her stellar record did not convince the state—they rejected her petition. So, despite her years of "faithful service," they ruled that she had to go.[59]

By making labor and character arguments, white supporters narrowly defined the meaning of black eldership, the interests of the state, and the place of black elders in it. To white patrons, black character was reduced to its ability to advance material production and maintain social stability. From their point of view, patrons conveyed an image of worthy African Americans who worked hard and were "faithful," which black elders symbolized to whites through labor over the long haul. Through their singular focus on black labor value, white advocates were generally much less concerned about what was significant to black subjects, whose words offered much more nuanced, multidimensional arguments and self-portraits. The arguments made by black elders reveal their complex understandings of their social relationships, relationship to the state, and expectations of what should come along with old age.

Nativity

As African Americans saw friends, neighbors, and family members die or get pushed into the slave market, those who stayed rooted in place and lived into old age developed deep personal bonds to the land and the people who survived. This prompted them to file petitions to remain in the state where they had been enslaved; these documents also portrayed slave elders as fully orbed individuals embedded in communities, figures who defied flat ideas of African Americans as being useful only for labor and material production. Their accounts attested to their intimate and intergenerational attachments, and they spoke a language of nativity to mark their time, which they defined not only through their forced material labor but also through their relationships and subtle connections to the land. Their petitions thus constituted part of a larger social and legal movement through which African Americans claimed "birthrights" and exercised what they understood to be their status as citizens.[60] Pointing to their birth and nativity, Black elders contested racist expulsion laws and made appeals to citizenship.

For example, Nathan Dunlap filed a petition to stay in Virginia with his family. Emancipated in 1834 by his owner Catherine Dunlap, the 50-year-old freedman wanted to spend his last years with his wife and five children. He had the support of local white citizens who vouched for his character and described him as "an honest harmless quiet industrious man." But going beyond this kind of work-related and respectability reasoning, Nathan Dunlap made a nativity, kinship, and longevity argument, claiming that he was "very desirous to remain with his family in the county in which he was born and in which he has constantly lived for nearly 50 years."[61] Though the documents do not reveal the outcome of his case, Nathan Dunlap's contention still points to black political arguments about the ties between old age, nativity, and rights.

African American appeals to nativity and birth constituted part of multipronged arguments made by black elders, which conveyed the long span of their life cycles. For instance, Ackey White had been possessed by different owners over his life course, first being the property of the father of Martha Parks and then of Parks and her first husband. Parks allowed White to hire his time, which enabled him to buy his freedom in 1824. When the freedman turned 60 in 1836, he was one of the few draymen in Norfolk, Virginia. In her affidavit on behalf of White's petition, Parks argued that "the great drain of the negro population by the South" made his labor indispensable to the city.[62] The account describes how, while the domestic slave trade depleted the city's work force, White stayed in Norfolk with his wife and children, whom he bought and emancipated. But White made his plea not only on the grounds of his labor value but also based on the two ends of his life cycle, birth and old age. The petition implied that "If now in his old age he be compelled to seek an asylum in another state it is but too probable that poverty and all its lingering train of evil await from which death only could relieve him." He also identified his nativity to make his case, asking to have the right to "spend the remnant of his days in the land which gave him birth," a case the commonwealth deemed to be "reasonable."[63]

The idea of nativity advanced by black elders carried with it ideas about a depth of relationships that could only be forged over time. At 70 years old, Gabriel Jones of Richmond had no apparent ties to family, but he still had close social bonds that gave him a sense of place. Perhaps he outlived his family or maybe, like so many other black Virginians, he lost them on the auction block. But he still had local connections that he wanted to preserve. And he sought to make good on his owner Simon Abrahams's will that liberated him. Abrahams added a provision in his 1838 will that upon his death Gabriel Jones, along with Nancy Hicks, 60; Hannah Cox, 60; Randall Henry, about 45; Tom Bower, 80; Aggy, 60; and Tom, 60, should be granted their freedom.[64] By the time Gabriel Jones filed his petition in 1851, they were possibly the friends he referenced when he challenged the government's demand of him "without even the means of transportation to leave his native state, his friends and his home, for some place he does not know where." Having lived a long life and being a native, he stood as one "now nearly three score and ten and cannot expect from the cause of nature to live anywhere long,"[65]

Looking back at his seven decades, Jones defended his claims to Virginia as his native state.

The longstanding connections that black elders had to family and home did not guarantee mercy from the state. For example, the Virginia assembly rejected the aged Jenny Parker's appeal to stay in her land of nativity. Parker had been a slave of Josiah Wilson, who included a provision in his will that she would gain her freedom upon his death. A year after he died in December 1812, she filed a petition with the Virginia legislature through Surry County for an exemption from expulsion. After all, she asserted, her "faithful and correct conduct" entitled her to freedom. She had also accumulated a long record of work. Beyond that, her family ties and age bound her to Virginia, her "native state." She had children, one of whom was free and owned two of Jenny Parker's children. Framing her family, age, and nativity as the grounds of her appeal, she wrote "Your petitioner being advanced in years and believing in the ordinary course of things that she cannot long continue to live and deeming it oppressive at her advanced period of life to be compelled to desert her native state children and friends to seek a residence in some to her unknown quarter of the country."[66]

In the case of the free black Sam Johnson of Virginia, he linked his appeal to old age and nativity to a request for his daughter Lucy to have the right to stay in the state to offer him elder care. He wrote that "He is getting old and feeble," would soon become dependent, and envisioned becoming "forced in a short time to rely [on her] for daily sustenance." Looking backward and forward in time, he informed the state about his life of "incessant toil" that enabled him to secure "a small cottage and garden where he had hoped to close his eyes in peace attended by his child—his only child." He added that his ties to his daughter Lucy as well as to the county and its people were "strong and unalienable." At the end of his life and under the expulsion law, Sam Johnson found himself trapped. The petition concluded that "he could not at his advanced age and with his feelings [move] to another soil and another people and yet without his daughter and alone how could he live here."[67] The state disagreed with his reasoning, rejected his petition, and left him vulnerable in his old age, as the law of racial order drove a wedge between him and his daughter.

Likewise, the state rejected the petition for Sam and Sookey, who claimed nativity. The two saved enough of their wages from hiring out their time to buy their freedom and live the rest of their years in Virginia, though the law stood in the way. With Sam being older than 70 and Sookey at 68 when their owners filed a petition on their behalf in 1857, they faced expulsion and forced migration to Liberia. Appealing to their old age, the petition states, "They are too old to attempt to emigrate to a free country, and they desire to spend the short remnant of their days in the country of their nativity, the home of their affections, and the land of their birth."[68] Though not supported by the state, their appeal demonstrates the role of aging, identification with place, and intimate relationships in their personal and political identities.

For some free black elders, their sense of place was established through the acquisition of property, which they sought to defend and bequeath. For example, John Caruthers Stanly defined his attachment to the land through the lens of the property that he acquired over his long life. After years of "long, faithful and meritorious services," Stanly attained his freedom from his former owners Alexander and Lydia Stewart, who got a license to free Stanly in the Craven County court. But Stanly wanted security to protect the freedom and property he acquired over his long life. In his 1798 petition to the North Carolina assembly, he told the state that "by honest and persevering industry, he has acquired a considerable real and personal estate," and he wanted the state's protection in case "some accident may deprive him of the evidence of his emancipation." Thus, he wanted the assembly to pass a law to "confirm, establish and secure to your petitioner his Freedom."[69] Realizing that living on property was not enough to secure his freedom, the aged Stanly successfully pushed the state to recognize his emancipation.

When black elders secured their own freedom and property, they made cases based on their old age to pass their property to the next generation. Molly Horniblow, the grandmother of Harriet Jacobs, faced that barrier after she accumulated property as a free black businesswoman in Edenton, North Carolina. Seeking to keep the fruits of her labor in the family, Horniblow bought her son with the goal of emancipating him and bequeathing her property to him. In her petition, she attested to her own character by showing that through "prudence, industry and economy, she has become the owner of considerable property" and that her son Ramsey had been "honest, industrious, obedient, faithful and attentive." Raising the fact of her old age, she continued that "She is now nearly seventy five years old: that there is no one to whom her property can descend: that it is advised that her son cannot take either by will or gift, but on the contrary will himself be and continue a slave, at the death of petitioner unless liberated by your honorable body." Horniblow thus aimed to turn her eldership, knowledge of legal and moral codes, character, and acquisition of property into resources for her son.[70]

Through decades of forced labor and through their personal relationships, black elders identified with the land, reasoning that only death should force them from their "native" states. Black elders supported their claims to residence by going back to their personal origins of birth, providing personal narratives about work on the land and stressing the unique significance of their family relationships in old age. Though they stood on the margins of Southern labor and commerce, African American elders saw the land as their home and felt entitled to live their final years on it rather than on foreign soil. Through their individual and collective stories, their petitions provide a lens into the politics and meaning of age by showing how they had aged on the land and making a clear demand that they be able to live on it over their few remaining years.

Afflictions

In old age, antebellum black Southerners looked back in time, pulled on their birthplace, and recognized the labor they performed while younger to define their native status. They also suggested that forced labor created an accumulation of infirmities in their bodies. African Americans who reached old age conveyed that afflicted, wounded, or infertile bodies should be exempt from expulsion laws because they could not to withstand the pressures of being uprooted from their family and native land. Thus, the idea and experience of an aged body became a shield against actions by the state. The petitions of black elders not only spelled out how they came of age and described the circumstances that led them to seek redress but also brought up infirmities to serve as a defense. They also provide a window into gendered and racialized modes of elder care among black Southerners.

When black elders raised the condition of their health to appeal for exemptions, they were not seeking sympathy alone. Rather, they implied that their old age and infirm bodies evinced that they had earned the right to stay in place. For example, Rachel Collins made her case to remain in the Commonwealth of Virginia by highlighting her strength of character that deserved credit and her "afflicted" body that demanded recognition. Born a slave around 1776, she worked as a domestic in the Herbert family household. She attended to her mistress, who promised Rachel her freedom, a promise that was betrayed. When Mrs. Herbert died, her financially insolvent husband sold Collins to Captain Robert Steed in 1796 under the condition that Collins could buy her freedom. She eventually did and lived out her life as a free woman in Norfolk, Virginia. Over the course of her long life, she paid her dues to the state. She paid her taxes and fed the militia during their defense of the town during the War of 1812. More importantly to Collins, she formed bonds of friendship in the community "during the active and useful part of her life." Looking at her life in retrospect at the age of 60, Collins said that she had an earnest right to stay. As she put it, she "expected to end her few remaining days there with the respect and approbation which necessarily attend a life well spent." Drawing on a bank of respect that came from living her life well, she sought enough social credit to stay in Virginia in her old age. Collins also stated that she was "somewhat afflicted and infirm." Given that she "was a poor old harmless and inoffensive Female" who would not live long, she argued for the right "to spend the sad remainder of her days in the Commonwealth amongs those who have known her in her days of usefulness." Collins grounded her argument in the cumulative value of her life experience—work, taxes, usefulness, and friendship—and the pain of an aged body that was too fragile to move someplace else. Being poor, childless, infirmed, and close to death made her particularly vulnerable, but Collins turned those factors into a reason to stay and maintain her ties of affection. The assembly granted her some relief, deeming her argument to be reasonable.[71]

The free black Virginian John Elson also raised the issue of his infirm body and his need for care from his family. Over the course of his life, Elson acquired "a sufficient property with which to maintain himself and family in comfort and independence." He bought his wife, his son, and his daughter Clemensa, holding them in slavery as the best way to preserve his family. Setting them free would mean they would have to leave the state. By the time he filed his petition in 1837, he was "far advanced in life, of very infirm health, and of a feeble constitution," and he depended on his daughter Clemensa to care for his aging body.[72] Before Elson bought her, she worked as a domestic in the household of Joseph Mays, but Clemensa left Mays to "live with her parents, both of whom being very old and infirm required her attention." Elson wrote that "She has hitherto been a comfort and a solace to his declining years," and he wanted permission to emancipate her on the condition that she could stay with him. With Clemensa performing the work of elder care, a lot that normally fell on black women, he argued that she ought to inherit his free status, a petition that the assembly referred to the Virginia Committee for the Courts of Justice.[73]

The case of Hannah and her mother Phillis also bound up infirmity with an appeal for residency and exemplifies the role of black women as caregivers to the aged. The aging and infirm Phillis, her daughter Hannah, and the rest of her family sought relief from the Commonwealth of Virginia. Their owner James Scott put a provision in his will that upon the death of his widow, Hannah, Phillis, and their children would not only go free but also inherit "a tract of about three hundred thirty acres, constituting a valuable farm." Forcing them to leave under the expulsion laws would mean financial hardship by forcing them to sell their land below market value because they could not hold out for the highest price. It would also mean family hardships. Hannah had four children—Celia, Charles, Elizabeth, and Porter—with her husband who was owned by John Cowan. Leaving the state would thus separate wife, husband, and children. And the condition of Hannah's mother Phillis also became a point of contention. With Phillis being "very far advanced in life, and extremely infirm, and in the common course of nature cannot expect to live but a very little longer," forcing her out of the state would be especially unjust, they argued. They added that Phillis, "almost on the brink of the grave, will be compelled to undergo the fatigues and difficulties of removal, which if undertaken in her aged and infirm condition, may prove fatal to her."[74] With Hannah playing a leading role in the petition, she most likely performed the work of elder care in this multigenerational household.

Along with caring for each other, African Americans also performed the work of caring for aged slaveholders, and this experience entered David Ward's petition. David Ward spent the bulk of his working life attending to the personal and business affairs of his owner John Ward. As a single man and the owner of a substantial estate of land and slaves in Pittsylvania County, Virginia, John Ward leaned on David Ward to manage his property. David Ward kept the estate's lodging running by attending to guests, handling their luggage, and managing financial transactions. Beyond that, David Ward oversaw agricultural production on John Ward's property, and for twenty-five years he slept in his owner's bedroom, taking care of his bodily needs.[75] As John Ward's servant, David Ward along with his sister Nancy Ward took care of him in his old age, especially when he became subject to life-threatening, suffocating "attacks."[76] According to his petition, David Ward displayed unceasing loyalty and portrayed himself as a moral exemplar.

He argued that he sacrificed himself caring for others while young, and when he became old, he deserved to stay in Virginia. He wrote that he spent the "prime of his life" in "fidelity and obedience to his master, [showing] respect for others and reverence for your [the state's] laws." In old age, he expected an exemption, not to be forced to "part with his pittance awarded to him by his late master (for long tried services) as a support for his feebleness of old age." He urged the state to "not drive him, with a little property into the hands of speculators and sharpers." In old age, after years of loyal behavior, and with the prospects of feebleness, David Ward fought against the threat of being sold down the river. His fight did not matter to the state, which rejected his petition.[77] The state did not extend to David Ward the right to hospitality when he was past his "prime" that he extended to his former owner, reflecting the arbitrary nature of the legal system's treatment of black elders.

Since most slaves did not have a precise record of their birth or age, some black elders made arguments for inclusion by exhibiting signs of old age in their bodies. For instance, the free black Titus Brown used his graying hair to verify his old age. He filed his petition in 1834 in the wake of being notified to leave the commonwealth. The 60-year-old argued on the grounds of kin relations to stay in Virginia—he was married to Diana, "about four or five years younger than himself." And he also tendered his aging body as evidence. The petition states, "His head furnishes the best proof of his advanced age, being almost entirely white." With little time left in his life, he hoped the state would "relent from the rigor of the law" and allow his family "to live the remnant of their days in the land of their birth." The assembly viewed his petition favorably and "recommended a bill be passed in support of him."[78]

Grounded in changes in his body and laboring capacity, the declining property value of Isaac Harris created an opening for his petition. Harris's owner Bennett Taylor said on his death bed that he wanted Harris to be freed. Unfortunately for Harris, Taylor never included his dying wish in his will, leaving Harris to depend on his own word and the verbal testimony of others to gain his freedom. Conjuring up the wishes of his aged former owner, Harris also made the case that his own old age should be taken into consideration when deciding on how he should be treated by Taylor's heir. Harris doubted whether "the immense fortune left to the masters infant son will suffer a perceptible diminution in the emancipation of a slave who is growing old."[79] With an aged slave being owned by an infant, the ways that chattel slavery allowed such distorted relationships surely was not lost on Harris. But that is what he faced as an old man. Given his limited options, Harris reasoned that "growing old" diminished his financial value, attempting to turn his old age to his advantage.

Black elder petitioners made even more complex arguments about their changing bodies when they discussed their reproductive capacity. In the case of a group of white North Carolinians who supported the emancipation of the slave Abraam Smith, they painted him as innocuous because of his old age. His owner Jacob Smith filed a petition to the North Carolina State Assembly concerning him, noting he was "about sixty five years of age" and deemed him a worthy candidate for emancipation "for his faithful services through a long life." A host of neighbors signed a statement attesting to Smith's character, arguing that because he was of "an advanced age" he "can not increase the species of population in our midst." His advocates claimed that his aging, infertile body justified his entitlement.[80]

Will of Virginia pulled in related threads, appealing not only to his own work history, physical infirmity, and family ties but also to his wife Mourning's infertility. Will lived in Campbell County, Virginia, and, like many other slaves, had an abroad marriage. By the time he filed his petition in 1815, he had been married to his wife Mourning for about twenty years. When he was younger, Will was physically able to visit her. But, when he filed his petition, he "was advancing in years, and becoming somewhat infirm, so as to render it inconvenient to visit his wife, who resided at the Distance of between twenty-five and thirty miles from where he lived." Given the physical difficulty he had in visiting Mourning in old age and his isolation and desire for "comfort and consolation," Will proposed to use his life savings to buy her freedom so she could live with him. He wrote that he had lived a life of "uncommon merit and fidelity," had spent years saving up money he earned through "honest industry," and faithfully paid back a loan extended to him to buy her. He added another argument about old age, which was that Mourning was "believed to be so far advanced in life, that she will not probably have any more children."[81] Will's owner Bowling Clark supported the petition, reassuring the state that "Mourning is a woman of between forty and fifty years of age, and is not likely I imagine to have any more children."[82] Tamping down the specter of increasing the size of the free black populations, Will used his and his wife's old age to create an exception to the rule. Hearing this argument, the assembly forwarded it to the committee for courts for review.

Trapped in a bind between a longing to stay connected to the land and expulsion laws designed to limit the growth and viability of the free black population, some black petitioners conceded similar ideological ground about the fear that Southern whites had about free blacks. They had the choice of leaving, staying illegally, or using whatever resources they could to legally remain at home. Given this dilemma, some black women argued that their infertility made them candidates for exemptions. For instance, Amy of

Chesterfield County, Virginia, filed a petition grounded in a logic tied to old age, family, labor, generation, and infertility. Amy was manumitted by her owner Mary Cox, who stated in her will that she wanted Amy to have the right to stay in the commonwealth. But since owners did not have the final say and since Amy faced the threat of expulsion under Virginia's law, she filed a petition with the assembly. She opened the petition by attesting to her former owner's desire for her to stay in Virginia. Amy also recognized her family ties, saying that she was the "mother of many children, all of whom [were] slaves" and lived in the county. She reasoned based on individual moral and labor principles that her "fidelity" and "good conduct" should allow her to enjoy the "fruits of her labor" by staying in the commonwealth.[83]

Her argument became more complex when she raised her old age and infertility and pointed to the original intent of the expulsion laws. She asserted, "The object of the law, as she is informed, was to prevent the increase of free negroes—not so much in the persons of those who were or should be manumitted, as in the descendants of each." In other words, the point of the expulsion laws was for the state to prevent a new generation of free-born African Americans. The petition added, "Your petitioner is now rapidly approaching the end of her mortal career, and at farthest will be a sojourner here but for a little while" and that "she is too old now to multiply and have increase." She closed her petition by pointing to her old age and asking permission to "spend the evening of her life in the enjoyment of freedom, where, in her declining years she may reap consolation and comfort from the hands of those, to whom she gave birth." Amy had limited options and within those limits sought to use her old age to turn the tables on the state's overarching concept of black women's reproduction. Since the colonial period, the planter class defined the children of black women as "increase," and Amy well knew this racialized and gendered concept of black childbirth.[84] As the term generally applied to enslaved children who were thought of as an "increase" in slaveholders' property, the state also applied the concept of "increase" to the children of free blacks. By displaying her old age and inability to "increase" the free black population, she used her old age and gender to find a loophole in the law.

Other African American women made comparable arguments. At 65 years old, Dolly Woodson filed her petition in the city of Richmond. Having been manumitted and having inherited property from her mistress Ann Pritchard, she did not reap the benefits of that potential boon because Pritchard's estate got caught in legal wrangling in the courts. By the time she made her case, Dolly Woodson was "subject to fits of frequent occurrence," a claim that she had backed up by two different doctors who treated her.[85] Realizing the white anxiety about a growing free black population, she assuaged the commonwealth by saying that she was too old to give birth, a point supported by Doctor Chamberlayne, who wrote that she "would never add more than herself to our [free] population."[86] Old, infirm, childless, and poor, she did not have the resources to relocate; the assembly agreed, ruling her plea to be reasonable.

Yarico also made this case. Her owner, Fontaine Wells, filed a petition in 1835 seeking the right to free Yarico. By then, Wells had already been subject to different legal entanglements. After his father died insolvent, Wells bought Yarico, who had been allowed to hire her time and earn her own wages. But that right was revoked by "the policy of our laws forbidding the going at large of slaves, or hireing themselves out" in the wake of Nat Turner's slave rebellion. The expulsion law was yet another barrier to her freedom, and Wells made the case for an exemption. He argued that Yarico, "from her age, has been long beyond childbearing, and . . . that her character, as far as they know or believe, is that of an honest and unoffending creature." Though unable to bear children, she could still work on her own, and the petition asked for her to be granted the right to be freed and stay in the state "upon such terms, and under such restrictions to prevent her hereafter becoming chargeable to the public or in any way obnoxious to society." Though old, the petition argued, there were still conditions under which she could maintain her roots in the states.[87]

Within black families and communities, the appearance of aging bodies called others to respect them. They took on a different meaning on the pages of petitions, as aging black bodies became a way of getting individual justice from the state. With gray hair, having less geographical mobility, being unable to live independently, being less physically able, or being beyond childbearing years became markers that distinguished not only black elders but also reasons for their appeals. In pleas that had multiple dimensions, black elders gave voice to their character, local connections, and flesh to exercise political power.

Time

In their petitions, black elders reflected on the broad scope of what they did in the past—they worked, made connections to the land, bought property, experienced loss, and developed reputations. They gave voice to their present state, especially the condition of their aged bodies. But old age was also about the future, as black elders saw a small window of time ahead of their current age and had an immediate sense of their mortality. Reflecting on their limited opportunity, black elders wanted more than anything else to spend time with their family and friends. And in doing so, they testified to the pressure on and the resilience of those bonds of love, tenderness, and care.

Confronted with the possibility of expulsion, the aged sought to spend their few final years with their loved ones. As in other petitions, they gave multiple reasons to back their appeals, but the goal of having time for kin was paramount. For example, John Dunn Scott looked at the entire arc of his life in his request for an exemption. Through work, saving hard-earned money, and through "meritorious" service, Scott earned his freedom, which the superior court of Wake County, North Carolina, recognized. He then purchased and wanted to secure the freedom of his wife and only son. An old man when he filed his petition to the North Carolina assembly in 1832, he claimed a debt owed to him for having "scrupulously performed his duty to his master and who now as a freeman bows with reverence to the laws of this country." Peering into the future, he wrote the assembly that he was "now advanced in the journey of life and . . . at best can only hope for but a very few years," a plea that the assembly sent to committee for review.[88] The longevity of black elders like Scott gave them a personal vantage point on the value of time that they incorporated into their petitions.

Similarly, Denis Comer pointed to his long life and labor contributions and predicted how little time he had left. Born in the era of the American Revolution, Comer acquired his freedom from Edward Washington on May 1, 1806. According to white neighbors who vouched for him, Comer exhibited "extraordinary good conduct through his life," and he worked to establish the financial grounds for his life as a free person. By the time he filed his petition to stay in Virginia, he had acquired a two-hundred-acre farm. Just as important to his close-knit community, he earned a solid reputation for his work. His white neighbors supported his petition, praising him for "his good character" and for being "extremely useful as a blacksmith." Beyond accounting for his past work, Comer recognized that his time was running out. Comer, his petition wrote, sought to "be allowed to pass the ballance of his life (and he is now more than sixty years of age) where he was born." With the reservoir of his life's time running low, he drew on a reservoir of his labor contributions to remain in the commonwealth, which the assembly recognized by sending his case to the committee for the courts of justice.[89]

Others were more explicit about their desire to enjoy their family bonds in the limited time they had left in their lives. Sterling survived the colonial and revolutionary eras of Virginia and was 50 years old when he filed a successful petition. He lived a long life but lost an early opportunity to become free. His mistress Mary Mann "bequeathed him 50 pounds to purchase his freedom," but she died in 1798 or 1799 after the commonwealth passed its law limiting slave emancipation. He remained committed to gaining his freedom and earned wages as a carpenter. By the time he filed his petition, he had a wife and nine children owned by Major Thomas Beaufort. Having saved $550 for his self-purchase, he sought to buy his freedom, stay with his family in Virginia, and "enjoy the blessings of his liberty and his family for the few years of remaining life that he has to spend." Faced with limited remaining time, Sterling defined liberty in terms of family.[90]

Old age, emancipation, and family connections, however, offered no guarantee of protection from the state. The case of Robin demonstrates the apparently arbitrary nature of the law when it came to the aged. Born a slave in Virginia at the start of the American Revolution, Robin gained his freedom from his owner Benjamin Ferguson, a legal status which did not end his troubles. The emancipated Robin left the land of his birth and moved to Ohio in compliance with Virginia's expulsion code. But his lifelong attachment to the commonwealth and his love for his wife and children drew him back home to Culpepper County in defiance of the law. He simply could not be "reconciled to live without his wife with whom he had lived happily for many years." Such was the bond that he was said to "prefer returning to slavery to losing his society with his wife." He continued to work, maintaining a good reputation in his community as a handyman. On Virginia's soil he had been raised, worked, and loved, and it was where he wanted to die. Using his age to assuage the state's concern, he foresaw the time before his death "cannot be long as he is now 60 years of age." Despite his argument and supporting statements from white citizens, the state rejected his appeal to stay in Virginia. No matter his age, family status, work ethic, or time left in life, the state still deemed him to be an outsider.[91]

Edmund Briggs appealed to the particular significance of old age and argued that he wanted to spend the limited amount of time he had left with his "kindred." According to his 1850 petition, he took care of his owner Thomas Beince "during his old age and particularly during his last illness." Beince's will granted Briggs his freedom, and he sought an exemption from expulsion. A resident of Monroe County, Virginia, for twenty-two years, Briggs was 69 years old and had deep attachments to people and place when he filed his petition. His wife was still enslaved, and he could not "think of now separating" from her. Seeking relief, he beseeched the state to allow him to live the "remnant of his days in this his native state, among those who have always been and will continue to be his friends." The alternative was "severing his ties with his kindred and seeking an asylum in his advanced age among strangers."[92]

Forecasting that they had a short time left in life, which they wanted to share with kin, black elders pressed their cases with a sense of urgency but were not promised a favorable decision from the state, which had varied responses to their petitions. For example, Hill Ballard was emancipated in the will of his owner Willis Ballard on March 25, 1809. With his wife and children being "the most endearing and affectional" to him, he made his case to be able to remain in the state with them. In his 1812 petition, he pled on the grounds of his old age, informing the assembly that he was "now old and infirm," and he wanted to live his remaining life through "acts of bounty and beneficence, exercised either in giving pecuniary aid, or in imparting to his children his skill and judgement." The petition was referred to the committee for the courts of justice and rejected, putting his legal status in the state at risk.[93] The free black William Strother's case had a different result when he filed his petition in 1830. Having worked into old age and nearing 60 years old, Strother was known in Rockingham County, Virginia, for his work skills, which earned him his "alias Billy Carpenter."[94] His white supporters noted his financial independence and that "his labor has been highly beneficial to the part of the county where he resides."[95] As important as his labor was to the white community, his connection to his aged wife went deeper, and he wanted to be able to spend his last years with her. He sought to stay "4 or 5 years when in all probability his wife may sink into the grave, when your practitioner can say I have no wife, no child, no father, no mother, and will feel in duty bound to depart."[96] His petition considered reasonable, Strother likely stayed in Virginia alongside his wife during her few remaining years.

As the clock wound down, other elders struggled to bridge the divide between slave and free and looked to preserve their kinship ties. For example, Ben looked to maintain his family connections in old age, a case that the assembly forwarded to the committee for the courts of justice. Because the fruit of Ben's labor had paid for the education of his owner Bolling Vaughn, he sought to liberate Ben, who was "upwards of 60," for his decades of labor to the Vaughn family. As an aged man with a wife and seven children owned by another master, Richard H. Mann, Ben deemed separation from them to be "worse than slavery to him." Caught between slavery and freedom, exemption and expulsion, his case highlights the challenge of maintaining mixed-status black marriages, made especially acute in old age.[97]

Considering the limits on time and defining the significance of their past and future became keys for aged petitioners who aspired to stay with kin. With only a short "remnant" of time left, Arthur along with Amy and Richard made their appeal by invoking time, labor, family, and age. Arthur gained his freedom through his mistress Mary Cox's will. His old age meant that he could count past years of "good conduct and service" toward his argument. But being an elder also meant something about the future. More than 60 years old, Arthur sought to "live the short remnant of his days surrounded by those who are near and dear to him by the ties of blood and affection." The prospect of maintaining his connections stood in contrast to a future of exile, where he feared that he would "become a wanderer in a strange Country, and, now, in his old age, burdened with its cares and its infirmities." Reflecting on his limited time and seeking to spend the "evening of his life" with his wife, children, and friends in the country that he called home, Arthur demonstrated the centrality of his kin relations. Rather than be exiled to Liberia, his prayer was to live the "remnant of his life spent with his own family in the hope of dying in the arms of his children," a prayer that the assembly answered by referring it to the committee for the courts of justice.[98]

Though usually lacking in depth, the petitions nevertheless provide brief narratives about the aged that open a window into their individual lives and reveal their broader understandings of time and family. For example, Lucy Crawford's case highlights the meaning of family, Diaspora, and age from the point of view of black elders. Lucy Crawford and Delila joined forces in their petition, and they wanted the commonwealth to take old age into consideration. Having been slaves of Captain Robert Craig, they received their freedom upon his death in 1834. Aware of the meaning of old age, they told the state that their emancipation constituted Craig's "last solemn act of his life." When they filed their case in December 1835, Lucy Crawford was 65 and Delila about 40, facts that they combined with their sex in saying they "are females, the one already having attained and the other rapidly approaching old age." Crawford tied her old age to her status as a slave mother, telling the state that "her children are slaves and dispersed by distribution and otherwise in different parts of the world." In this case, the state explicitly sided in favor of these women elders, deeming the petition to be "reasonable."[99]

Across the antebellum South, a host of black elders like Lucy had their children "dispersed by distribution and otherwise in different parts of the world." With bodies that had signs of old age and families disrupted by slavery, black elders wanted to be surrounded by a circle of care, the remaining friends and kin to whom they belonged. They pushed their cases through the legislatures, acts of defiance that were grounded in an expectation within slave families and communities that they deserved a degree of recognition and had earned a stake in their land of birth. Young slaves learned the lesson at an early age about the authority that black elders commanded. They drew on that ethic to make demands from the state. And those expectations also took root in growing antebellum Northern free black communities.

CHAPTER 4

Communities of Care and Concern

The aged Belinda wanted to live her final years in dignity. Raised by her parents along West Africa's Volta River before being kidnapped and trafficked through Atlantic slave trading routes, she survived fifty years of slavery and the American Revolution in Massachusetts. After her Loyalist owner Isaac Royall fled from his property during the war, she filed a petition with the state in 1783 for a portion of Royall's estate. In making her argument, she raised the issue of age. The petition stated that before she turned 12 years old, "She was ravished from the bosom of her Country, from the arms of her friends—while the advanced age of her Parents, rendering them unfit for servitude, cruelly separated her from them forever!" She also described how she had been treated over the course of her long life. Slavers transported her across the Atlantic on "floating worlds" where she witnessed "scenes which her imagination had never conceived of." In North America, she felt the constant overhang of her enslavement, a status from which she came to believe "death alone was to emancipate her." A half century of forced labor showed in her body, leaving her "frame feebly bending under the oppression of the years," while her owner Royall acquired "immense wealth, a part whereof hath been accumulated by her own industry." From her vantage point as an aged woman, Belinda recalled earlier times when she made her plea, seeking to enjoy the fruits of her past labor. She also stood in the present and peered into the future, petitioning the state to grant her income from Royall's estate to "prevent her and her more infirm daughter from misery in the greatest extreme, and scatter comfort over the short and downward path of their Lives." Belinda's petition began a seven-year struggle with the state, all in search of support for her daughter and the right to enjoy her few remaining years.[1]

As unusual as her case was, Belinda's material circumstances and aspirations in old age reflected larger patterns among African Americans in the North after the revolution. Black elders offered care, exerted authority, and sought support from their families and communities. They simultaneously struggled against the state and capital, which used age markers to define and mobilize black labor. Belinda's case also exhibited a larger political debate throughout the Northern and mid-Atlantic states about the terms of emancipation, which linked the age of black people to their legal status. Considering this changing legal environment, this chapter explores the tension between black family and community formation and the economic demands on different African American age groups. It considers the political context of gradual emancipation and how its age-based policies created generation gaps among Northern blacks. I examine how within that context African Americans coped with the quotidian struggles of growing old and dying in the antebellum North, with a focus on Philadelphia. The chapter also examines the practices, belief systems, and institutions through which elders tried to exercise power and influence in antebellum Northern free black communities. It demonstrates how such elder power and influence operated through the frames of class and gender, creating different avenues and destinations for men and women, for strivers and the working class. Closer to death than birth and as they struggled to survive, elders through public and private actions were instrumental to the formation of Northern free black communities in the nineteenth century.

Gradualism

From 1777 to 1804, northeastern and mid-Atlantic states passed laws that set forth the terms of slave emancipation, codes that used age to draw the line between unfreedom and freedom. Once enacted, the laws gave new generations of African Americans a legal status that placed time limits on their terms of forced labor. Vermont's 1777 law set males free at the age of 21 and females at the age of 18, though they could be "bound by their own consent after they arrive to such age, or bound by law for payment of debts, damages, fines, costs or the like."[2] Pennsylvania's 1780 gradual emancipation law had more restrictions and gave masters more control over black labor. Slaves born before March 1, 1780, remained slaves for life. But the law's "free womb" provision meant that if a slave mother had a child after March 1, 1780, that child would be forced to work for their mother's master through the age of 28.[3] New York's 1799 law had a similar "free womb" requirement but mandated freeborn females to labor through the age of 25 and freeborn males through the agc of 28.[4] In 1804, New Jersey followed suit by emancipating freeborn females after 21 years of age and males after 25.[5]

And while in principle the laws set boundaries between slave and free status, the lines proved to be illusory in practice largely because emancipation's gradualism was designed to compensate slaveowners through command over black labor during their most productive years. As one prominent historian of gradual emancipation argues, gradualism enabled slaveholders to recoup the costs of rearing young freeborn African Americans through forced labor in their teens and early twenties, allowing masters to reach a financial "break-even" point.[6] Gradual emancipation thus rested on a familiar logic of giving masters control over young black labor, whose social and political status was more akin to slavery than freedom. Defined by historians as "statutory slaves" or "slaves for a term," the freeborn had a subordinate and liminal legal standing.[7] They were bought, sold, or kidnapped in a drawn-out process that stretched a forced labor system comparable to slavery well into the nineteenth century.[8] As emancipation's rules of gradualism unfolded, a dual system of legal standing emerged that on the surface split the legal status of African Americans along generational lines, between young and old, between slaves for a term and slaves for life. But the implementation clouded such legal distinctions. Some slaveholders relegated the children of slaves for a term to the same status, keeping multigenerational black families within the master's domain.[9]

From the vantage point of aged slave parents and grandparents born before the emancipation laws, the uneven effects of gradualism were apparent, as many African Americans remained bound to the master class. In many cases, slaves' freeborn children and grandchildren had limited social and geographical mobility.[10] Furthermore, the social and political turmoil of the revolutionary era kept the aged in a vulnerable position. For instance, when the British evacuated New York City at the close of the revolution, the United States Commission of Forfeitures sold young slaves seized from Loyalists but freed the aged, who became a public charge. In addition, some slaveholders broke from colonial-era laws that required them to guarantee material support to aged slaves as a condition of emancipation. Masters from New York and New Jersey "freed aged or sick chattel and then abandoned them in the streets of New York City" in the 1790s.[11] Thus, gradual emancipation exposed the ongoing entitlement and interests of masters in young black labor while leaving the aged vulnerable to further exploitation or neglect.

The dual systems of slavery and freedom in the early republic thus left African Americans in a bind. The different legal statuses and labor expectations of the young and old clashed with the aims of African Americans to build bridges across generations. In some cases, their only recourse was support from allies such as the Pennsylvania Abolition Society (PAS), which provided legal aid to African Americans in the wake of the state's emancipation law.[12] For example, the PAS worked on the case of the aged Betty, who became free by virtue of her owner's will. Rather than being able to exercise her right to freedom, she got re-enslaved, as were her "5 children and a grand child . . . [who] was left to be sold." Richard Waln of the PAS took her case to the New Jersey Supreme Court, hoping that the court would side with Betty and her descendants and seeking habeas corpus for her release. And while the outcome of the case is not clear, it indicates the strains that the dual system placed on multigenerational black families like Betty's.[13]

Given that African Americans faced these kinds of threats, elders could be critical in grassroots abolitionist struggles by having the right information, maintaining the right connections, or knowing who to trust, which could make the difference between slavery and freedom. Intuiting the dangers around her, the aged Sarah Prior reached out to her daughter for a copy of her owner's will. Over her long life, Prior surely came to understand the importance of such documents as a potential form of legal protection, and she mastered discrete forms of communication that allowed her to build an inner circle of trust. She wrote her daughter Hannah, asking her for "the Coppy of my Master's Will which I sent you last summer." Prior added, "I wish you would send it back to mee as it is of great consequence." Warning Hannah of dangers that lurked ahead, Prior told her, "I do not wish you to come down to see me until something which you know is settled my dear child."[14] Knowing the significance of circulating legal documents, Prior used them as the tender of her and her daughter's freedom. And she used her elder authority and knowledge to protect her daughter and herself.

Still, the in-between status of blacks could reverberate across time and generations. For example, one unnamed slave woman was carried with her child to Lexington in Rockbridge County, Virginia. Decades later, the case came to the attention of the PAS, which possibly based their advocacy on the 1788 Pennsylvania law that placed restrictions on the movement and sale of slaves across state lines.[15] The woman was entitled to her freedom, they argued, because "all slaves brought into the state of Virginia and sold there, were entitled to their freedom." Despite Pennsylvania's antislavery law, she was labeled and treated like a slave, being "sold to what was then called a slave trader or Georgia Dealer in slaves." By 1819, she had both children and grandchildren who were being held as slaves.[16]

This woman's experience of growing old legally free but held as a slave reveals the problem of emancipation's gradualism because of what it meant not only for her but also for her descendants' legal status. The PAS sought to counteract the ambiguity by doing sleuth work in Philadelphia's probate records. They found that her owner Bordley had assigned her to Arthur Bryan on March 17, 1794, and they suggested that further records might be in Baltimore that could prove her free status. By the time the case reached the PAS, she was old, and her descendants were being held with her as slaves. Even as the PAS sought to free her, they asked whether the right of manumission would "extend beyond the children of the parents there named so as to include grandchildren."[17] The status of her descendants depended on the advocacy of abolitionist allies, the information about her legal status in the written record, and her family's collective memory. And while the PAS records do not clearly indicate the case's outcome, the experience of this aged black woman reveals the ways that slaveholders sought to maintain their capture of black labor across generations and over time, as African Americans sought to step on the path toward freedom.

Gradual emancipation was defined by the politics of age, granting different rights to African Americans across generations. However, the different legal status of the black young and the black old did not completely sever their intergenerational ties; in some ways, African Americans pulled on connections across generations to challenge the differences in their legal standing. Through the gravity of family ties, aged black parents and grandparents remained in relationship with their descendants, creating complex kin networks that cut across the legal status of older slaves and younger slaves for a term. In such ways, African Americans saw the transition to freedom as a collective project even as legal differences set them apart by age. Over the course of the late eighteenth century and into the nineteenth century, this system of legal differences continued to shape the experience of the black aged. Their history under forced labor and the ongoing presence of various modes of labor continued to impact the material lives of the black aged, even as some became free.

Makeshifts

African Americans in the North in the wake of the revolution and into the nineteenth century faced a range of material obstacles that had a significant impact on their lives in old age. Like other poor people in the early modern world, African Americans used an "economy of makeshifts" to survive.[18] But in some ways, they faced more constraints because of the nation's racial division of labor. Held in slavery permanently or for a term, pushed out of or excluded from skilled labor positions, migrating to find short-term work as tenant farmers, or living in substandard housing were among the many unique barriers black Northerners faced during this era.[19] Given these obstacles, they improvised and cobbled together support from different resources to make a living, a strategy that the black aged had come to master after long lives on the economic margins. They saw varied results from their efforts, but most black elders in the North struggled to make a living.

Richard Allen was an exception. By the time Allen reached his final years, he had married his beloved Sarah, been a successful artisan and entrepreneur, helped found the African Methodist Episcopal Church, and worked in the antislavery movement. By the measures of his time, he had a meaningful life that touched thousands of others in his adopted hometown of Philadelphia and beyond. And his legacy continued well beyond his death. But his ascent was not guaranteed. Born as slaves, he and his brother convinced their owner to study the Christian gospel, which influenced him to grant the Allen brothers a path to freedom.[20] Looking back on his long life, Richard Allen reflected on a moment when the prospect of growing old served as a personal crossroads. After purchasing his freedom, Allen turned his faith into service by preaching the Christian gospel, and word spread about his abilities. In 1785, Methodist Bishop Francis Asbury evangelized along the eastern seaboard and invited Allen to join the mission, but Allen declined the request. Asbury didn't offer Allen wages—only food, clothing, and transportation would be the free black Allen's material reward. Such was the sacrifice expected of him to spread the gospel. Allen refused, reasoning with Asbury that "People ought to lay up something while they were able, to support themselves in time of sickness or old age."[21] By the time he reached old age he did "lay up something" after surmounting one obstacle after another, working with his hands cutting wood and making bricks, mobilizing free blacks as public health workers in Philadelphia's yellow fever epidemic of 1793 and breaking from the Methodists to establish an independent black Christian denomination.[22]

In contrast to Allen, Jarena Lee entered the religious movement but had a much different personal trajectory and life in old age. Born free in Cape May, New Jersey, she converted to Christianity and moved to Philadelphia where she joined the African Methodist Episcopal Church. Previously denied access to preach by Allen, who followed the rule that it was not women's station to do so, Lee seized an opportunity, took the pulpit, and preached a dynamic sermon at a church service when the presiding minister stumbled during his sermon. Witnessing Lee's ability to interpret the Bible, Allen not only authorized her to preach but also traveled with her to Methodist conferences. During the height of her career as a preacher, Lee delivered hundreds of sermons and trekked even more miles each year.[23] But unlike Allen, she fell into obscurity and into the margins in old age. By the time she reached her seventies, Lee's life mirrored that of most black women elders in mid-nineteenth-century Philadelphia who struggled to survive. An 1863 report by the PAS indicated how much Lee's status had declined. The society recalled that Lee "for many years has laboured as a preacher amoungst the Methodist." But in old age, the report added, "She endeavored to support herself as long as she could."[24] The 1860 census indicates how. With a personal estate worth $50, Lee worked as a "washerwoman."[25] Allen's story was remarkable, an exception occasioned not only by his faith and individual tenacity but also through his exercise of male church authority. Most free blacks were not able to break out of the economic margins. Like Lee, they faced a precarious economic life in old age, placing severe limits on the full exercise of their freedom.

Black elders did the prosaic work of making a living and pushing for their rights to do so, with some engaging in intellectual pursuits. Such work sustained Benjamin Banneker. Though achieving iconic status and being remembered for his mathematical and scientific work and his contest with Thomas Jefferson, Banneker waged struggles for economic rights in concert with his intellectual contributions. In his fifties, he wrote his first almanac, sent his manuscript off to other experts to verify his calculations, and awaited a response. While he defined himself as being "among the beginners in Astronomy," Banneker stood by the accuracy of his almanac. He argued that "The greater and most useful part of my Ephemeris is so near the truth that it needs but little Correction."[26]

Understanding the need for white allies to get his work in print, Banneker got the backing of Elias Ellicot. In one letter of support, Ellicot gave Banneker's background, saying, "He is a Black Man about 56 years of age. His father was a Guinea Negroe." Ellicot defended Banneker, saying that he had become a self-taught astronomer who sought to have his almanac published in Philadelphia. But at the time in 1790, Ellicot added, Banneker "was a poor man and would be pleasd with having something for the copy but if the printer is not willing to give any thing he would rather have nothing than not to have it published." Banneker wanted to promote "the cause of Humanity" of black people by making the case about their intellectual capacity.[27]

Having worked long and hard on his almanac and still poor, the aged Banneker used his relationships to get his work into the public domain and to reap the fruits of his intellectual labor. He performed highly accurate astronomical calculations that caught the eye of whites, and he struggled to protect the rights to his intellectual work. Seeking not just public recognition but also to earn money from his discoveries, he farmed the text out to different printers. He sold a copy of his almanac to William Goddard for three pounds, a sale that gave Goddard nonexclusive rights to print it. Banneker maintained that granting Goddard exclusive rights would be "unreasonable in him to expect, after reflecting on my indigence as also my labor and loss of time in the Calculation." He negotiated upfront with Goddard for him to pay out an honorarium from almanac sales. But Banneker reserved the right to pursue other printing outlets. When Banneker broached the idea of printing his text with a Philadelphia firm, Goddard "expressed neither unwillingness nor dissatisfaction." Banneker pointed to the precedent of other texts being printed by different printers. As such, Banneker understood that he should retain the right to have his book printed through various outlets, with a printer in Georgetown on the Potomac printing copies, an agent working to have it printed in Philadelphia, and his pursuit of two printers in his home state of Maryland.[28]

Banneker continued to press his case. He wrote that he wanted to have his book printed in Philadelphia, because he doubted that those printed by Goddard would reach that market.[29] The financial value of his work was also subject to negotiations, with Goddard asking Banneker's advocate James Pemberton for advice on "what would be a liberal ample compensation to the sable Astronomer."[30] And his reputation created other opportunities, such as a commission he received to produce tide tables.[31] Banneker fought over both ideas and compensation for those ideas; the income was needed because of his "indigence," and since he was around 60 years of age. A witness to the material lives of the people around him, a student of the natural world, and an expert in cycles, Banneker realized where he stood among them and drew on his intellect in his struggle to stay afloat.

The longevity of other elders positioned them to be intellectual workers, as in the life of the elderly "Black Alice." Included in an early nineteenth-century volume titled *Eccentric Biography*, which gave stories of exceptional women as exemplars as well as cautionary tales about gender roles, Alice's story appeared first in the book because of the coincidence of alphabetical order. She had deep roots in Pennsylvania and, according to her biographer, was "a sensible intelligent woman" and had a "good memory." With parents brought from slavery in

Figure 5. "Alice," 1804. Courtesy of the Library Company of Philadelphia.

Barbados to the colony, Alice lived among Pennsylvania's founders. Providing information about the state's history to public audiences, "She remembered William Penn, the proprietor of Pennsylvania, Thomas Story, James Logan, and several other distinguished characters of that day."[32] And while Banneker received an income from his intellectual work, the slave status of Alice meant that she did not. Nor did her work end there; she performed physical labor well into old age. Like Betsy Bailey, she worked as a fisherwoman; even after she became blind, Alice "would frequently row herself out into the middle of the stream, from which she seldom returned without a handsome supply of fish for her master's table." She also worked collecting ferry tolls.[33]

A few could escape the trap of old age poverty, using institutional means as an exit. That is how Richard Allen made his exit, and so did his partner Absalom Jones. As Jones came of age, he ascended as a master craftsman and church and community leader. In 1794, Rachel Nixon bound "her son to Absalom Jones to learn the trade of nailing." They came to terms on an agreement—her son James Nixon would serve four years as an apprentice in Jones's nail-making shop, receive board and clothing, have access to night school, and receive freedom dues of clothing.[34] Complementing his artisanal projects, he also worked to advance black education in post-emancipation Philadelphia. The PAS tapped Jones to oversee the recruitment of twelve scholars for community schools. Trusted as a church leader and male community elder, Jones supported a cohort of students taught by a black woman on Cherry Street in South Philadelphia. Jones recruited students and handled the scholarships; while the experiment had mixed results with students dropping in and out of school, he served as a stabilizing force.[35]

Belinda Lucas also discovered a degree of stability in old age. Lucas had been kidnapped in Africa, carried to Antigua, and bought by a ship captain who took her to New York. She was traded several times before she bought her freedom at the age of 40. She lost a child and three husbands, and she lived without family after her last husband died when she was in her late forties. Without immediate family, she built community ties through caring for the poor and the sick.[36] She went to a Clarkson School and learned how to read the scripture and testified that "Though I can't read all the hard words in the Bible, I can read Matthew and John very well."[37] Unlike most other former slaves, she achieved financial independence, having bought church stock for $100 that yielded a $7 annual income.[38] She worked "early and late" and earned enough to build a house that included rental space on the second floor.[39] Living to 100, she took stock of a life that had yielded her relative comfort, financial stability, and longevity. Belinda reflected, "The Lord knew that I was to live a great while, and He put it into my heart to do so; and now I have plenty, and trouble nobody for a living."[40]

Though Belinda Lucas, Richard Allen, and Absalom Jones worked their way up the social ladder, to be old and black in the North usually meant poverty and working in old age. The condition of Black Alice, Benjamin Banneker, and Jarena Lee was the norm. For instance, as their bodies frayed, Billy and Jenny of New York kept working. Billy was born in New York around 1738, while Jenny was brought to the colony around 1744. They married and had ten children—nine boys and one girl. During the Revolutionary War, they were emancipated and went on as productive laborers until their bodies gave way. Billy's would go first, becoming disabled but, though no longer able to earn wages as a day laborer, still working in his garden. Jenny continued to work outside the home as a domestic and at home on the spinning wheel until she became blind and "enfeebled by age."[41] The aged Nancy Poulson and Julia

Morris of Philadelphia eked out a living by sewing "rags when they can get them." And like Morris and Paulson, the 75-year-old widow Hannah Jones made it through by sewing clothes even while suffering from rheumatism.[42]

Such labor marginalization and bodily transformation forced some of the aged to seek public or private charity. In part, the African Methodist Episcopal Church filled this need, taking regular Sunday school collections and reserving a portion of their monthly income for the church's steward to distribute to the poor.[43] In the winter of 1835, the board of the church extended a gift of firewood to Sarah Green and Ann Munro, and they extended "immediate assistance of fifty cents per week" to another woman in need.[44] They also added Elizabeth Moore, Mary Waterford, Mrs. Adkins, and Sister Robinson to the "poor list."[45] In other cases, the aged had to rely on more informal charitable systems. The 101-year-old Sarah Easton, born in Delaware, a widow for more than two decades, and "quite feeble and hard of hearing," scraped together support from her daughter and from charity. According to a report by the PAS, Easton's daughter "pays her rent of four Dollars per month and does what else she can for her mothers support but the latter is mainly aided by the benevolent."[46] The report also noted that the former African Methodist Episcopal preacher Jarena Lee's "last days depended upon the contributions of others." They added, "This was so distasteful to her that a short time before her death she remarked, 'she wished she was done with begging.'"[47]

The black aged felt the sting of economic insecurity and worked close to the point of death. In a context of United States property ownership and the collection of rents of various sorts, black Northerners found themselves with few resources other than their labor. Whether it was Jarena Lee working as a washerwoman, Billy tending to his garden, Jenny working as a domestic, Benjamin Banneker performing his calculations, the blind Black Alice going out to fish, or the arthritic widow Hannah Jones sewing together rags, the black aged scuffled. With limited incomes and few financial assets, they also struggled to find space.

Space

As with their financial prospects, free blacks faced housing insecurity, an experience that could vary over a person's life cycle and according to one's gender and class. For example, both Richard Allen and Jarena Lee went from state to state to spread the Christian gospel and relied on the kindness and generosity of strangers for lodging. About his short stay at the home of Caesar Waters in Radnor Township, Pennsylvania, during the early years of his ministry, Allen recalled, "Never was I more kindly received by strangers that I had never before seen, than by them."[48] Jarena Lee also relied on strangers when she followed her calling. Rev. Winston paid the bill for her night at an inn in Chambersburg, Pennsylvania, and in Wilmington, Delaware, she spent two days and nights at the family home of Captain Rial.[49] By the end of their lives, however, Allen and Lee lived in different circumstances. With an institutional base at Mother Bethel African Methodist Episcopal Church, Allen had stable quarters in Philadelphia, living at his home at 150 Spruce Street from 1791 until his death in 1831.[50] But as Lee grew old, she stayed on the move. At the age of 57 in 1840, she lived with a roommate in Philadelphia's Walnut Ward.[51] In 1850, she cohabited with Eliza and Charles Wilmore in Philadelphia's Third Ward.[52] By 1860, she had moved again, staying with the 56-year-old cook Afilinda Lone in the Eighth Ward.[53] By the time of her death in 1863, she had returned to the Third Ward, possibly staying with Eliza Wilmore once again.[54] Geographically mobile but remaining in the black working class, Lee like many other free blacks relied on community networks for housing in old age.

As widows, widowers, refugees from slavery, or parents whose children had been snatched away by early deaths or the slave trade, many black elders could not rest on familial support for housing. The long-range consequences and legacies of slavery presented a major obstacle to black kinship-based elder care. And for the aged poor, homeownership was no option. As a result, black elders like Mary Brown and Lamar White adapted through cohabitation. A native of Duchess County, New York, Brown struggled to gain her freedom. But before her emancipation, she was "four times sold and has had six children all of whom are deceased." An impoverished widow with no children to offer her material support, the 96-year-old Brown shared a room with the 80-year-old Lamar White, who was born a slave in North Carolina, where her seven children remained in captivity.[55] Such were the long-term, downstream effects of enslavement on black Northerners that they led elders like Brown and White to improvise, relying on work, friends, or charity to put a roof over their heads in old age.

With meager incomes from domestic work, the aged poor inhabited spaces that reflected their economic standing. Like Jarena Lee who spent her last days living with friends down an alleyway, other aged black people pooled their resources by rooming with others. Nancy Poulson and Julia Morris of

Philadelphia cohabited in rough quarters with "dilapidated stairways" and "very small windows alowing but little light to enter the room."[56] Similarly, Beckie and Betsy lived in a "low, murky room, in one of the dirtiest and most dismal alleys in the city of Philadelphia."[57] And while the young working poor might experience similar living conditions, the aged did not have much of a prospect to escape and felt an acute sting of exposure to the elements.

Given their dim working prospects and bleak living conditions, some of the aged turned to the Philadelphia Almshouse. Along with city-born black residents, migrants with weak family ties in the city entered the almshouse when they had no place else to turn for support. The home held 868 whites and 106 blacks when Hannah Barton was admitted to the surgical and syphilis ward of the Philadelphia Almshouse's Lunatic Asylum in 1837. At 80, she was by far the oldest in the ward, surrounded by women ranging from their teens to their forties. The ward housed women like Maria Richardson, 40, who was born in the West Indies, landed in poverty because of illness, and deemed by the staff to be intemperate. And there was the 28-year-old Virginia native Catherine Miller, who was impoverished because of mental illness, as were Ruth Johnson of Maryland, Louisa Jackson of Louisiana, and Sarah Ann Gibbs. The black aged also occupied the incurable and working ward of the almshouse. Born in Delaware, the widow Hannah Barton became impoverished, according to the records, because of "old age." The 70-year-old widow Eve Turner of Maryland landed in poverty because of a "debility," as did the 69-year-old Lavinia Rix of Virginia and the 60-year-old widow Sarah Child of Jamaica. The 100-year-old Ann Taylor of Maryland was said to have been pushed into poverty because of blindness, and the widow Ann Dunbar, from the West Indies, fell into poverty because of "old age." So did Aminta Smith, the 61-year-old widow from Maryland.[58] Defined by almshouse managers as having mental and physical ailments including "old age" that prevented them from living on their own, these working-class black elders received basic support from public charity.

Black people from the region, from the South, and from the African Diaspora who sought refuge in the North might grow old there, spending their working lives until death in cities like Philadelphia and New York. Recognizing these labor dynamics, called by Christian duty, and identifying the specific housing needs of black working people in old age, a group of reformers opened the New York Colored Home for the black aged. One of the residents was Peter Bensé. Born in the Caribbean, he became the valet for a British official, who took him first to England and then to St. Petersburg. While there,

Bensé married and bore children with a Russian woman before being separated from them upon his and his master's departure. Captured by the French and held as a prisoner of war in Paris, he returned to London after his release. Hearing a rumor that his family had moved to New York, Bensé received permission to move to the city, but he never found them there. Even on his deathbed, he had hopes of reuniting with them and was haunted by memories of his family, conjuring up images of his young wife as if she was still present. Alienated from his family and having moved about, Bensé lived out his final years under the roof with a broader community of aged African Americans.[59]

Bensé had a unique path to old age in New York, meandering as it did from the Caribbean and through Europe before he arrived in the city. But his journey and destination reflected a larger history of domestic labor, forced migration, displacement, and family separation that left working-class African Americans in the urban North housing insecure at the end of their life. Some like Richard and Sarah Allen and Belinda Lucas could count on space of their own. But it was more common for the black aged to move from place to place, live with friends and family, or rely on charity for firewood, rent money, or room and board. They fully felt and experienced the afterlife of slavery, which was a strain that they carried in their bones.

Illness and Death

Illness struck across the age spectrum, but the aged suffered from specific infirmities and embodied physical conditions that constituted a distinct feature of their identities as elders. The narratives about residents in the New York Colored Home demonstrated how the institution supported black bodies that had broken down over time, suffered from chronic illness, and showed signs of old age. The text described Hercules Schureman as having a "large muscular frame, indicating great physical strength." But in old age, he had become less mobile and "confined to his bed by sickness and infirmities."[60] Sophia was blind, and her body had transformed. Observers noted that "a more emaciated frame was seldom seen," apparently because of her distaste for the food offered by the home.[61] Amy Jordan, one of the first residents of the home, entered once she became infirmed and remained there until her death.[62] The author also portrays the blindness and illness of Betsey Johnson, whose "eye became dim and her physical force abated."[63] The same was true of Peter Bensé. When he walked in the street, he carried himself with dignity and with the aid of a "large *brass-headed* cane," and he also had a head full of white, bushy hair. But as time wore on, "anxieties, and the infirmities of age broke down his health."[64]

Such painful, chronic bodily and mental afflictions marked the daily lives of black elders, limiting their spatial mobility and ability to work. Writing her daughter Hannah, Sarah Prior said about herself that "Your poor old Mother is Got old and so troubled with rheumatic pains that she is not able to walk to meeting," but she maintained "hope and trust in the Lord."[65] The biographer of Alice noted that she continued to work as a fisherwoman after she temporarily lost her eyesight in old age.[66] The PAS encountered Mrs. Bogg, widow of an African Methodist Episcopal preacher, who had a stroke and tried to live independently but struggled to care for herself. They also met Anna Maria Hall, about 50 years old and described as "delicate" and needing support from her friends. Even more afflictions beset Amelia Webster and her kin. At the age of 85, she had a "deranged" 60-year-old daughter who had been hospitalized. Well into old age, Webster was able to work for a living but fell out of the labor force because she suffered from "Rheumatism, Cramp and Dizziness."[67]

The afflicted did not always face their suffering alone, as black communities in the North sprang to collective action to care for the ill. The day-to-day experience of manual labor and environmental forces took their toll on black bodies. And care for their bodies became the grounds for black community formation and a driver of African American institutional and leadership development in the late eighteenth and early nineteenth centuries. They formed mutual aid and benevolent societies to care for the sick, and they found over time that they needed to attend to age and eldership as factors of community and organizational health.

Early mutual aid organizations created opportunities for grassroots leaders to organize and steward collective resources so community members could make it through hard times. But they did not always make explicit reference to the age of their members, beneficiaries, or leaders. The Friendly Society of St. Thomas African Church of Philadelphia formed to attend to members and their widows and orphans. Founded in 1797, the organization collected dues from members, distributing the funds to care for members in need, pay the burial expenses of indigent members, and support widows and orphans. The society evolved over time, with elected officers handling the finances and making investments in real estate or other commercial ventures to sustain the organization.[68]

The Daughters of Africa used more modest means. Membership dues became its lifeblood, creating collective funds that circulated back to members who were ill or grieving. Guided by the principles of "Liberty and Equality," words written in the Daughters of Africa's account book along with the names and payment records of its members, the organization helped African American women like Ann White, Elisabeth Matthews, Harriet Fausett, Pheby Lewis, and dozens of other working-class Philadelphia women save in case of sickness or financial trouble.[69] When Hannah Morris, who would also serve as secretary, fell ill, she drew on the organization's treasury.[70] So did rank-and-file organization members like Leah Adams, Ann Morrow, Amelia Rice, and Lydia.[71] But for Leah and Lydia, receiving funds during their illness was not enough to keep them alive; the Daughters of Africa paid for their funerals a month after paying out Leah's and Lydia's sickness benefits.[72] Fellow Daughters could relate to E. Wilkins, who lost her child and drew on the treasury for their burial.[73] And they lent money to Mary Brown and "Margreett White" for the burial expenses of their children.[74] For members and nonmembers, they sought to provide relief through the life cycle.

While the Daughters of Africa did not make a clear link between their organization and the problem of age, members of the African Female Benevolent Society did, reaching out as elders to mobilize community resources. The society was founded in Troy, New York, home of a relatively small but historically significant black community. The town attracted prominent black abolitionist Henry Highland Garnet, who called Troy home in the 1840s, several years after the benevolent society was founded. Among its many purposes, the society promoted youth development through intellectual and moral education. And it did so through its elder members and appeals to age. In a direct message to the youth, Elizabeth Wick reminded them that their condition in old age was determined by the moral actions they took while young. She warned them that "Although you are young and in the full enjoyment of health, and the fair promise of many years to come yet remember what many are to day you may be tomorrow."[75] Pointing to the possibility of becoming ill in old age, Wick gave moral guidance to the youth of Troy to save for that exigency.

Working in parallel with the moral argument about aging were other practical concerns. The society depended on dues-paying members to pay benefits to the sick, and to stay viable it needed to gain new members. The organization tried to make the case to young people that they needed to live a moral life and avoid the moral pitfalls of "seducing arts [that] deceive the incautious heart."[76] But even virtue did not protect people, young or old, from the inevitability of illness, and the society cautioned the youth to be prepared. In her 1834 annual report on the society's financial condition, the secretary Eliza Dungy informed members that the organization had grown from ten to sixty-five members in the previous year. Dungy noted that most of the new members joined in name only and were in arrears on their dues. She called out young people who would "run well for a while and then turn back" by failing to pay their dues. She engaged them first with the question "Think ye the rough hand of sickness will ever visit you? Why not then prepare for the worst?" She then warned them that the society would stand by its constitution and if need be "enforce that clause which cuts them off from any relief" if they did not keep up with their dues.[77] Raising the specter of illness or old-age poverty, the African Female Benevolent Society centered their middle-class position and authority as elders to organize the community and the next generation for collective care.

Through such efforts, African Americans in the North cared for each other and sought to keep each other alive. Living with limited financial means and often separated from family connections by slavery and its legacies, the black working class improvised through makeshift methods of personal relationships, charity, and mutual aid organizations for care in old age. They pooled their resources to create a safety net for times of illness, with the fortunes of the sick and the healthy, of the old and the young being bound together. But death came, and it yielded a range of responses.

Death

Black and white Northerners could interpret longevity and death among African Americans in radically different ways. For instance, the medical sciences used data on longevity in census and death records to generalize about racial and gender inequality. In Gouverneur Emerson's 1827 study "Medical Statistics of Philadelphia," published in the *American Journal of Medical Sciences*, he explores mortality in Philadelphia over two decades and conveys a picture of the city's population. He compares age cohorts of men and women, including blacks and whites. The census data showed that women outnumbered men in the city and suburbs by a 111 to 100 ratio. But when Emerson disaggregated the demographic data using a combination of racial, gender, and age categories, he found a number of other differences that he sought to explain.

Table 1. Race, Gender, and Age Ratios in Philadelphia in 1820

	Whites		Blacks	
	Females	Males	Females	Males
Under 10	96.7	100		
Under 14			100	100
Under 16	100	97.6		
Under 26	100	91.2	100	70
Under 45	100	90.9	100	72
45 and older	100	74	100	69
All Ages	100	89	100	71

Source: Gouverneur Emerson, M.D., "Medical Statistics: Being a Series of Tables, showing the Mortality in Philadelphia, and Its Immediate Causes, During a Period of Twenty Years," *American Journal of the Medical Sciences* 1 (Philadelphia: Carey, Lea and Carey, 1827), Table II.

Interpreting the gender differences within the white population, he argued that work explains the gap, pointing to the theory that older white women outnumbered their male counterparts because of "the greater risks of life encountered by the male sex in the various occupations and pursuits."[78] He made a similar argument about the ratio between black females and males, saying that the difference was "owing to the circumstance of the services of females being in more demand in cities than in the country, and partly to the greater mortality of the males."[79] Along with his analysis of gender ratios among black and white Philadelphians, Emerson also disaggregated the city's mortality rates according to race. He reported a dramatic difference across the color line, with 1 in 19 black people dying per year in comparison to 1 in 50.89 whites.[80]

The difference between white and black working conditions could have easily explained the difference in their mortality rates, a labor theory that Emerson used to explain gender ratios in old age. But he drew a different conclusion, one that was shaped by assumptions in the collection of his evidence. The census used different age ranges to count black and white people, and this is reflected in Emerson's study. When it came to the level of precision that the census used to categorize people by age, first came white males, then white females, then black people, who literally and figuratively were counted for less.[81] His 1827 table of the city's demographics set different parameters for age cohorts according to race and sex.

The age categories for his 1831 study were even more skewed, breaking whites into 13 cohorts while organizing black Philadelphians into only six age cohorts.[82] Of interest is not only how he measured blacks and whites

Table 2. Race, Gender, and Age Categories for 1820 U. S. Census

White Males	White Females	Black Males and Females
Under 10	Under 10	Under 14
Of 10 and under 16	Of 10 and under 16	
Between 16 and 18		
Of 16 and under 26	Of 16 and under 26	Of 14 and under 26
Of 26 and under 45	Of 26 and under 45	Of 26 and under 45
Of 45 and upwards	Of 45 and upwards	45 and upwards

Source: Gouverneur Emerson, M.D., "Medical Statistics: Being a Series of Tables, showing the Mortality in Philadelphia, and Its Immediate Causes, During a Period of Twenty Years," *American Journal of the Medical Sciences* 1 (Philadelphia: Carey, Lea and Carey, 1827), Table II.

differently and what differences he found but also how he *explained* the data. He found that while black people constituted less than 10 percent of Greater Philadelphia's population, the records indicated fourteen black men and twelve black women were older than 100 while there were only seven white women and four white men who reached that age, a difference he attributed to "the difficulty which frequently occurs of ascertaining the ages of blacks with certainty," making it "possible that more of them are reported among the instances of extreme longevity than are entitled to the distinction."[83]

At the same time that he was skeptical about the claims about black longevity, he was confident that the substantial difference in black and white mortality rates could be explained by innate racial differences, arguing that the statistics proved that blacks were inherently inferior to whites. In contrast to the labor argument that he used to explain why women outnumbered men in Philadelphia, he argued that the makeup of black people explained their mortality. Stating that between 1820 and 1830, the black annual mortality rate was 1 in 22, about double the 1 in 42 rate for whites, he concluded that "The fact last mentioned is of itself sufficient proof of some peculiarity in the African constitution, which distinguishes itself from that of the white."[84] To Emerson, the numbers on the longevity and death of black people reified his racial thinking about an "African constitution," an idea that echoed but flipped concepts about "lusty" black constitutions that shaped the preferences of Atlantic slave traders for young people in previous centuries.

While figures like Emerson used numbers and ideas about race to conjecture and speculate about the meaning of the black aged and dead, African American communities faced the everyday work of attending to the dead. In doing so, they created institutions and developed roles as elders along the way. For example, the United Benevolent Sons of the Mother Bethel African

Methodist Episcopal Church did the regular duty of extending death care to its members. The society embodied principles of self-governance and efforts at democratic practices within the church, and elders held key positions. They elected church elder Morris Brown as president to lead the important work of caring for the sick, the dead, and survivors.[85] On one occasion, they paid to the widow of member Samuel Valentine a "gift in consequence of the Benezet Society having paid his funeral expenses."[86] As part of their community-wide effort that divided labor along gender lines, Sarah Ash did the grim work of preparing the dead for burial, with the board moving for her to "attend to the dead of the Union Benev. Sons of Bethel and Union Church."[87] The most prominent of their late members was Richard Allen. After his death, Brown called the membership together to recognize and attend to the last rites of their fallen leader. He reminded his fellow sons of "the charitableness of the Bishop in not receiving aid from the Society during his late and long protracted illness." Given that they did not give Allen any financial assistance, they were called to display their support through their physical presence. Brown called on members to assemble in their meeting hall and "form a procession to attend the funeral of the Late Bishop." They also organized a testimonial to show their "respect for the memory of there lamented fellow member Richard Allen."[88]

The work of burying the dead could also glue organizations together, because the income that church cemeteries generated could be substantial. In the 1830s, money brought in by Mother Bethel's burial grounds averaged around 25 percent of the church's weekly income, and in several instances that number was much higher. For example, on September 12, 1832, the burial grounds brought in over half of Bethel's weekly revenue. The church created this space for the living to envision their last rites, offering members dignity in death.[89] Through such quotidian acts, preparation for death became the grounds of Northern black organizational life, in many cases led by local elders.

As much as it was a place of care for the living, the New York Colored Home for the aged served as a site for black elders to have a dignified death. Separated from family members, they could not experience a "good death" in the way that white middle-class families expected.[90] Rather, faith and their aged friends offered them support in facing death and going through its last rites. For Hercules Schureman, he "died in the faith in which he had lived" and was "gathered into the heavenly garner" at the age of 105. Tommy Warner's dying wish was to be buried next to his roommate Henry. When Warner died, other residents of the home assembled for his last rites in the home's hallway. The residents sang one of Warner's favorite songs, "Jerusalem, My

Happy Home." After remarks and a brief service, the elders accompanied his body to the grave. The account of the home reported that Warner's corpse was "followed by five of the oldest female inmates, and all the old men who could walk," and "he was conveyed to his final resting-place, and laid by the side of his friend Henry."[91] Through this act, his fellow residents served the role of extended kin and afforded Warner a good death. Blind Sophia, whose body wasted away, had parting words for one of her caregivers, who stood in as a surrogate family member. "Oh, God will bless you, dear Missy," Sophia said soon before her death. Having refused medicine because she longed "to be at *Home*" in death, Amy Jordan died at 76 with the last words, "Christ is near me; I want nothing more."[92] Betsey Johnson had Katy Schenck as a roommate, and they accompanied each other in the last phase of their journey. "Intimate friends in the latter days of their pilgrimage, by death they were not long divided."[93] For Peter Bensé, it was the thought of his family that he carried to the grave, as he hoped to reunite with them until he took his last breath.[94]

Having reached old age, black elders saw death around them. They survived the high mortality rates that took most black people to the grave before they reached old age. They struggled to meet their material needs, working into old age, sharing space with friends, relying on private or public charity, and pooling their resources to manage hard times. A few broke out of this system into middle-class status. But the majority had limited material resources to live out their old age. And whether the aged suffered from economic deprivation or acquired property, their experience was not defined solely on material terms, as African American elders made claims on spiritual power that came along with their years.

Piety

Biographies, memoirs, and accounts of black elders link their old age to religious piety. Narratives of the black aged imply that the keys to longevity were their early conversion, religious devotion, and faith in salvation in the afterlife. In their youth, the culture sexualized black bodies or saw them as vehicles for material production. But as those bodies aged, they fell in their estimation as objects to fulfill sexual or material desire. In the popular imagination, as discussed in books and pamphlets that circulated among literate audiences in the early to mid-nineteenth century, the black elder often became associated with religious piety and virtue.

The vignette of the pious black elder became something of a genre in the nineteenth century. According to her profile in *Eccentric Biography*, Alice was a lifelong Episcopalian. Being illiterate, she showed her exceptional piety by having her friends read her the Bible. She was "temperate" and "careful to keep the truth." The biography adds that in old age, "She was so zealous" about her faith "that she has often been met on horseback, in full gallop, to church at the age of 95 years."[95] Alice continued to work and attend church services well into old age, and the biography implies that her religious devotion translated into vitality and favor well into her old age. The biography of Zilpha Montjoy of New York also explores the interlocking nature of faith and old age. Born a slave and emancipated later in life, Montjoy lost both of her children and her husband. But, the biography continues, she stayed connected to the Methodist church and grew in devotion in old age. At the age of 68, she enrolled in an African Clarkson Society mission school, established by Quaker women in New York City to help African Americans make the transition to freedom.[96] The narrative recounts, "The teachers endeavoured to dissuade her, telling her she was too old to begin."[97] Yet she persisted, claiming that, "We are never too old to do good."[98] As she believed that "the Lord would help her," her faith and piety served as a shield against age discrimination. The biographer also notes that even as Montjoy's health declined and "her understanding failed," she remained devoted. Before her death and interment in the New York African Burial Ground, she declared, "If it is the Lord's will to take me, I am willing to go, but I must wait my time."[99] The biographies thus examine the lives of black elders to suggest the buoying power of piety.

The narrative of Beckie and Betsy further elaborate on this motif of the pious black elder. According to their collective biography, Beckie and Betsy had purified spirits. Beckie purified her spirit through material restraint. Rather than indulge in buying and displaying on her body the latest fashions of the day, Beckie wore simple clothing. And when she had cancerous growths on her ankles in her final year alive, she refused to take opiates. Thus, she signaled that she relied not on the material world but rather upon "the one ever living Helper."[100] By the power of her word and embodiment of restraint at the end of her long life, she provided spiritual leadership to others, especially her spiritual sister Betsy. She carried on Beckie's work, turning her bereavement into service. The narrative recounts that Betsy "was resorted to by many of her own colour as a counselor in both spiritual and temporal matters."[101] Even her white Philadelphian patrons "rejoiced in the opportunity of visiting this humble, cheerful, though, in her own estimation, least and weakest of her heavenly Father's children."[102] As she aged, she became blind and physically disabled, but she still felt compelled to "carry the Lord's message" to the poor, the sick, and the suffering. The text implies that her aging body could still be a religious instrument. After Betsy became paralyzed and lost her speech, another black woman elder comforted her on her deathbed. This "aged coloured woman" (as the pamphlet described Betsy's visitor) would say to Betsy, "Do ask Master to give thee steadfastness of mind."[103] Such biographies suggest that black elders, and especially black women elders, possessed exceptional spiritual power.

Hagiographies of pious black elders spoke to larger audiences and concerns, promoting the benefits of Christian virtue. For instance, Phoebe Jacobs embodied virtues of a Christian woman—prayerful, humble, forgiving, generous, churchgoing, an ardent student of scriptures, happy, and unafraid of death. Certainly, the narrative concludes, she paid her way to heaven by virtue of her faith and conduct.[104] The narrative of "Uncle Harry" also fits into the mold of the pious black elder, as he was represented in a text that was at once biography and promotional literature. The tract characterized Uncle Harry as the embodiment of religious devotion and piety and one who responded to the scripture through a posture of praise, with hands clasped in his lap and his head turned upward. Having been exposed to Christianity by an acquaintance who was converted by George Whitfield, Harry held his own in his knowledge of scripture when a Catholic priest sought to convert him. In telling the story of the black elder, the author expressed his own belief about the transcendent power of the Christian faith. Witnessing Harry's piety, the author "was made to appreciate the value and Excellency of that religion, which could take a poor slave, and so transform him, that he was well nigh fitted to be a companion of saints in light, and of just men made perfect."[105] While many of the narratives explored the laity, a number highlighted the piety and example of black preachers. The account of the New York Colored Home included the biography of Hercules Schureman, who served as a Methodist minister for half a century. Even in the home, he was known for his devotion and "would pour forth from the desires of his soul in a strain of fervent prayer."[106] In these ways, the activity and image of black elders became vehicles to spread the faith.

The black elders who were represented publicly in books and pamphlets had their counterparts in the private lives of African Americans. Elders stood at the center of religion, family, morality, and praise, and they held the fragile bonds of generations together. For instance, the aged Sarah Prior sought to influence her daughter Hannah by putting her devotion on display. Sarah wrote that it was "a beautiful thing to serve the Lord" and urged Hannah to "attend to meeting and keep no bad company." Writing for the rest of the family, Sarah let Hannah know that she was cared for by her father, her brother Warner who had plans to visit, her sister Nancy who wanted a gift, and her sister Sally, who sent Hannah "all the love she has to spare." Sarah Prior closed the letter in the spirit of elder piety and devotion, sending her well wishes to Hannah and her brothers John and David. She added a final prayer, "May God be your Guide and Jesus Christ your Savior."[107]

Belonging

Along with the claims to piety came a moral impulse directed toward more worldly concerns. African Americans grounded their well-being, material security, and prospects in long-term, multigenerational relationships. Such interests had a broad reach, as black Northern political and religious leaders explained their work with generational reasons. In a convention call by Henry Sipkins of New York, he charged "every free man of color to employ his utmost energies towards our moral elevation in this country. It is a duty he owes not only to himself and family, but to posterity; and monstrously delinquent must he appear who shall neglect to perform it."[108] Similarly, a contributor to the African Methodist Episcopal Church's periodical the *Christian Recorder* spelled out the proper role of elders in the lives of the next generation. "Let the children be cared for," the essay argued, because that care creates blessings that the caregiver will reap later. When children receive care, "they will not only bless you in after years," meaning in old age, "but they will also bless you in the grave." The author pinned the blame of elder neglect and poverty on the way the aged treated their children. When "aged fathers and mothers" become destitute, "the reason, and the only reason to be assigned for this state of things, is, that such parents have not trained up their children in the way that they should go." From this vantage point, being a good parent meant two things—caring for your children and being cared for by them in old age.[109]

The logic of intergenerational moral and material bonds called for by elders at the organizational level also operated at intimate, kinship levels. The aged free black man Hector and his wife gave shelter and care to an orphaned child with whom they developed moral and material ties. Hector convinced his wife to take in the child, believing that he might have been sent "to take care of us in our old age." By the time he was 8, they apprenticed him to a chimney sweep, which gave him the means to contribute to the household budget. Even after Hector's wife died and he went into the city's almshouse, his adopted son fulfilled intergenerational social ties, providing both visits and financial support.[110]

Such moral and material bonds between elders and young people proved to be critical in navigating the day-to-day affairs of living on the social margins and in the transition from slavery to freedom. Given that gradual emancipation laws freed newborns while leaving older generations enslaved, elders made pleas to the younger generation for help. For example, when Hannah Van Buskerk (Grover) reached out to her only son, Cato Way, in 1805, she had not seen him in two decades. She tried to reconnect, asking him to visit, send her money so she could visit, or update her on his personal situation, his family, and his livelihood. And she also sought him out in hopes of freedom. She wrote, "I am a poor old servant. I long for freedom. And my master will free me if any body will engage to maintain me." She closed with a plea for help, writing, "If you have any love for your poor old Mother pray come or send to me" payment for her transportation so she could visit him.[111]

While Sarah Prior and Hannah Van Buskerk struggled in old age to maintain relationships at a distance, other elders lived under the same roof as their children and grandchildren. When Billy and Jenny reached their seventies and their working lives ended around 1815, they "were removed to the habitation of one of their sons, where they were boarded, and remained until death."[112] Moses Gillingham of the PAS also provides an example of an intergenerational bond in the case of a slave woman who was being threatened with sale. When her owner fell into debt and faced pressure from the local sheriff to find assets to settle with her creditors, she considered putting her slaves up for sale. It came to Gillingham's attention that she was willing to part with the slave woman for $200 if the PAS could pay it; otherwise, she would likely have to go to the auction block. The appeal indicates the intergenerational nature of this slave woman's experience. She not only had "2 small children," she also had "the grandparents living with her" and a husband on a nearby estate.[113]

In informal ways that were grounded in a broader moral code of respect across generations, young people looked out for elders when needed and elders looked out for young people when called upon. For instance, Stephen Dutton of Wilmington, Delaware, advertised in the *Genius of Universal Emancipation* that his granddaughter Eliza Boyce had been kidnapped by slave traders. He called on people to see if they could find her among the slave coffles heading through the South.[114] Lydia York advocated for her niece Hetty, whose mother Sarah Batson "died in Virginia and left said Hetty under [Lydia's] care." Seeking the PAS's support, York tried to protect Hetty from employers who had "not used [her] well."[115] And Isaac Johnston looked after his children and grandchildren, using his knowledge as an elder to aid their emancipation. He informed the PAS that his daughter-in-law Levina was "freeborn" on the Eastern Shore of Maryland near the Virginia border, close to "Daniel Mifflins Mill abt 16 miles from Snow Hill." Her father was named Littleton, and her mother was Rachel Stevens. He added that others in the community—"James Knox, a Taylor, Tho Millburn Green, Levin Townsend, Ralph Millburn, John C Handy Clerk of Court" and others—"all living in Snow Hill know that Levina is free born." Johnston recalled that Levina married his son Isaac, and they lived for about seven or eight years in a community along the Maryland and Delaware border. But she and her children Rachel and James were kidnapped. Using his knowledge of family relationships, Johnston asked the PAS to interview Philip Lee, Levina's uncle. Johnston informed them that Lee could be found at his job at a grocery store in Baltimore's lower end, "near the Brickyard." Johnston assured the PAS that Philip Lee was "acquainted with Levina and those who can testify to her right to freedom."[116] As a walking atlas and genealogist, Isaac Johnston drew on his knowledge to fulfill his duty to his family; being a family elder was essential to his daughter-in-law Levina and to his grandchildren.

With a host of threats facing them, African Americans tried when they could to move across space and thresholds to maintain intergenerational bonds. Jarena Lee tried to stitch these thresholds together, visiting the deathbeds of the ill and aged. She periodically visited her aged mother; on one visit, Lee found her 78-year-old mother "happy in the Lord, and my sister also."[117] In the last decade of her life, Lee visited former African Methodist Episcopal Church parishioner Rebecca Cox Jackson on January 1, 1857, as an act of reconciliation, repentance, and closure. Jackson and Lee had both started in the African Methodist Episcopal tradition, but Jackson split with the denomination in the 1830s and became a Shaker eldress, while Lee had stayed loyal to the African Methodist Episcopal Church. A conflict during their time in the African Methodist Episcopal denomination led them to become estranged. Jackson recalled that Lee had been "one of my most bitter persecutors." But the mood during Lee's 1857 visit took on a different tone, with Lee embodying a "kind and friendly spirit" on that New Year's Day. Lee spoke and then "sung a few verses and kneeled, and prayed a feeling prayer."

Jackson offered the same in kind, and, she says, "When done, I rose and went to her, and embraced, and kissed her."[118]

Turning their piety into action, black elders had concerns about the here and now. They tried to maintain bonds of mutuality and belonging over space, time, and multiple generations. With the social pressures of low-wage or slave labor arrayed against them, elders offered care and protection to future generations when they could. Younger people responded in kind, caring for elders when they had the means. Complementing their individual religious sensibility, elders set their moral compass toward care of family, neighbors, and friends. Out of this collective vision emerged organizations through which they exercised community leadership, ones that were not free of underlying tensions; outward conflict, status seeking, and gender politics; and struggles for power, resources, and position.

Power

For the black poor in the antebellum North, reaching old age and becoming an elder involved various material, social, and ideological struggles, as they improvised to live on the margins. Their old age and the idea of eldership could enhance their social and spiritual status, even when they were poor. But the idea of the religious black elder took on another form, one linked to church authority and that implied but was not necessarily dependent on old age. The idea and practices of black eldership took an institutional and masculine form in the African Methodist Episcopal Church. Within the organization, the church elder served as a nominal and ecclesiastical figure, whose authority rested on experience, title, and place in the church hierarchy. Through an intersection of their relative seniority, religious power, manhood, and middle-class status, elders had considerable power in the church. Its founding and governing documents bear this out. When the church set up its articles of association in 1799, it developed a structure of black male grassroots leadership upon which rested the authority of the white elder of the Methodist Episcopal church. At the base, black men had full membership rights—originally, women did not have the right to vote for trustees. The male base elected trustees, who in turn elected the officers of president, treasurer, and secretary. The trustees had substantial authority to run the church—they had the power to override vetoes of the elder on financial matters, controlled the church's revenue, and passed bylaws. In essence, on temporal and material matters, the all-black male trustees were in charge.[119] But on ecclesiastical matters, the elder had greater authority—he had the right to the pulpit of Mother Bethel on Sundays, to nominate and license preachers, and to judge cases concerning personal conduct of members.[120] In short, though it would be over the property that the trustees exercised control, elders had power over religious matters.

These institutional roles created the grounds for conflicts, such as when the African Methodist Episcopal Church fought against white Methodist elders. The African Methodist Episcopal Church conference, male and female, passed a unanimous resolution to incorporate the church property independent of the white Methodist Episcopal hierarchy. Even as they got control over their temporal affairs, they still felt the sting of white ecclesiastical authority. The white Methodists insisted on sending ministers to the black church, but they underserved the community, prompting a tussle over resources. One year, a white Methodist elder visited the black church only five times, leading the trustees of the African Methodist Episcopal Church to cut his salary. In another instance, the congregation physically blocked access of a white Methodist elder to the pulpit, which was being occupied by their own preacher. All of this pushed the membership of Philadelphia's Bethel church to join black Methodists from Baltimore and elsewhere to form the independent African Methodist Episcopal Church.[121] Their organizational structure placed a premium on the role of ordained elders, who among many things were responsible for serving as liaisons to the broader community and for enforcing church discipline.

In their *Doctrines and Discipline*, the church spelled out ground rules for personal conduct, which elders played an important role in maintaining. This was part of the larger moral ethos of the church that promised to cleanse individuals of sins and be of service to the poor.[122] They not only performed rituals such as church services and marriage ceremonies; elders also operated as judicial functionaries in the church. The church empowered them "to receive, try, and expel members, according to the form of discipline."[123] Being enforcers of moral codes meant that they had to withstand the scrutiny of the church community. It took at least eight years in the formal ministry to attain the title of elder. On lower rungs, licensed preachers served at least four years before they could be promoted to deacon. They had to then serve as a deacon for four years before ascending to the position of elder, a step below bishop in the church hierarchy. At each step, congregation members had the opportunity to weigh in on the character of the candidate through a public inquiry. During the ordination of deacons, for example, the bishop asked the church,

Figure 6. "Bishops of the African Methodist Episcopal Church," 1876. Courtesy of the Library Company of Philadelphia.

"Brethren, if there be any of you who knoweth any impediment or crime in any of these persons presented to be ordained Deacons, Let him come forth in the name of God, and show what the crime or impediment is."[124] A similar public ritual of moral scrutiny attended the ordination of elders. To be an elder and hold the community together meant to be above reproach, which was essential to the larger moral ethos of the church and its work of providing for the poor and carrying out Christian ideas and practices to "cleanse the thoughts of our hearts by the inspiration of the Holy Spirit."[125]

The codes of behavior and structures of authority spelled out in the church discipline, as detailed as they are, do not fully reveal the nuances and complexity of the daily lives of church members in relation to elders. Members argued about the proper role and behavior of church elders, who had a critical position in church governance. Their role in adjudicating appeals cases on conduct charges meant that their judgment could determine whether a member charged with misconduct could stay in the fold or be expelled. For example, during a debate over whether the church should add new administrative roles of presiding elders appointed by the bishop to judge cases at the annual meeting, J. M. Brown objected to the centralization of judicial power, preferring that some power of appeal be kept at the local level. He thought that elders who operated at the local level played an important role in administering justice. Using a hypothetical example of a conflict between a young preacher and a member, he argued that the preacher "would prefer the advice, counsel, and example of a wise and experienced elder to preside in his quarterly conference" to resolve the issue at the local level rather than have it adjudicated by a presiding elder at the annual conference. Thus, J. M. Brown perceived the knowledge, judgment, and wisdom of local church elders as essential to just rule, church governance, and discipline in church communities.[126]

This approach was consistent with his earlier, generational vision about how to set men onto the path of church eldership. While he praised past generations for breaking from the white Methodist church, establishing an independent church, expanding the denomination, and practicing their faith with zeal, Brown argued that current times required different qualities in the ministry. Bemoaning the intellectual decline of the church community, he called on a new generation of more highly educated clergy to receive three years of college education. "I want to see young men come up, filled with the Holy Ghost and cultivated minds. They must build upon the foundation thus laid by our venerable fathers. The names of those noble-hearted pioneers will long be born in mind. Generations unborn will call them blessed." Through the intellectual development of male clergy, the church can be revitalized, Brown claimed, and he also argued that his old age gave him this perspective. He felt especially devout, saying that as time goes on, "The cause of my precious Master grows better and better to my view. The older I get, the sweeter I find him to be."[127] Brown thus made the case that a strong foundation of knowledge ripened with age and enabled religious authorities to render judgments and enforce social norms.

Through moral authority that rested on their years of experience, male clergy and elders in the African Methodist Episcopal Church had the power to decide who did not belong to the community, holding positions that enabled them to respond to internal conflicts and hear the cases of members brought to trial. The elder and all-male committees ultimately determined the fate of defendants. This was a case for Nancy Collins, who was brought to the church's bar of justice by Solomon Tate. After hearing both sides, the committee led by Richard Allen found Collins guilty and expelled her from the church "for imprudent conduct." For the elders, violence was beyond the pale. One member was charged by Clayton Durham "for fighting his wife." The committee found him guilty and "judges him not a fit member of Society and therefore he is disavowed from Society."[128] The threat and fear of violence also played out in the case between Charles Bohanon and Abraham Morton. Bohanon charged Morton with threatening to "knock him down" for defending his sister and other women in the community. The church expelled Morton from its membership.[129] And D. Diggs faced charges of "beating and abusing his wife and makeing use of profaine language." While the defendant failed to attend the hearing, the committee took the testimony of Kitty Miller, who overheard the verbal abuse. Abraham Morton also testified that he asked Diggs about his conduct, and he "acknowledged that he did beat his wife and made use of profaine language." Hearing this testimony, the committee, led by the elder Richard Allen, concluded that the defendant was "not a fit member of the Church of God and is accordingly disowned."[130] They also decided the fate of Hannah Harris, who faced a grave charge of terminating a pregnancy. Matilda Black brought the case, claiming that she knew how a pregnant woman looked. Black also insinuated that Moses Hancock was an accessory, dumping the remains from a chamber pot and hiding Harris in his house. Harris denied the charges and brought character witnesses to her defense, who attested to her personal conduct. Led by Richard Allen, the committee found her not guilty of the charge.[131] Relied upon for their knowledge and experience, elders heard cases and determined the fate and standing of church members.

The case of Anthony Davis and his sister Phillis Bohanon demonstrates the patriarchal role African American male elders could play in family disputes. Davis asked the church committee to save his sister Phillis Bohanon's reputation. Her husband Charles Bohanon traveled to attend a church meeting in Baltimore and asked African Methodist Episcopal exhorter Andrew Tilgh to "take charge of his wife untill he returned." Davis feared that Andrew was getting too close to Phillis, visiting her day and night. Gossip started to swirl. As Davis put it, people were "talking in the street." Phillis and Andrew defended their reputation, with Phillis responding that Anthony "never saw anything indecent of me" and Andrew stated the same. Because there had "been so much bad report," the committee put Phillis Bohanon on a three-month trial, and Andrew Tilgh was banned from exhorting "until the next quarterly conference."[132] The church elders thus defended Davis's right to oversee his married sister's behavior.

Taking a posture of religious piety, elders enforced the discipline and regulated the day-to-day behavior of members. In this way, they used words carefully and demanded the same of others in a church culture of interpersonal surveillance. The nature of some of the records reveals their verbal discretion and secrecy, where the precise details and offenses went unspoken. They tell us that Sophia Benson was put on trial and Sarah Brown was expelled for "imprudent conduct."[133] Likewise, Mary Hamilton was examined and found guilty of "a charge of Immoral Conduct."[134] In other instances, they tried to prevent the misuse of words. Using "sinfull words" could land a person before the committee. Samuel Valentine brought Isaac Cook to the church's committee to be disciplined for "saying that the Trustees and church might go to hell." Cook admitted to saying the words but clarified and contextualized his statement. He was responding to an internal conflict in the church that he deemed to be petty, so Cook said, "Before he would trouble his brains any further, that the trustees and church might all go to hell."[135] Even with this explanation, the committee found Cook guilty. On the other hand, a case against Stephen Smith was dismissed. Rev. Joshua Eddy brought a charge against Smith for saying that "If the Corporation adopted a certain amendment to the bylaws of the Constitution that in 2 years they would have it in the Discipline and the Discipline would be a Slavish Discipline, then we the members of said church would be perfect slaves."[136]

In these ways, words and conduct could create or tear apart the bonds of community, and congregants called on church elders to mediate interpersonal conflicts. For example, Henrietta Randolph claimed that Sarah Gordon spread gossip that Randolph was having an affair with Gordon's husband Henry. The church queried a set of witnesses, including Henrietta, her mother Ellen, and Henry Gordon. No one denied the gossip but could not trace the source to Sarah Gordon. Ellen came to the defense of her daughter, saying that the rumors were "too much for any one [to] bear. Such reports will have to be stop[p]ed." The court sided with Sarah Gordon, not seeing any evidence to substantiate Randolph's claim that Gordon slandered her reputation.[137] Words also cemented financial relationships, as in the case of agreements between landlords and tenants. Alford Laurance brought a grievance against a church "sister," Margret Fussom, who was $13 behind on her rent, a case heard by Rev. W. D. W. Schureman. He set up an agreement for her to pay it in twelve months, working to reconcile the differences between the two.[138] The church made similar arrangements for Rev. Joshua Eddy, who brought Peter Burtin before the elder to get repayment on a loan. Upon arbitration, the church set up a one-year payment plan for Burtin to repay his debt.[139]

Elders in the African Methodist Episcopal Church played a leading role in practicing grassroots methods of justice, reconciliation, and enforcement, an ethos that was reflected in other contemporary black organizations. The Union Benevolent Sons of Mother Bethel African Methodist Episcopal Church expelled members for nonpayment of dues, as was the case with one member who was "expelled from the Society for his [arrears], and all that he has paid are [forfeited] for the use of the same/Society." At the same meeting, the organization fined another member "for sleeping."[140] The Daughters of Africa also placed limits on its benevolence. Given the precarious nature of black working-class women's lives, the Daughters of Africa aimed to support its members during periods of economic hardship; but given the small scale and limited resources of the organization, the actions of individual members could affect the whole. So, they tried to collect from members who fell behind. If a Daughter did not pay, the society kept a record and went after members in arrears. They took a harder line at their June 11, 1824, meeting, when they approved a resolution that all members in arrears should "be notified to come forward at the next stated meeting and pay up or be expelled."[141] Faced with ongoing challenges of compliance, they later made delinquent members ineligible for benefits.[142] Members of the Daughters of Africa ran afoul with their sisters not only by falling into arrears but through other forms of "misconduct." Financially desperate women Hester Brown and Bethany Blanton were charged with "immoral conduct and theft."[143] Otherwise, the record books did not specify what kind of behavior could land a member in trouble. The committee found "Mrs. Stewart to be disorderly" and the conduct of Ann Clinton and Elizabeth Hemmons to be "disorderly and improper in the extreame."[144] They later moved to expel Hemmons from the society for "immoral conduct."[145]

In the overall scheme of these organizations, there were few cases to resolve. Perhaps some community members worked things out before they made their way through the official channels. At the top stood elders who sought to bind people together. The cultural idea they represented as moral exemplars was critical, allowing them to withstand scrutiny while mobilizing their communities, judging the behavior of others, or castigating members who had run afoul of community norms. In the Daughters of Africa, women office holders required members to adhere to the rules, and male elders and leaders in the African Methodist Episcopal Church exerted moral pressure on its members. And while elders tried to maintain control over their organizations, they faced opposition from peers and from marginalized groups, particularly women and the young.

Conflict

They may have tried, but church elders could not monopolize institutional power. For example, in 1854, the presiding elder of First African Presbyterian Church submitted his letter of resignation. For a reason not clearly stated, the elder stated that he had "become unacceptable to the congregation." He reassured parishioners that he was not leaving for the sake of "gratifying any private whim" but rather to prevent division in the congregation. By virtue of his resignation, he demonstrated the important unifying role the elder had to play in church affairs, and if the elder failed, he should leave for the sake of the whole.[146] It also demonstrates that individuals did not have permanent and unassailable authority; rather, the institution and its norms had primacy. In this regard, it shows the fluidity and, at times, instability of the role of individual elders and how free black communities wrestled with authority figures.

Looking at free black communities from the vantage point of eldership and generation offers insight into day-to-day gendered and class relations among African Americans. Even as they were outnumbered in the urban North, male figures held more institutional power, having the ability to enforce moral and organizational codes of behavior. For example, the male trustees, preachers, elders, bishops, and other authority figures in the African Methodist Episcopal Church tried to build a shared community of purpose, and the *Doctrines and Discipline* provided a unifying code of conduct to maintain order among and connection between church members. This organizational structure, codified in the text and incorporated by the state, helps to explain the ongoing growth and development of the church. As fissures within the church arose, the *Doctrines and Discipline* became the instrument through which church leaders aimed to resolve internal conflicts. The minutes of Mother Bethel African Methodist Episcopal Church also demonstrate how elders and trustees exerted power, how they and others struggled over resources, and how elders created hierarchies and categories of insiders and outsiders to build the church community. But as much as the church's *Doctrines and Discipline* and common purpose established a binding agent that enabled the church's longevity, neither elders nor others in the church maintained a constant united front.

This was the case when the Bethel and Wesley congregations merged. In 1822, church elders met, and "it was unanimously resolved by the corporation of Bethel Church and the trustees of Wesley Church that the two churches should be united."[147] They held a mass meeting to ratify the decision, which revealed internal rivalries that broke the peace between the two communities. At a meeting held at Bethel church and with only a few dissenters, the members of Bethel and Wesley churches voted in favor of conjoining their congregations. After closing the meeting with singing and prayer, Richard Allen announced that he would walk over to Wesley church, which stood next door to Bethel. To symbolize the union, Allen led a group of Wesley trustees and Bethel leaders and congregants to the Wesley church building. A small faction of Wesley members who opposed the merger blocked the church's entrance, and when the procession tried to enter, the opponents "engaged in pushing and pulling the people off the steps." With the aid of Wesley trustees, Allen and the procession eventually made it into the sanctuary. After Allen took the pulpit, he "demanded silence in the name of the commandments" and preached a sermon. But the conflict escalated. According to the Bethel minutes, "Wm Perkins," one of the Wesley dissenters, "behaved very bad indeed, he ran up into the gallery and jumped out of the gallery into the pulpit and sit upon the pulpit along Rev. R. A. during the time of worship and disturbed the congregation very much, he spit several times on the Rev. R. A. while preaching."[148]

Even as internal conflicts and challenges arose, the church grew because of its highly disciplined organizational structure, with elders and bishops at the top. Given the size of the church, the relative paucity of cases that ended up before the committee demonstrates how much congregants saw moral discipline as essential to their individual and collective liberation. The exceptions proved the rule, as was the extraordinary case of trustee Henry Brooks. The church owned residential property to bring in auxiliary income to support its work, and they authorized trustee Brooks to collect rent from their tenants. Problems arose when the church tried to collect back rent from some tenants, only to discover that they had already paid Brooks. Supported by other witnesses, the church discovered that Hester Johnson paid her rent to Brooks, even paying by express mail when she traveled to the countryside. Brooks took advantage by skimming money from her payments and altering her receipt book. After hearing a range of testimony from Johnson's family and neighbors, the church found Brooks guilty of fraud, and he was expelled from the church.[149] In another, less extreme case, the church trustees found Rev. Joshua Eddy to be past due on his rent of church-owned property. They presented a bill to Rev. Schureman. The parties brought in arbiters, and the church brought in a third party to negotiate matters. Before the arbitration went forward, Eddy made payment.[150]

Struggles over church finances reflected other tensions about roles and control, and eldership could be at the center. At Mother Bethel African Methodist Episcopal Church, a faction of trustees challenged the selection of Elder John Cornish to lead the congregation, having been appointed by the church bishop. Cornish was received by a majority of the church trustees, but a minority countered by holding a convention to nullify his appointment and select a new minister. With the majority supporting Elder Cornish, they tried, convicted, and impeached the dissenting trustees for violating church discipline. In retaliation, the "rebel" trustees barricaded themselves in the church. A legal battle ensued. Cornish's faction hired a lawyer to get possession of the pulpit and the case wound its way through the courts up to the Supreme Court of Pennsylvania, which ruled in favor of Cornish's faction.[151]

The elders of Mother Bethel also resolved conflicts over the election of trustees, which was essential to the longevity of the church but also created the potential for succession disputes. For example, Osborn Spriggs brought charges against Rev. Eddy, arguing that Eddy did "deprive them of their constitutional rights of nominating and electing their officers of the temporal affairs." After Eddy pled not guilty, the church committee went through a set of documents and testimony. Unconvinced by the evidence and after Schureman gave his statement in defense of Eddy, the committee dismissed the case.[152] In another case, the presiding elder J. B. Campbell brought charges against trustees Nelson Gordon and Benjamin Harris for obstructing the transition of three new trustees into their positions. The specific charges included interfering with a new trustee during Sunday collections, not recognizing the legitimacy of the new trustees, sowing dissension, claiming Elder Campbell had "usurped and taken away the rights of the members of Bethel Church," and rejecting efforts to remediate the conflict.[153] Schureman testified that the African Methodist Episcopal Church's General Conference passed a rule that empowered elders to nominate trustees in the case of vacancies. Henry Gordon testified that members had voted on the nominees, and Rev. Eddy attested to the obstruction of the collection. In their defense, Gordon and Harris brought witnesses who challenged some of the claims. Abraham Morton claimed that only 12 or 14 of the 150 members present actually voted in the election and Hans Shadd stated "That the though the Elder made the nomination, he did not call a motion." Moses Jones and George Custas made similar statements.[154] In these and other ways, the precise role, rights to title, and authority of elders did not go unchallenged.

Though male elders monopolized control over positions of public authority, church women pressed to exercise institutional and spiritual power.

For instance, the Bethel church fell into debt to its women's auxiliary organization and authorized the formation of a committee to "settle the books between Rev. Richard Allen and the Corporation and also afix the seal of the Corporation to a bond with the Corporation to the African Female Benevolent Society of the Bethel Church for money which the Corporation borrowed of the said Society on interest."[155] The United Daughters of Tapsico made a similar extension of credit to Wesley church. Withdrawing cash from their bank account, they resolved to loan the church "$100 carried at six per cent interest."[156]

The role of women in the day-to-day affairs of the church during its early years was not lost on succeeding generations. In her *Appeal to the Females of the African Methodist Episcopal Church*, Mary Still celebrated the role of early church women to mobilize her contemporaries and younger generations. Still argued that the church should build upon the work of the church's founders and improve the condition of African Americans, slave and free. Looking back in time, she reasoned that the church owed a special debt to women for their years of sacrifices, writing that women had, "like the women at the Sepulchre, were early to aid in laying the foundation of the temple."[157] And while many of these early church women had died, she wrote, "Some still linger on their staves watching with intense interest the ark as it moves over tempestuous waves of opposition and ignorance."[158] Not only did women build the foundations of the church, they also performed honorable deeds by establishing mutual aid societies to "alleviate each other's sufferings."[159] Still thus invoked the contribution of elder women to inspire young church women's work.

While Still worked within the church, Old Elizabeth's *Memoir* demonstrates the tension between women who received a call to preach and the church's male elders. Elizabeth's experience was by no means singular and reflects a larger phenomenon of the ways that women preachers had to negotiate the gender politics of the church. Her conversion narrative follows a familiar arc—being separated from family, feeling alienated, suffering physical or emotional afflictions, and then being led by a spiritual force. At her moment of conversion, Old Elizabeth "saw the Savior standing with His hands stretched out to receive me. An indescribably glorious light was *in* Him, and He said, 'peace, peace come unto me.'"[160] After her emancipation, she got called to preach after being led to the Bible passage, "Gird up thy loins like a man, answer thou to me. Obey God rather than man." Called to "gird up thy loins like a man," Elizabeth used the language of manliness to step into a religious role but still faced opposition from male clergy. When she held a prayer meeting with a group of women, it was broken up by a watchman, and it met with the disapproval of the male church elders. Even "old sisters" shrank from the pressure and fled the meeting.[161] Rejected by male religious elders, she continued her preaching and served as an itinerant minister for another four decades and well into old age.[162]

As she understood it, the Light and the Spirit were constant companions, and as she became old, she came to understand them as a shield, a form of protection. When whites and blacks came to one of her meetings to "hear what the old colored woman had to say," one "great scripturian" came to record her words, but she recalled, the Spirit moved through her so powerfully that not only did the congregant "cast away his paper and pen," he also paid for her transportation. As an aged preacher, an elder without the formal title, she counted on the "Lord's power" for strength and support.[163] The self-trained preacher Katy Schenck rested her ministry on similar grounds. After her conversion at the age of 28, she believed "that the Lord has fast hold of me." From that point until old age, she preached the gospel that she learned, in her words, from "the school of Christ."[164] She thus claimed a direct transmission of knowledge, working around the religious authority of male elders.

Along with the gendered conflicts about religious authority and eldership, periodic, low-grade tensions simmered across generational lines in black institutions. We see this in the quotidian world of the prominent First African Presbyterian Church of Philadelphia, where bickering arose between a younger generation and a group of older church members. The church included emerging black Philadelphia leaders like Jacob White, Jr., who was a member of the church's Singing School Association. While he and other association members were devoted members of the congregation, a criticism from older members pushed them to lodge a complaint. Led by White, the Singing School Association addressed the church elders because they had been "subjected to insult and ridicule from some members of the church who appear to be in a very high degree dissatisfied with the manner in which the singing is performed in the devotional exercises." They asked for relief and for the church leadership to "oblige us by protecting us from those whose age is an invulnerable shield behind which they place themselves with the most perfect security and heap upon us scorn, abuse, and insult with the utmost impunity."[165]

The Benjamin Banneker Institute engaged in a similar, albeit secular intergenerational struggle. Like other African American organizations, the Banneker Institute wrote bylaws to set the group in motion. On April 13, 1854, members adopted their bylaws, which among other things required members to be 19 years of age or older.[166] They held regular business meetings and launched their mission to enlighten members. They held lectures, assembled a library, commemorated Benjamin Banneker's birthday, collected a copy of the Banneker-Jefferson correspondence, and took seats at a lecture by Frederick Douglass at the Library Company of Philadelphia.[167] But amid this work, they, like the Daughters of Africa and the African Female Benevolent Association, struggled with the day-to-day operations of the organization. Soon after its founding, the institute faced the problem of delinquent members. The president reported "that several members have been expelled for delinquencies and neglect of payment of their monthly dues."[168] The situation became dire, with the secretary reporting that nineteen members had been expelled or were delinquent and eight were out of town, leaving only fifteen active members. This led the president to plead for members to support the organization and to "improve themselves in mental view and to exert such an influence as shall tend to enlighten and elevate that class of people with whom we are identified and who have so long [been] subjected to ignominy and disgrace by the more favored sons of America."[169]

The institute played not just gender and class politics. They were a self-conscious youth organization. Shortly after its founding, members reached out to E. J. Adams for support.[170] He wrote the institute, praising members for their efforts and saying that he was "happy to learn that your Institution is composed of young men whose age bespeaks a susceptibility rarely found in any Institution, whose minds have not yet been made and rendered incapable by advanced old age and stupefied by semi-barbarous ideas that hang like a midnight vale to the vision of our ancestors."[171] Whether in African American religious or intellectual organizations, young people and elders could be at odds and wage battles over the direction of their culture or community concerns. Even as black Philadelphians engaged in common struggles against racial and material barriers, differences along gender, class, and generational lines created social fissures and became the grounds for competing individual and small group interests.

While eldership became a site of class, generational, and gender conflict in the antebellum North, especially as institutions emerged, the daily lives of most elders involved a basic, often private struggle for material support and a longing to care for and be cared for by loved ones. They worked until death, improvised, and depended on personal connections for food and shelter.

Organizations—mutual aid societies, churches, homes for the elderly, or almshouses—filled in the gaps of support; but most faced a high degree of instability and uncertainty. Benefactors took some comfort in their beliefs about pious black elders who may have suffered materially on earth but were deemed to be exemplars of moral conduct with a reward that awaited them in the afterlife. Self-reflections of black elders confirmed such popular notions. They also performed roles of moral exemplars in their institutions, which both created bonds and shared interests but also created tension within and across generational lines. Waged in their private lives and in public domains, the black struggle of eldership and generations in the North foreshadowed what was to come during and after the Civil War.

CHAPTER 5

Home for the Aged

When Union forces entered Confederate territory, black elders served as walking reminders of slavery's violence, and their presence and bearing also showed their defiance of the system. The Northerner Lucy Russel learned those lessons when she came to Tennessee with her father, who set up a law practice and took over a plantation in the late stages of the war. She looked condescendingly toward the black workers that her father employed, believing that "the black folks ought to stand up and take care of themselves now, white people had done so much for them," but her cook Irene set her straight by teaching Russel about an aged slave woman also named Lucy. The violence of the system, in Irene's words, "cowed and cowed" slaves "till they have learnt to be afraid." She used the experience of Lucy "being whipped and whipped, her Master sitting by and telling the overseer that he did not hit hard enough and she was on her bed three weeks bathed with oil before she was well." Irene added other stories, including a description of a log that slaves were tied to and how her husband's nephew "plowed three weeks in the field with the fifth chain on his neck and feet."[1]

But slaves remained defiant—the aged Maria offered another example. Russel wrote, "There is an old Aunt Maria here who was nurse to some of the family. She has a very expressive face and moves about the grounds with the stateliest step leaning on her cane and looking more like the proprietress than anyone here."[2] Russel glimpsed into a range of elder experiences—one had the memory of being brutalized by her master and yet another walked the land as if she owned it. Focusing on the experience of black elders and the role of generational dynamics during the Civil War and Reconstruction, this chapter explores the tension that the experiences of Lucy and Maria exemplified, analyzing how age and eldership were sources of struggle and regeneration for black families and communities in the transition from slavery to freedom during and after the Civil War.

Flight

The pressures of the war required the planter class to adopt new ways of organizing their labor force while maintaining its focus on the young. For example, William Tayloe's estate sought to isolate young people from the conflict. Their overseer wrote a list of "Negroes taken from Mount Airy Dec 16th and delivered to Wm. Tayloe Dec. 24th 1861—for safe keeping."[3] They included thirty-three "field hands" between 12 and 40 years old and fifteen children ranging from 6 months to 12 years old. Those who Tayloe's overseer left behind included aged slaves like the 62-year-old field cook Franky, 67-year-old slaves Minny Page and Fanny Bragg, and 86-year-old Sukey.[4] At the start of the war, Tayloe thus replicated the pattern of intergenerational separation characteristic of the domestic slave trade, with the war reinforcing the slaveholders' idea of age and slave value.

In his farm diary, the slaveholder Thomas Maguire recorded similar observations during the fall of slavery on the outskirts of Atlanta in 1864. He tried to maintain the status quo and force slaves to raise wheat, spin cotton, or make syrup, but there was no keeping the slaveholding order together. As cannons bombarded Atlanta in September 1864, he recalled "hands not doing much" work on his plantation.[5] Later that month, he made a note to himself about how hard it was to get his slaves to work for him, with "every body grunting." He added that "We have lots of rumors of Negroes trying to get to the Yankees."[6] And that wave of discontent caught up with him, as Maguire later found that his slaves "Isaac Merritt Louis and Peter" fled captivity. Seeing that they were "missing this morning," he would "supose they are gone to the Yankees."[7] So did two black women who fled "from the back of the old House." While he "gave them a good hunt," he came up empty handed.[8] After having had control over his slaves, Maguire found that such instability was "a very troublesom life to lead."[9]

Within the context of such wartime movement and flight as the Union lines reached Confederate territory, some black elders got left behind. For instance, in Gloucester County, Virginia, after the Emancipation Proclamation and under the threat of imprisonment, the black contraband "Jack and Dick Pope came down last week in the night and carried off all their masters negros, except a one arm negro, and two old women." A week earlier, the "*faithfull* servant" Peter went to Dr. Byrd's plantation where his spouse lived and "carried off his wife and 15 others." They left Byrd with "only one man (Joe) a worthless old man, a woman and two or three children." In a context where African Americans had newfound mobility, such as the sixty-one slaves who escaped from the Clarke estate, the aged had less.[10]

Viewed from a grassroots level, black flight during the Civil War was largely a young people's affair. For example, Jacob, Jerry Glasgow, Richard Thomas, Elias Harrod, and Issac, all between 24 and 40, fled the Tayloe plantation to Union lines in December 1861. In 1863, Peter Richardson, 28, and Urias, 34, also took flight. But one outlier, the more aged 47-year-old mason Edward made his escape with Urias.[11] In terms of the age demographics of flight from slavery during the Civil War, the forced labor system collapsed at the center. Yet, black elders could be counted among those who fled, such as in the mass exodus of slaves from Richard Eppes's Hopewell and Appomattox estates. Of the thirty-one fugitives who escaped, ten were older than 40, including Madison Ruffin, 50; George Oldham, 58; and Jenny Oldham, 73.[12]

As they panicked about the loss of their property, some planters feared that the aged would also escape. On Christmas Day 1862, one week before the Emancipation Proclamation, Overton Bernard complained of the unrest that the Civil War in Virginia had caused among slaves. They had been, in Bernard's words, "seduced from their homes" and flocked in town. They went in motion, "dreaming of freedom by first of January."[13] Once the Union Army made incursions into Confederate territory, slaveholders tried to stem but could not stop the tide of slave flight, including acts by the aged. Maxwell Clarke's father reported from Gloucester County, Virginia, in 1862 that slaves were fleeing to Union lines, leaving plantations bereft of labor: "Oh!! My God my dear son you little dream of our wretched condition here. Our negros are all leaving, in a week I doubt if there will be a hundred negros left." The fugitives from Clarke's estate included William, who had one leg and managed to break into their stable, take two horses, hitch them to a wagon, and take off toward the coast. Seeing what was transpiring around him, Clarke's father wrote, "I am satisfied my dear Max that I shall not have a servant left in a fortnight even the *old and infirm*."[14]

Slave elders took flight, shattering planter illusions about their dominion. While they sought to preserve what they had, planters saw their control erode as the war unfolded, and with that loss of control came an erosion of their sense of self. Having invested in the idea of lifelong ownership of slaves, they were surprised by the reality of slave rebelliousness. The actions of slave elders further challenged planters' beliefs. Responding to the crisis, the slaveholder Maxwell Clarke saw it as only a matter of time before he lost a hold of his slaves. Fearing the role of kin networks in fomenting slave resistance,

Figure 7. "Contrabands Escaping," 1864. Courtesy of the Library of Congress.

he believed that if his slave "Jordan went, Dublin, Jim, Dabney, Nell, Rachel, and her children would go." He added, "Sterling and Charles will go if the wives take offense or for any cause should propose to go." He risked losing the aged as well, with Clarke speculating that "Even Fanny would go, if Old Isaac wished it." Seeing a fugitive in every slave, Clarke concluded that "In short there is not *one negro* in *all the South*, who will remain faithfull *from attachment to their master and mistress*—not one."[15]

The word of emancipation and movement of black people during the war transformed the South. Though young people were more apt to fight or flee during the war, African Americans also worked collectively in response to their new political status. And the collective struggle of African Americans, whether in political meetings or jubilee celebrations, challenged the social order. For example, the Virginia planter Richard Eppes took the added measure during the first year of the war to ban slave meetings, especially at night, even though they had already been prohibited by the state.[16] But as the Emancipation Proclamation took effect in areas under Union occupation, such prohibitions became meaningless, and African Americans claimed the right to assemble by holding mass meetings and celebrations. In Portsmouth, Virginia, on the eve of January 1, 1863, African Americans held an all-night meeting at the African Methodist Episcopal Church and then held a "jubilee procession" on New Year's Day to mark their freedom.[17] A year later, African American men and women on the Sea Islands reaffirmed their freedom.

Union Major John Emory Bryant observed on January 1, 1864, about freedmen and women that "hundreds of these people came together from the different plantations on these islands and had a day of jubilee." Over time, the meaning of the proclamation became more apparent, with Bryant saying that while in 1863 "few understood the importance of the change," "now very many more do."[18] Ella Gertrude Thomas of Augusta, Georgia, remarked in her diary that on the day she heard an official announcement about the end of slavery and that planters had to agree on labor contracts with freedmen and women, "All afternoon Yankee soldiers and Negroes were promenading the streets."[19] But as former slaves contemplated their new status and as their movement across space took shape, it took a generational turn as young people were more likely to make their escape. Some of the aged fled to the Union forces, making it to contraband camps or the cities, but the majority remained in the countryside. And when Union officials entered the South, they encountered and learned lessons from those black elders.

Encounters

In a mission trip to Memphis, Tennessee, in the final year of the war, Rev. Edward Wasmuth met the freedman Rufus Campbell in Webster Hospital. Until the war, Campbell "had been a religious man 40 years and a preacher of the ME Church." When he heard of the Emancipation Proclamation, he "told his master that as soon as he found a place he would take his freedom with his family." Old age proved to be no obstacle to Campbell's dreams of claiming and fighting for his freedom, saying that "He was too old to enlist but did so for example's sake. Was going to do all he could for the government and the colored people." At the end of their encounter, they made a symbolic gesture of religious elders by "promising to meet in heaven through Christ."[20]

Wasmuth got an education about the meaning of slavery from another former slave, one who had converted to Christianity after realizing that he had been living as an "ole hypocrite." He did not hold back about slavery, telling Wasmuth about Nathan Bedford Forrest. The slave trader Forrest defrauded a slave buyer when Forrest coerced the slaves he put up for sale to lie by saying that they had skills as a chambermaid, a carriage driver, and a field worker. Once the buyer set them to work and discovered that they did not know those trades, he returned them to Forrest's estate, where they received a "breaking." This local memory worker also told Wasmuth "some dreadful things concerning the treatment of the master toward the female slaves. They are all stripped of clothing to be examined when about to be sold."[21] In these ways, black elders introduced Wasmuth to the historical legacy of the antebellum South. Wasmuth was not alone in sharing intimate moments with black elders. For example, one elder stayed with a dying Union soldier in his last moments. In her diary, Margaret Grimball wrote that "One young man had an old negro man who sat by him & fanned off the flies." As the wounded soldier lay there, "the servant remained with him until he died, and then after preparing his body for the grave, bundled up his things, put them on his head and went off home."[22]

Union officials on Roanoke Island also encountered black elders, and their interaction reveals the continuing significance of old age and its intersection with gender in the black experience in the process of emancipation. After capturing the island, Major General J. G. Foster ordered Union forces to establish a black settlement on the island. With a location protected from Confederate forces, the settlement was both a refuge for noncombatants and the source of African American recruits for the Union Army. By the summer of 1863, about one hundred young men had enlisted. The enlistment of the young had the unintended consequences of turning the island into "an asylum for the wives and children of soldiers, and also for the aged and infirm, where the children might be educated, and all, both young and old, [could] be trained for freedom and its responsibilities, after the war."[23]

The settlement's superintendent Rev. Horace James met black elders who informed him about the long shadow cast by slavery. James recalled that "An old Roanoke negro told me he had built eight houses for himself on his master's plantation. His heartless lord would give him a building spot, and suffer him to live there until he cleared the land around his dwelling, and then would drive him out, to repeat the process in a new location."[24] Reminded by this elder of the significance of control over land and housing during slavery, James instituted a policy that extended to black families the right to own homes on one-acre lots. He recalled, "It was affecting to hear the old men and women declare how fervently they blessed the Lord, that their eyes were permitted to see this unexpected sight."[25] While they rejoiced at the news, James remained cautious in his approach, seeing in their old age a reason to grant them rights to homes and not farms. He reasoned that "Invalids, aged people, and the soldiers' wives and children cannot be expected to improve more than a single acre."[26] To James, economic development required young men, and their numbers were not optimal in his eyes. By 1864, females outnumbered males 1,796 to 1,295. He added that, of those males, "seventy per cent. of the adult males, are either in the immature period of youth, or in the decline of life."[27]

In the North, reformers also grappled with the presence of elders and the diverse ages of black fugitives who made their escape across state lines. In the early years of the war, as it had been before, Philadelphia became a refuge for runaways from the South. Planning to help get fugitives on their feet, the PAS's education committee set up a subcommittee on employment to match employers looking for workers and fugitives looking for work. The subcommittee was charged to "record the names of applicants for work as well as of those wishing to employ apprentices, laborers, etc. stating in each case the residence and references in regard to the first class, their age, nativity, etc."[28]

The generational pulls of the war shaped the age structure of the refugees who made it North, requiring different responses by abolitionists. With very young "contraband" unable to enlist in the Union Army, they joined groups fleeing their plantations, with some making it to Philadelphia. For example, the PAS "received word from Eliza Bates at Hampton that Col. Kinsman proposed sending to this city about 50 orphan children and desired that places be found for them." The society also placed notices in the *Friends Intelligencer* and *Friends Review* asking for support. The Quaker Louisa Roberts visited Washington, D.C., and returned with "30 women and children," who boarded in separate lodgings or at the Home for Friendless Colored Children. Demonstrating their vulnerability, a rash of illness broke out among the refugees, causing one of them to die soon after their arrival and others to be quarantined until they could get placed in more stable living situations. Another set of "about 60 children and adults arrived from Fort Monroe in [Schooner] George Leary . . . and were taken to the Home for the moral reform of destitute children from whence 27 children were taken to the Shelter for Colored orphans untill places could be found for them."[29] In addition, the PAS engaged local black leadership. Early in the war effort, the society recruited the black abolitionist stalwart William Still to lead a grassroots labor bureau. He sprang into action sooner than he expected when in the spring of 1862, "91 'contraband' or 'freedmen' (who appeared to have been forwarded by someone connected with Gen. Banks division of the army in the Potomac) rendered it necessary" to start before the society planned. The contraband ended up "scattered among the colored people of our city," and the society worked with churches to get the word out about the labor agency at William Still's store at 107 North Street. While the antislavery movement found job opportunities in Philadelphia for working-age refugees, abolitionists found it harder to support those on the ends of the age spectrum, especially the aged. The society reported about one group of fugitives, "Several families remain unprovided for, among whose younger members sickness has prevailed, and the 'old Lady' is reported 104 years of age." Not planning to care for the aged or unemployed, the society withheld support because its members "did not feel themselves authorized to spend any of our funds for that purpose."[30]

During the Civil War and with the collapse of the Confederacy, black elders sought to reshape their lives. They tested social and geographical boundaries, defying the limits imposed by enslavement. An "old Lady" made it to Philadelphia among the youth. Figures like Maria walked with a regal bearing as she claimed her freedom. Others on Roanoke Island sought to build households. While the capacities of their bodies differed from young people's, they had a common aspiration of freedom. As African Americans entered the era of Reconstruction, age continued to shape their individual experiences and their strategies for survival. Consequently, black elders and intergenerational relationships played a significant role as they and the country sought to rebuild in the wake of the war.

Wages

During the onset of Reconstruction, African Americans forged bonds across multiple generations, especially when they faced the tide of violence from fallen Confederates. The tense state of race relations struck contemporary observers, including one Union soldier who served in Savannah and had prescient concerns about the postwar South. Regarding his time in Savannah in the fall of 1865, he wrote that ex-Confederates were "assuming an independent, arrogant manner, as if they had conquered, not we." He continued that they had "a way of disposing of the Negroes by shooting one occasionally."[31] Given this threat, African Americans organized across generational lines to protect their new status. In their mass political meetings, distinctions between ages blurred. John Emory Bryant noted that they usually held meetings "on the Sabbath after church service. From two to three thousand colored persons frequently attend these meetings and the *Loyal Georgian* is read to them by one of the members. Thus they may be instructed even if they are not taught to read and write."[32] In one mass meeting in August 1867, described as a "glorious success," the attendees felt free to speak "what they thought, without fear or favor, hit who it might."[33] Such mass meetings created the grounds for multigenerational black political struggles.

Seeking to break the patterns of domination from the antebellum period, many freed men and women moved in groups across the land. Georgia slaveholder Thomas Maguire kept record of labor losses, first of his neighbors and then his own, after the surrender of the Confederacy. He recounted that "3 or 4 of Mr Lees Negroes went off this morning to the Yankees." While he tried to maintain control of African American labor and keep his farm alive in the wake of the war, an undeniable change was unfolding in his midst. Having visited a nearby town, he reported that one freedman named Andrew had "gone to the Yankees, with the Lee Negroes, we have a bad state of affairs, how much worse the times will get is hard to tell." He also recorded a case of "300 Black yankees at Lithonia with 700 Horses and mules bound for Augusta."[34] The planter Peter Davis noted that while some of his former slaves entered into contracts to work with him, he "could not take all on this plantation and some are scattered."[35] Landless, former slaves had to find work where they could, doing so while trying to maintain or rebuild multigenerational relationships from the antebellum period. Moments of displacement and labor struggles show how age and generation influenced the black experience during Reconstruction.

As emancipation unfolded, former slaves carried connections with and memories of family members that stretched across generations. In what may have been an oblique reference to the aged, Hannah and Sam of Georgia negotiated a four-month labor contract with landowner Green H. Brewer for food, clothing, and medical care for themselves and "for all the nonworkers and the infirm and helpless ones now living on the plantation."[36] John Emory made a clearer observation. He noted in his diary on July 1, 1866, that he encountered "an old colored man from Beaufort" who came to Augusta "on the evening train to look for his son who had gone away with concert man 'Prof Bird Carleton,'" an instance that highlights the intergenerational bond that the aged father had and expected to maintain with his son.[37] Madison Ruffin had a similar bond with his daughters. Born in 1812, Madison and his wife Harriet lived on Virginia's Eppes estate and had six children—Paulina, James, Agnes, John, Samuel, and Indianna.[38] In the latter stages of his life and the aftermath of the war, he reconnected with two of his daughters. In his diary, Eppes wrote "Madison returned from Norfolk today having been absent 3 1/2 days, he brought back with him his two daughters Paulina and Agnes."[39] In old age, Madison reunited with his descendants who had been scattered.While a freedman such as Madison traveled a short distance to reunite with his family, longer distances and geographical immobility presented a particular obstacle for black elders who sought to reconnect with kin. For example, the elder Frank Martin tried to repair a family that had been broken nearly two decades before. Martin spent the bulk of his years in slavery, being raised in Virginia before being sold into slavery in Claiborne County, Mississippi. Recalling that he "used to belong to Mr. James Fisher," Martin was married to Lucy Anne Martin (Brooks) before he was sold in 1855 and separated from his wife and six sons. After the war, he remarried and had two daughters and a son, and while he maintained "good health" in old age, he remained in poverty. Though he formed a new family in Mississippi, the memory and hopes of reconnecting with his sons remained. Writing his former owner, he asked, "Please let me know where they are or when you only could let me know something of one of them, you would do me the greatest favor any mankind could do to me, and my thanks, which I can give to you where I am so far from you. I will send in prayer to heaven." He added, "I am as poor [as] I was when a slave, might be a little poorer but I would [forget] age and poverty in the joy to hear something from my boy, which, I hope you will be able and kind enough to give."[40]

The family of Preston Hedrick waged a similar multigenerational struggle of spatial mobility. Before the war, Hedrick was a slave on the estate of Jacob Hedrick in Pittsylvania County, Virginia, where he had a wife, Sonia, and a son, Adam, as well as a daughter and a 45-year-old mother-in-law, Phillis Jefferson. After the war, he originally stayed on his former owner's land but then migrated to West Virginia in the spring of 1867 in search of work. Having found employment but being separated from his family, he wrote to the Freedmen's Bureau for help with transportation costs to bring his family to him. The needs of his aged mother-in-law were particularly acute. He wrote, "I forgot to mention that my mother in law is in bad health and has been confined to her bed for twelve months, up to the time I left home."[41] Hedrick was essential to her elder care and support, and their kinship strategy reveals the challenges that multigenerational families faced in a world with new modes of labor mobilization and orientations to space.

White Southern landowners in the aftermath of the war tied labor, age, and gender together. During slavery, age and gender shaped the ways that slaveholders determined the monetary value of or production expectations for slaves, and landowners similarly used age and gender to set wages in the postbellum period. For example, the Thomas family paid a girl, Anna, $4 a month to milk cows and tend the yard and paid a young woman, Dinah, $7 to wash, iron, and do housework, but the aged Harry scraped by on $3 a month for cutting wood.[42] On the Eppes estate, they paid out wages primarily from $10 to $15 a month to young male laborers. On the high end of the pay scale, Alfred James made a monthly wage of $15 while Charles Anderson made $10. Children earned less, such as the boy Tom, who pulled in $5 a month for his labor.[43] Other young people likely worked without wages. For instance, as black day laborers and workers on monthly wages cultivated the Eppes estate, the daughter of the "Month Labourer" Gabriel Scott went to work. Without noting any wages, Eppes recorded in his diary that he "had Gabriel's daughter Matilda to bring water to the hands in the fields."[44] On the other end of the age spectrum, the aged Madison and Harriet Ruffin made lower wages than younger workers, operating as a family unit as they stayed on as wage laborers on Richard Eppes's estate. Madison earned $10 a month and Harriet took in $7. Meanwhile, their 17-year-old daughter Paulina and 15-year-old son James made $5 per month.[45] With lower wage prospects, the Ruffin family depended on collective efforts and contributions of the young, a phenomenon that shaped black labor and intergenerational relations more broadly. One observer noted that among some former slaves in Virginia, "They are very sharp to get children who are old enough to earn something and to hire them out. In such cases their parental and guardianship discipline are very severe."[46] Trying to maintain households, expecting young people to comply with their demands, or wielding social power or authority, black elders might expect a share of the labor of the next generation.

Given the paltry wages, elders struggled to become independent. For example, in the outskirts of Atlanta, the aged Will scuffled to create an independent household. In the fall of 1865, after leaving his former slaveowner Thomas Maguire, Will returned looking for work. Maguire wrote in his diary, "Old Will is at work again, he came up yesterday after finding a home for his family." But by the early part of 1866, Will's household arrangement apparently fell apart. Maguire recounted that "Will came up today and wishes to be let to stay here." The landlord Maguire continued that he "promised him his old patch, his food and clothing for his work." Without close ties to kin, and perhaps too old to have much bargaining power for better wages and too tied to his locale to enter a different labor market, Will was vulnerable to a labor arrangement in which he merely eked by.[47]

In the day-to-day life of the Reconstruction South, black elders generally lived on the economic margins, providing an inexpensive labor force. For instance, the Northern minister William Matton relied on the convenience of an aged black worker. Matton came South to spread his faith. Pushed out of Southern pulpits by ex-Confederates and their claims to church property, he then struggled to find housing. In one instance, he was overcharged for lodging because, as the owner put it, his reputation was "*endangered by keeping a Yankee*." He ultimately found a room and furnished it with a table, a few chairs, some blankets, and a mattress. And he relied on an aged black woman's labor, writing in his memoir that he "*hired an old Colored woman to cook for me*."[48] Others observed the role of black elders in domestic labor. When Marcus Sterling Hopkins traveled through postwar Virginia looking for a place to stay, he saw light coming from the home of General Tries. He "knocked at the Kitchen door and presently an old crippled colored woman came and asked what I wanted. I told her I must come in and she rather suspiciously admitted me to sit down by her fire." Hopkins added, "After a little while she took some fire up in the General's room and told him to get up, that there was a man down stairs. The General soon came down and welcomed me in his usual cordial manner and took me up stairs where we chatted till breakfast time."[49] The former slave Leah also worked as a domestic, though she had some spatial mobility, using it to search for employment in different households. She worked in the Demmings's household and then looked for a job as a cook for the Thomas family. After a one-day trial period, where the "elderly mulatto woman named Leah" proved her skills, they asked her to get a refence from the Demmings family before hiring her full time. For reasons the Thomas family did not discover, Leah never returned.[50] Perhaps she had fallen out with the Demmings family. Perhaps she was able to get a better offer. In either case, like many aged black women, she performed domestic labor.

Such dire economic conditions kept alive their vision of land redistribution, which echoed beyond William Sherman's meeting with black elders in Savannah, Georgia, in early 1865. In Memphis, Tennessee, in 1868, one "old" freedman had hopes of land ownership. During the 1868 campaign, the idea still circulated among African Americans that the government was going to live up to its promise of forty acres and a mule. In the case of the freedman Guilford, "when he went to the polls, [he] carried a *piece of rope to lead his mule with*." Guilford also had "selected his '40 acres'" from his former mistress's estate "that he *was going to have*."[51] Leaving the polls empty handed, Guilford likely returned to the ranks of the aged black poor.

While in most cases the aged stood on the lowest economic rung, that was not always the case for other aged African Americans. In the immediate aftermath of the Civil War, Richard Eppes paid laborers $0.50 per day. For example, the freed men and woman John London, Beverly Gill, and Charles Anderson earned those wages. But so did "Old Man Jackson," who earned the standard wage. Jackson had some economic clout in his community. His son John Jackson worked on the same plantation, and the elder Jackson took charge of their negotiations over wages. Eppes wrote that after one period of closing the books that the elder "Jackson applied for a settlement for himself and his son." The elder Jackson also lent money to the freedman Bob Likes. When Eppes tried to pay $5.87 1/2 in wages to the elder Jackson with $6 in cash, Jackson owed Eppes some change and didn't have it on hand. So, Eppes wrote, Jackson said that "Bob Likes owed him $.50 and requested [Eppes] to deduct $.12 1/2 from [Likes's] wages." But in other ways, the aged found themselves in the same position on the low end of the wage scale. For example, the cook Elisha James and "Old Man James" made half the monthly wages of the average field worker on the Eppes estate.[52]

When elders died, they left behind families who grieved, and they also made claims to their backpay. For example, in the summer of 1866, Alfred James and his family pressed Eppes to pay "for the services of his father previous to his death as the old man James would never receive any money whilst in any service either during or after the war." Seeing the "account is a troublesome one to settle," Eppes wrote that the late elder James "was very old quite 70 years but very industrious for his age." James's unrequited work during and shortly after the war included attending to the garden and feeding livestock until he died on November 12, 1865. His family came to Eppes to settle their deceased elder's account.[53] In the case of York Stevens of Liberty County, Georgia, he claimed property passed on to him by his grandfather while he was alive. Stevens had been a slave of the Winn family before being bought by a Mr. Cay before the war. He submitted a request to the Southern Claims Commission for having his property seized during the war. He testified, "My grandfather owned the horse and when I got married he gave me the horse and a sow pig. This was 4 years before the war."[54] In such ways, some elders built modest legacies, and they continued to benefit succeeding generations in material ways.

The experience of the black aged took new shape after the war, as freed women and men were tasked with maintaining or reconstructing intergenerational ties, which were pressured during the antebellum period. The work of Reconstruction included their signing labor contracts, trying to buy land, and getting involved in politics. And it also meant stitching together relationships that spanned multiple generations. Elders relied on family members and young people to address material concerns. They continued to work into old age. And they also relied on local governments and federal authorities as they made the transition from slavery.

The State

During Reconstruction, the state responded differently to African Americans depending on their age. While governments developed schools or negotiated labor contracts for younger people, the position and status of the aged prompted a different set of relationships to and policies by the government. For example, the experience of "Old Evan" highlights the role of local governments in caring for the aged poor. In the antebellum period in King George County, Virginia, whites far outnumbered blacks on the rolls for poor relief, and many of the poor whites were orphaned youths. For example, orphans from the Staples, Crismond, Berry, Rollett, Hudson and Dodd families inhabited the county's home for the poor. In contrast to these sibling groups, the black poor were more socially isolated, such as the blind African American man "Old Evan" who lived in the poorhouse in the mid-1850s.[55] He remained in the poorhouse after the war along with eight poor whites.[56]

Aged African Americans sought other kinds of state support, including relief from taxes. For the year of 1868, Freedmen's Bureau agent C. G. W. Clelland petitioned the county on behalf of Absalom Signal, 73; Henry Thompson, 80; Phil F. Lucas, 64; Isaac Washington, 73; Anthony Robinson, 78; Benj. Rose, 64; James Gray, 77; Dennis Johnson, 64; and Hansen Pierce, 63, that "In view of their ages [and] indigent circumstances . . . that they be exhonerated from the payment of all taxes." Others seeking tax relief included Stephen Grimes, 95; Samuel Gordon, 87; Edward Scott, 64; Benj. Johnson, 74; and John Cohen, 75. Making note of their ages, the petitioners' plea for tax exemption demonstrated the early position of the federal government on elder care and how African Americans waged political struggles on the grounds of old age.[57]

The Freedmen's Bureau geared aid directly to the aged, paid for by taxes on younger male workers. In the early years of Reconstruction, the bureau oversaw poor relief in Virginia, which operated through county governments. Depending on local government officials to distribute relief, they barred counties from discriminating against the black poor. For example,

Drummondtown, Virginia, Bureau agent Lieutenant George French ordered that "No discrimination is made by the laws of the state in extending aid and support to the destitute of either race." He aimed for relief to go to people "when age or sickness or infirmity disables them from gaining their own subsistance." The poor relief would be paid for by a head tax at the county level on all "male persons" over the age of 16.[58]

The bureau had less concern for the young and "able bodied." Seeking to enforce a work requirement, Norfolk's bureau superintendent pushed local officials to assign "a portion of *Land* on the *Poor_Farms* for *cultivation* by the indigent *Freedmen*" and have the fruits of their labor "be applied for their comfort." Admission to a Freedmen's Hospital didn't spare African Americans from work. The order mandated hospitals to set aside vegetable gardens to be worked by convalescents.[59] In some cases, they made provisions for landless and destitute freed men and women, such as those who migrated to Richmond in the wake of the war. One Union general in the bureau in Dinwiddie County ordered, "When destitute colored people in the county cannot be cared for by their former masters or procure support by their labor," the bureau "will provide for their care and support at suitable places in the county." But the order also imposed limits, stating that "They will be neither brought nor permitted to come to this city, where they can obtain no labor and are liable to be contaminated by city vices." In contrast to the city where freedmen couldn't live off the land, in the countryside they could subsist by working for others or "cultivating patches of land and raising vegetables for their own use and for the market."[60] Captain Asa Gregory reported other strings attached to federal support. He informed Brigadier General McKibbin of an order from their major general that "No 'destitute Rations' be issued to any able bodied man unless he has a family of his own," who had to show "undoubting evidence of their destitution and that he cannot procure *any sort of employment*."[61]

While trying to create a capitalist marketplace for labor that centered on mobilizing the young and able bodied, the Freedmen's Bureau considered the capacity of black elders and offered them more relief than the young. For example, James Chaplin Beecher organized aid for aged freed men and women who struggled to survive in the immediate aftermath of the war. There was a 60-year-old Tabitha Henry, who was "starving for lack of rations."[62] The 61-year-old freedmen Jeffrey worked for a Mr. Crackin but had "nothing to eat."[63] The same was true for the 65-year-old Tinah Wilson, who worked on the Wilson plantation but, it was said, "gets nothing to eat." Likewise, the 79-year-old Jack and his wife Sarah had nothing to eat.[64] Beecher made inquiries to intervene with their landlords and eventually issued them rations.

The distribution of rations changed over time and came to tilt more heavily toward the aged and the very young, reflecting broader ideas about age, gender, and African American labor. In a November 1865 distribution in Charlotte County, Virginia, the bureau gave over thirty of the seventy rations to freed men and women who were in their twenties and thirties. Mostly women, they were deemed eligible. Just the following month, the beneficiaries changed dramatically. Among freed men and women given rations on December 13, 1865, thirty-two out of fifty-eight were 13 or younger, and twenty-one were 40 or older. Being a widow also made a difference—35-year-old Rose Ella and 32-year-old Eliza received government support. The infirm and blind 104-year-old George stayed in the barracks and regularly relied on the bureau for rations.[65] Even with the bureau's material support, the young and old worked to access government rations. For instance, 30-year-old Hal and 40-year-old Phil got full rations for their families for cutting wood for the barracks, while at 75, Tom got "rations allowed his family for cutting wood for Destitute in Barracks."[66]

When African Americans sought aid from the bureau, they worked across multiple generations. For example, bureau agents in Farmville, Virginia, found destitute aged former slaves in need of relief, and the bureau coupled with family members to distribute rations. Bureau agent William E. Ganaway wrote "a list of proper objects of charity around me." Everyone on the list—Patty Clay, Sarah Smith, Ara Walton, Celia Clapton, John Green, Phoebe Green (wife of John), and John Brown—was listed as being 70 or older. The agent gave the list to Sarah Smith's son John Smith to pick up their rations.[67] The freedwoman Malvia Robinson called for even more help. Distressed from caring for her aged sister and infirm niece, Robinson told a bureau agent "that she has supported her sister Cynthia Benois aged 70, very decrepit, and her daughter Sivia King aged 30 been sick with the consumption for nearly a year . . . and is unable to support them any longer wants the Bu. to take care of them."[68] Even as African Americans leaned on family support systems for care in old age, individual caregivers could reach their breaking point.

The aged also reached out to the bureau to intervene in disputes over guardianship of younger kin or to reestablish bonds between generations. Lucy Williams wanted the bureau to act on behalf of her grandchildren, who were being held by "James Henry Edmunds who lives near New Baltimore, Fauquier Co., Va." She complained that Edmunds unjustly held "her two

Grandchildren, named Moses and Ellen Woodson, which he refuses to give up to her or their parents (Gibbert and Betsy Woodson,) who live at Marriottsville with Mr. Wm. Davis, and are able and willing to support them."[69] Amy Young, the grandmother of Ephraim also came to his aid. After the war, Ephraim had neither a mother nor a father. Perhaps they ran away or died during the war; perhaps he had been separated from them by the slave trade. With his grandmother as his closest relative, the bureau ordered that "As the boy Ephraim (Cold) has neither Father or Mother living, his grandmother is entitled to the boy. You will therefore deliver the boy Ephraim Taylor (Colored) to Amy Young Freedwoman forthwith on receipt of this order."[70]

Elders came to federal officials for other kinds of support, revealing a particular exposure African Americans faced to white Southern domination in the postbellum era. Because of the demands placed on their labor and role in the Civil War, younger people were particularly vulnerable to violence. But the aged did not escape violent attacks. James Chaplin Beecher reported that the elderly Johnnie was assaulted by Joseph and James Marvin. Johnnie had "his head split and otherwise damaged," leading Beecher to issue arrest warrants to the Marvins.[71] Lydia Coleman also reported a case of elder abuse, which accompanied other forms of coercion by the planter class. Coleman accused Captain Shules of "keeping her boy" and threatening to "drive her off to leave her crop." She also informed Beecher that Shules had "threatened to take crop from old freeman."[72] Likewise, Isaac advocated for an aged freedwoman in his circle. He, Monday, Betsy, and "old cook Betsey" contracted to work on a plantation after the war. But it changed hands, and the new owner "planned to order him off the place."[73] Isaac got Beecher to negotiate for them to have the right to stay through the harvest, showing both the tenuous status of the black aged and their dependence on social support systems.

Seeking relief from county governments or local Freedmen's Bureau offices, the black aged pushed the state to respond in ways that resonated with their antebellum strategies. They often worked in concert with family members, using a collective strategy in their engagement with the state. The federal government took age into account when implementing policies at the local level, seeing the black aged as more worthy of support than the young. The state also acknowledged grandparents as the appropriate guardians of the young when the young lost their parents. But even as African American elders turned to the government after the war, local and federal governments offered limited support. Labor, family, and faith became the primary ground upon which they stood.

Faith

Elders were at the heart of the black churches that emerged during Reconstruction. Forged during slavery and expanded through missionary work, the religious tradition sustained African Americans as they rebuilt their lives after the war, and contemporaries noted the meaning of faith to black elders. For example, Edward Wasmuth performed missionary work after the war, making his way through western Tennessee, preaching in camps and hospitals. During his mission tour, he "asked an old colored man as to his faith in god." He responded, "Yes sir I have faith in God—that's all I have."[74] William Russel made similar observations about the aged in the postbellum South. He observed their responses to sermons about Noah's Ark, Pontius Pilate, and Jesus—stories of movement across the waters, betrayal, and redemption that were analogous to the black experience. Russel was surprised that "the older people moaned and cried about what I could not tell." In contrast, he noted, "The younger listened stolidly."[75]

As black Southern churches came into the public and expanded during Reconstruction, elders played an outsized role in advancing the faith, even as churches and schools became sites of rituals and ceremonies that blurred the lines between generations. During a summer holiday, youth from Belmont, Georgia, Sunday schools performed a series of skits to display what they'd learned. It was clear that they had been trained and disciplined by their teachers. They "marched into the white people's church and had prayer alternating with singing." And while young people were the main characters on stage, remarks by an elder from Augusta set the tone for the occasion. Amid the festivities and youthful play, the elder brought up questions of mortality, remarking that "Beyond the grave we knew nothing." Through his words, presence, and bearing, he added meaning and depth to the faith of the next generation.[76]

The underground religious work that slaves performed during the antebellum period paid off for their communities after the collapse of slavery, as former slaves who lived into old age transmitted their knowledge to others during Reconstruction. One aged man learned the scripture surreptitiously during slavery. While he was a slave, "He would lie on the floor, close to the door of the room where the children were learning their lessons aloud and listen, and when detected was severely beaten but he persevered and taught his fellow slaves." During Reconstruction, he was ready to support his congregation. On one Sunday, when the presiding preacher kept his sermon short because he was fighting an illness, the "old man" kept the spirit moving, giving "out the hymns, which he did, reading a line, first, which the congregation repeated, singing." The elder also offered a closing prayer.[77]

Such elders who emerged out of slavery served as religious and moral authorities in Reconstruction-era African American churches. Among their duties was to evaluate the conduct of other congregants and to lead rites of passage. David Franklin Thorpe observed in 1863 about one congregation in Fripp Island, South Carolina, that African Americans "cling to every form of ceremony and watch one another closely in order if possible to detect some delinquency." He added that among the congregation sat "about a dozen sagacious looking elderly elders" who were "always ready to search into any kind of shortcomings." With the island undergoing a revival and church meetings filled with "glorious singing," elders also oversaw the baptismal candidates and rituals. On one occasion, Thorpe witnessed nearly 150 people getting baptized. They came from nearby and across the island, meeting at the church in the morning. Candidates marched into the church and sat in the back pews, "dressed for the waters." Men, women, boys, and girls each "had their head tied up in a handkerchief." The baptism needed the assent of an elder to proceed. Thorpe writes, "After Mr. Phillips, the minister, had read their names and they had responded, and 'Old Pa Tom' had nodded his approval to their examination, the Pastor placed himself at the head of his flock and lead it down to the creek." On the side of the creek stood other members of the community, all wearing their "Sunday best" and "bright turbans and white turbans." As the sun shone down, family members surrounded the converts and offered physical support while the minister and his assistant baptized each one by immersion. Symbolizing their spiritual transformation, converts went into the bushes to cast off their old clothes and put on new clothes, and then they returned to the church.[78]

Elders provided spiritual stewardship of African American communities during Reconstruction. With traditions of respect being established in the antebellum period, elders continued to exude moral authority after the war. Every Sunday, young people could enter church and see members of the community with gray hair, perhaps leading hymns, offering prayers, or moaning in the pews as the preacher delivered the sermon. They held the high watch, helping to maintain a sense of order and stability in their communities. But as hard as they worked, both in material and spiritual production, they needed rest.

Rest

Among its many limits, Reconstruction failed to systematically address the specific needs of the black aged. Rather, federal and state economic policy focused on the conversion of former slaves to wage laborers for the maintenance of white Southern landownership. The material needs of black elders did not fit into this framework. After the war, most depended on friends, family, or living hand-to-mouth. Northern social reformers anticipated this problem and founded homes for aged and infirm African Americans in the mid-nineteenth century. It was a regional and urban affair; black elders in the South had fewer options than black Northerners, some of whom received philanthropic senior care. Among the most prominent was Philadelphia's new Home for Aged and Infirm Colored People. The institution provides insight into the culture of nineteenth-century Christian reform movements, the long-range consequences of enslavement, and the significance of multigenerational relationships to black organizations. In this instance, elder care became the glue for black community and institutional development. Reformers who organized the Home for Aged and Infirm Colored People in Philadelphia did so in the spirit of their faith. An extension of the African Methodist Episcopal Church and the religiously grounded antislavery movement, Christian ideology and practice infused the home, which followed the logics of other Christian reform movements. But the age of the clients altered the movement's ideological contours. Activists believed that service to the aged presented an opportunity to practice the highest form of Christian altruism. To some believers, support for the aged became the capstone of Christian practice, one also grounded in the abolitionist movement. The Philadelphia home emerged during the Civil War through a confluence of black and white abolitionist activity, black church leadership, and African American cultural traditions.

By the time of the Civil War, the PAS realized that black elders constituted a group in need of distinct forms of care. In March 1864, the society considered a proposal to support the establishment of a home for aged African Americans in the city. As the organization's chairman of the committee on schools, Joseph M. Freeman assessed the need for an institution for black elders. His report concluded that the aged had "whilst in health supported themselves and families respectably but from various causes are thrown in their old age upon the charities of their friends." Freeman thus recommended that the society should support a home for aged and infirm African Americans, who his committee deemed to be the respectable poor.[79]

Furthermore, Black abolitionists, church leadership, and cultural practices of care for the dead were essential to the development of the home. Over the course of the late eighteenth century and into the nineteenth century, black Philadelphians had invested emotional labor and financial resources into the development of cultural institutions that became resources to support the aged. For example, the African Methodist Episcopal Church gave support to its senior members to get admitted to the home and, quite fittingly, used its cemetery as a resource. African Americans in Philadelphia had a long history of being interred in separate burial grounds.[80] In the colonial period, African Americans in Philadelphia buried their dead in a separate section of the Strangers' Burial Ground. Their section, known as "Congo Square," was a meeting place for free blacks and slaves and served as a reminder of their ancestral legacy. Like African people in other parts of America, they left goods including food and drink on their burial ground, acknowledging the ongoing presence of the dead in the world of the living. Shortly after American independence, African American leaders set their eyes on more land to bury the dead. The Free African Society raised funds to bury its members, and with the emergence of black churches, congregants found their final resting place on church grounds or in church-run cemeteries.[81]

By the nineteenth century, African Americans held titles to burial plots and used collective and kinship strategies to claim land to bury the dead. The grieving mother W. G. Cooper paid a visit to Jacob White, Sr., a luminary in Philadelphia's African American community and director of the Lebanon Cemetery. She asked White to open her father's grave for the burial of her son.[82] The widow Eliza Baker transferred plots in Lebanon to Henrietta Duterte, one of Philadelphia's leading black undertakers. In the process, Baker reserved a space for herself and her sister Ann Wilson.[83] Duterte also handled the burial of a child, E. Ackerman, who was buried in the grave of her grandmother, who died six years before.[84] Grandmother and grandchild, grandfather and grandson, sister and sister were interred in Lebanon cemetery together. Like the black elders who shared cramped spaces to survive through old age, such women used communal approaches to space in their treatment of the dead. And such burial grounds also paid for African American elder care.

Soon after the founding of the home, Mother Bethel African Methodist Episcopal Church used its burial ground to support its aged parishioners. The decision was prompted when, in April 1867, the church considered selling its cemetery to pay for a new home for their minister. After an internal debate and set of negotiations that lasted over a year, the church's board of trustees agreed to lease the burial ground for ten years and use one-third of the income to pay off some financial obligations, one-third to pay for the minister's parsonage, and one-third to support the aged. They wrote in their minutes that "We the members of the 'Corporation' of Bethel Church, deem it our duty to provide for our old and infirm members that have borne the burden and the heat of the day and by the sweat of their brows purchased the burial-ground."[85]

As a culmination of the collective efforts of black and white social activists, the home was not simply a material form of care. It served as a container for broader social and cultural ideas about race, class, gender, religion, and age, carrying multiple meanings to its supporters and occupants. Opening its doors to its first resident, Susan Silvey, on March 7, 1865, black women outnumbered black men throughout its early development. For example, Nancy Poulson and Julianna Morris—who had cohabitated with each other—moved into the home. So did Amelia Webster, Sarah Easton, and Sarah Boggs, who had previously struggled to make a living. In 1871, Mary Anna Brown at the age of 101 was admitted to the home.[86] The imbalanced gender ratio in the home, from its inception through its first half century of service, reflected the history of black gender divisions of labor. With African American men around the city looking to farms and the seas for employment, black women found hard and low-paying yet steady employment in Philadelphia as domestic servants. By 1840, black women outnumbered black men in the city by a ratio of 1.63 to 1, an early pattern that set the tables for the gender demographics in the home.[87] The presence of aged black women, deemed by this period to be pious and the worthy poor, bolstered the religious foundations of the movement.

The founders of the home coupled their beliefs about old age and religious ethics by arguing that charitable work for the aged poor had an enhanced moral value. They first affirmed the significance of charity as a baseline Christian virtue. In its first annual report in 1865, the board pronounced, "It is one of the requirements of Christianity to administer to the necessities of the poor and destitute." Board members added that giving benefitted the giver, saying that "It is wisely ordered that in the attempt to benefit them, our own happiness is increased, and we experience that it is more blessed to give than to receive."[88] Edwin H. Coates echoed the sentiment, seeing the home as not only "an outgrowth of pure Christianity" but also a way for younger

African Americans to pursue their professions and become free from the constraints of elder care.[89]

But some benefactors claimed to transcend any hint of a selfish motivation for doing Christian works, and supporting the aged provided an opportunity to demonstrate pure altruism. Alfred Love reasoned that care for the aged had more meaning than charity for the young. In aiding the young, supporters could expect a material benefit to society through an increase in labor productivity. Caring for the aged offered no such material return. "In the case of the young, we may receive many returns," Love thought. But with the home, donors "can receive none save the prayers of the aged." This led him to conclude that "of all philanthropic works, this of taking care of the infirm is the purest work of all."[90] T. Doughty Miller echoed this sentiment, casting aside the idea of charitable reciprocity by saying "Pure charity is that which gives, expecting no return."[91]

In tension with their altruism were highly ritualized performances of religious piety by people who interacted with the home and its residents. Serving the black aged became a public act of faith. First, there were the public prayers. To open the 1868 annual meeting, African Methodist Episcopal Bishop Jabez Pitt Campbell "led the audience in a prayer for a blessing of the Home," and in the following year, Benjamin Tanner did the honors.[92] With the tone set by the clergy, aged residents also offered their prayers. In its 1883 annual report, the board recollected, "One old man, after an expression of gratitude for our care, and the pleasure of seeing us come to them with cheerful countenances, said 'Well, there is one thing we can do for you, we can pray for you.'"[93] Reinforcing the idea about the spiritual power of the aged, the 1887 meeting opened with a prayer by the resident John Gibson, "said to be 115 years old."[94]

And while the aged stood in for moral and religious power, the clergy predominated in shaping the overarching tone and attitude about how Christians should treat their elders. For instance, the white minister Rev. H. L. Wayland contrasted Christian benevolence with stereotypes about other religions and other parts of the world where they took the old to "the jungle and left [them] amid those savage solitudes to be devoured by the beasts of the wilderness." In comparison, Wayland claimed, the missionary spirit of the home took care not only of the material but also the spiritual needs of the aged.[95] But most ministers made deeper connections between their faith and the work of the home. For instance, black Southern delegates in Philadelphia for a Methodist Episcopal Church convention visited the home, testified that "They had never beheld such a charity for their old and infirm colored people," and "compared it to the comfortless Poor-houses of the South, where such as these would be consigned."[96] Local black clergy maintained ties to the home, seeing it as part of their ministry to their aged congregants who were admitted into the home. Both religious and personal bonds of care moved them to serve, and perhaps for this reason, when African Methodist Episcopal Bishop Campbell died, his remains lay in state in the home for the aged to pay their respects.[97]

In this flow of material and religious goods, the home's leaders characterized the aged not only as a class to be served and guided but also the embodiment of a particular kind of religious virtue, reflecting ideas about the black aged that had been honed over previous generations. Though beyond their working ages, elders served as teachers who demonstrated faith, the power of Christian witness, and how to live and accept impermanence and death. For example, resident Emmaretta Murphy proclaimed, "I love the Lord; I love everybody; I care nothing about the things of this world—I give them all up; I want you to pray for me; all I want is that when I'm done suffering here, I may get safe to my Father's house."[98] Suggesting the healing power of her faith, the 105-year-old Chloe Lloyd announced that she felt no pain, that she was "'just waiting for Jesus—Oh! I love Jesus,' and then her old hands and voice were raised in praise and thanksgiving."[99] The elder Phillis Hogwood was said to have "never failed to find delight in reading her Bible" and "singing her favorite hymns."[100] Old age and religious values became so intertwined in the minds of the home's leadership that they concluded in their 1890 report that the residents had "devotional and emotional natures."[101]

The habits of religiosity regulated the daily and weekly rhythms of the home, rhythms spelled out in its rules and regulations. Rule 12 required that in the morning and at night, "All who are of ability shall be assembled in a suitable room, and a chapter from the Bible read to them, after which an opportunity shall be afforded for silent or vocal worship." The home also held weekly religious services and opened its doors for residents to "be visited (with their consent) for religious purposes at any suitable time."[102] The home made good on its spiritual promise. The 1881 annual report reflected on the growing religious enthusiasm in the home, saying about the services that "They have been much crowded and we believe that they have been periods of great refreshing to all who have been present."[103] Creating the home as an ecumenical religious space, Methodists, Presbyterians, Baptists,

Episcopalians, and Quakers rotated in the heading of services. Seeing the home as an experiment of sorts, its leadership claimed that consistent religious practice not only lifted the spirits of the aged but also helped with their physical needs, believing that the services could "revive and prolong the lives of our aged pilgrims."[104]

As with the black church, where the aged had been culturally grounded, there was no religion without music, which created a bridge that spanned social status and generations. Annual convenings began with music, such as the 1882 meeting when the residents "sang a few verses and were followed in addresses by Rev. D. Walters of South Carolina and Rev. Sol. B. Hood of Lincoln University." Forging links between the generations, young students offered flowers to the residents and then "favored the audience with the singing of some beautiful hymns."[105] On another occasion, the aged "received much enjoyment from the thoughtfulness of a company of young persons who have several times come out to the Home to sing to them."[106] National black singing groups visited the home as an homage to the elders. The Carolina Singers performed at the home as did the New Orleans Jubilee Singers and House of Refuge Band.[107] While many of the occupants couldn't quite move or shout as when they were young, their voices still sought to move in harmony. With each visit, the harmonies momentarily bound together different generations of black people whose histories and current demands and abilities normally kept them physically apart.

Prayers, inspiration, and a sense of shared struggle kindled a communal spirit in the home, which also had to manage its day-to-day affairs. Its annual reports not only accounted for the home's progress—money raised, property acquired, employees hired, building improvements made, residents admitted, or new programs offered—but it served as a tool to market the home for current and potential benefactors. Linked to broader nineteenth-century patterns of urban development and institution building, the home used science, a pragmatic approach, and grassroots and gendered modes of leadership to maintain and grow the institution. In ways that reflected church structures, the institution operated along the lines of a gendered system of power and influence, with male officers providing oversight and women managing the day-to-day operations of the institution. They encoded this in their constitution, which said that its officers should include a "President, Vice-President, Secretary, and Treasurer," and "a Board of Managers of twenty-four, half of each sex; the twelve men constituting a committee to have charge of the real estate and financial concerns of the home, and the women shall be a committee on its internal arrangements."[108]

While many other nineteenth-century black institutions had short lifespans, the home endured through patronage and a culture of modernization and improvement. The African American feminist and poet Frances Ellen Watkins Harper recognized this in her poem titled "25th Anniversary of the 'Old Folks Home.'" Pointing to women like Ann Jess and Sarah Pennock for fundraising for the home, to Israel Johnson for serving as treasurer, and to the recently deceased President Dillwyn Parrish, Harper acknowledged that the religion of the home was one of doing.[109] She also recognized the work of Stephen and Harriet Smith, "whose hands, enriched with golden store, Gave of their wealth to build this 'Home,' And changed a narrow domicile, Into a grand and stately dome."[110] The Smiths were the home's biggest benefactors. Born a slave, Stephen Smith purchased his freedom, went on to have a lucrative career as an entrepreneur, and enagaged in politics as an abolitionist and by offering a safe house in the Underground Railroad. In one of their final acts and as they entered their own old age, the Smiths continued their work of providing a safe house for African Americans by buying land and paying for the construction for a new facility in west Philadelphia.[111] The move to a new home also reflected the city's progressive culture of science, medicine, and engineering, and the application of modern technologies had specific relevance for the aged. The construction of an elevated streetcar line in front of the home gave visitors from central Philadelphia greater access to the home's westside location and decreased the social isolation of the residents.[112] Incorporating technology that was particularly suited for the less mobile aged, the home built a fireproof wing with an elevator.[113]

While the home's leaders did not explicitly describe their philosophy or approach to elder medical care, they discussed its limits and made racialized and gendered claims about the bodies of black elders. In one strand of thought, they reported cases of elders with remarkable bodies. They reported that one aged woman, though bent over at the waist, "was much stronger than many of our *young men* now-a-days." In another report, the home's leaders said that the aged were "unusually healthy." In another mode, they recognized chronic disease and the vulnerability of the aged. The 1883 report recounted that "Several have been invalids from incurable diseases of long standing, causing much suffering, which death alone can relieve. A few have been brought

Figure 8. "Home for the Aged and Infirm Colored People," c. 1894. Courtesy of the Historical Society of Pennsylvania.

there so enfeebled as to be hardly able to reach their rooms, which they never after left."[114]

Other nineteenth-century reform movements had a religious bent, and other organizations had a culture of improvement. But the specific theology of altruism and age-based resources needed to care for elders distinguished the home from others. Furthermore, the weight of history and the racial politics of the present—forced labor, family separation, migration, gender ideologies and divisions of labor, and other historical forces—that the black elders carried into the home drove its institutional development. It was a progressive abolitionist and Christian project but one that had to reckon with the past and current social and political conditions of African Americans. Those forces intertwined to shape the political and cultural lives of the home's black residents.

Supported by local black churches and led by the African Methodist Episcopal Church, the home was a hub in a social and political network that connected the residents to broader black worlds. As the aged became less mobile and aged in place, the black world came to them, reminding them of both past and future struggles. Leaders and supporters who visited spoke about the past. For instance, Rev. I. D. Baker looked back to a conversation he had with an aged woman when he was waiting for a segregated streetcar. She encouraged him by saying, "I shall not live to see the day when these distinctions will be removed, but you, I hope, will."[115] In recounting this ephemeral conversation, Baker suggested the possibilities of change, a black hopefulness derived from an elder, with the relative status and rights of different generations being an indicator of clear yet uneven black progress. In addition, visitor Edwin H. Coates recalled stories of the Underground Railroad.[116] One of its principal conductors, William Still, upon being elected as president of the home's board, also addressed the residents. Connecting the home to the antislavery movement, Still presented an engraving of John Brown going to his execution and spoke about traveling to Storer College in Harper's Ferry, West Virginia, where he made a pilgrimage of sorts to the site of Brown's imprisonment and hanging. His remarks were followed by the singing of "John Brown's Body."[117]

Others talked about more contemporary politics. Ida B. Wells delivered a lecture as part of her antilynching campaign. The home reported that Wells "addressed the meeting and gave a sad account of the lynching of her people in the south, and of her own exile from her native state, on account of the publishing of the outrages in her paper."[118] Even as African Americans in the South were descending into the nadir, black elders, many of whom had been enslaved, could testify by their presence to the continuity of the black freedom struggle and the possibilities of social change.

Being based in the commercial, cosmopolitan city of Philadelphia enabled the home to connect with broader African and Diasporic communities. For instance, lecture circuits enabled residents to connect in consciousness with international black communities. The widow of the late president of Liberia, Joseph Roberts, visited the home. So did Edward Morris of Liberia, who assured residents that though distance separated them from Africans in Liberia, they were "united with them in the bonds of sympathy and nationality."[119] George Peabody, "a native African prince and graduate of Lincoln University," also visited and gave remarks to the residents.[120] Those Diasporic connections took other forms, as they also celebrated the fiftieth anniversary of British Caribbean Emancipation Day on August 1, 1884.[121] Most residents of the home had been born in the United States, principally in the mid-Atlantic and upper South.[122] But in the early years of the home's opening, a few came from outside the United States. Mary Edwards and Charlotte Durand were born in Africa (Durand was from the Congo), and Elizabeth Smith hailed from Jamaica.[123] Even with a small number of residents having originated from outside of the United States, the elders in the home maintained social and cultural ties to local, Southern, African, and African Diasporic communities. In these ways, the aged extended their political and cultural imaginations across time, region, and generations.

Even as some of their abilities declined, elders engaged the larger black world, connecting through the depth of their own experiences. And through those experiences, they and their advocates made their case for ongoing support. One line of reasoning was that the elders deserved support not only because it was in the charitable spirit of Christianity. Rather, they also deserved it because society owed them for their past labor. For example, when they opened the home in 1865, the board recognized that the aged had "labored faithfully, and contributed largely to the comfort of many wealthy families."[124] At another annual meeting of the home, the white reformer Edwin H. Coates pointed out the example of an aged woman who had her children sold away and then died impoverished before the home opened. He argued that slavery's larger pattern of family and intergenerational disruption left the old especially vulnerable. Suggesting his and his audience's complicity with slavery, he stated, "As we have permitted and encouraged this system, we owe it as a debt to them that they be provided for when unable to take care of themselves."[125] Recognizing the long-term effects of slavery, the home was meant to care for people such as the resident who had "seen 105 winters," had been "taxed without representation," and had along with other black people "been compelled to work with no compensation for their labors."[126] The abolitionist and suffrage leader Lucretia Mott agreed with this sentiment, saying that the home was "a small return for the wrongs done to the colored people."[127]

While reformers reflected on concepts of justice, concrete life stories supported these more abstract ideas about how African Americans should be treated at the end of the life cycle. They identified specific cases of injustice, such as the fate of the runaway slave Eliza Perry, who worked into old age and died in the Philadelphia Almshouse, a case that Philadelphia reformers looked back upon as a reason they opened the home.[128] The individual stories of residents bolstered their argument. While the home kept a regular census that recorded the names, ages, dates of admission, and in most cases birthplaces of the residents, they also recorded individual interviews of some residents. For instance, they profiled Mary McDonald, who was admitted to the home about a week before Christmas in 1887, when she was said to have been 108 years old. They were struck not only by her old age but also by her

Figure 9. "Mary McDonald," 1898. Courtesy of the Historical Society of Pennsylvania.

mental sharpness and industriousness. The interview reported that her "faculties were good and she spent much of her time in sewing carpet rags." Even more remarkable was her memory of the country's founding, a faculty that resembled that of Black Alice. McDonald recalled that she directed Revolutionary War soldiers to food in her master's home, for which one thanked her by saying "God bless you, little one, you have done well for me and my men, may you live long and do well."[129] Her narrative struck a patriotic note; in contrast, the account of Emmaretta Murphy offered a more sobering story about the long-term impact of slavery. Murphy "received a knock when a child that hurt her very much, after which her head was always tender." The lingering symptoms included "a running sore," from which "several pieces of bone came out," and "giddiness and dimness of sight." By the time she reached her seventies, she had problems speaking. And on an occasion when she joined visitors for dinner, "She went into the dining room and took her dinner with the family, but on going from the table fell on the floor, from which she was lifted after much exertion, and finally gotten up stairs to bed." She died soon after telling her story, on January 17, 1870.[130]

The stories of eldership, told through words and represented by the bodies of individual residents, made their case for the home and showed what the experience of slavery meant. It was meant for life and lingered on even after individual or collective emancipation. And with this, the home represented a last stop on the Underground Railroad, as former conductor and president of the home William Still saw it. In reflecting on the home, he said that it offered a lesson "to multitudes who have failed to realize the gross prejudices and heavy burdens which have for centuries been weighing the Africo-Americans down." He added that this was particularly the case for black women, "whose burdens, I will venture to say, are heavier to bear than any other class of women in the country."[131]

Even with its contradictions—the condescending attitudes of some supporters, the gender inequality in its leadership—the home offered an experiment in support to aged former slaves. The work of abolition continued, with the home providing real, material support to some of the most vulnerable in the African American community after the Civil War. As much as the home embodied a religious ethos and contemporaries talked about the virtues and transcendent power of elders, they had needs of the body, and the home and its supporters attended to those bodily needs. They built an institutional apparatus where workers, developers, and supporters labored to create a space of rest. While the number of occupants was low relative to the black population of Philadelphia, the home still had a substantial impact on black community and identity formation. Young people; visitors from the city, the South, and Africa; and black leaders made pilgrimages to the home. The home offered a space of black dignity and a bold statement that elders were essential to African American communities.

The success of the home played out in the context of the limits of Reconstruction. In a political environment where national leaders defined freedom as bargaining for wages, aged African Americans, and by extension their family members, were at a distinct disadvantage. No longer able to make the already meager wages that younger black workers could command, and with the federal government withdrawing its support from Reconstruction, the aged depended on friends and family to survive. When they had the resources, they played familiar roles as surrogate parents to children who lost their parents during the antebellum period or the war. Some made it into homes for the aged, which demonstrated a commitment to elder care that foreshadowed twentieth-century United States social insurance policies. But left without a systematic social safety net, the struggles of the black aged and the unresolved effort to bind together multiple generations of African Americans continued into the late nineteenth century and well beyond.

EPILOGUE

A Black Wisdom Tradition

The Home for Aged and Infirm Colored People in Philadelphia was part of a larger movement to address the specific needs of the black aged in the wake of slavery. Homes opened in other cities across the United States from the mid-nineteenth into the early twentieth century. Among them was a home for the aged in Baltimore, which became a source of "continued and increasing interest of the Colored People for this portion of their race."[1] Even more significant was the Harriet Tubman Home for the Aged and Infirm, which opened in Auburn, New York, on land that Tubman donated to the African Methodist Episcopal Zion Church on the condition that they develop and maintain the home. Though not as harrowing or widely recognized as her work to help slaves escape from bondage, the act of building the home realized Tubman's goal to alleviate the suffering of African Americans who carried the weight of slavery in their bodies. Realizing that the needs of African Americans did not end upon reaching northern soil or with the Thirteenth Amendment, her home created a refuge for the black aged that addressed the long-term social and material consequences of enslavement. It was only fitting that Tubman herself entered the home as a final resting place, surrounded by former slaves until her death on March 10, 1913.[2] In the South, the former slave Callie House led a different movement for the black aged, a petition drive that pressed the federal government for pensions for elderly former slaves.[3] While Tubman's and other homes eventually closed and House's movement came to an end, elders continued to inhabit a distinct place in black cultural and intellectual life well into the twentieth century and beyond. The elder has served as a muse for black artists, writers, and thinkers, anchoring their ideas about community, morality, care, and human dignity. They could be visionaries and healers, and they stood up for bedrock values, teaching younger generations about the principles by which they should live.

In writing about black elders in history, I have been informed by memories, insight, and inspiration from elders who intervened at critical moments of my own development. There was Helen Byrdsong, who, after I spent a year drifting from my path, took me under her wing during a summer school English class at the end of middle school; I continued to work with her in high school. And there was George "Bob" Golson. When my father drove me to college, we stopped in his hometown of Fairfield, Alabama, on the outskirts of Birmingham. It was my second visit there, the first one happening when I was in elementary school. While I had not spent much time in the Deep South, I grew up around black Southerners, and I heard about aged family members like Aunt Mamie, who had a reputation for her energy and ability to walk the hills in and around Birmingham. During our stop, we stayed with my grandmother and my grandfather, the latter being bedridden from cancer and, unbeknownst to us at the time, in his last year. He had lost his ability to talk and other functions—but he reached out to stroke my arm. In conducting this encounter with my elders, my father took me to see my Uncle Bob and his wife. As I sat in their living room, with their radio in the corner that they used to listen to Atlanta Braves games, Uncle Bob offered me words of encouragement: "I'm so glad that you're going to college." Pointing in the direction of nearby steel mills that had been transformed by new technologies, he continued, "A young man used to be able to make a living using his brawn. Nowadays, you have to use your brain." He stood in a longstanding black wisdom tradition.

The tradition carried African Americans through enslavement and lived on after emancipation, with black elders serving as the ultimate teachers through the power of their knowledge, character, and presence. The son of African Methodist Episcopal Minister Benjamin Tanner, Henry Ossawa Tanner encoded this idea of the black elder as teacher into his painting *The Banjo Lesson*. Confronting racist minstrel performances that caricatured and ridiculed black musicians, Tanner's work directly challenged this stereotype. In the painting, a young boy sits in the lap of a gray-haired and balding old black man, who holds the banjo with his left hand. Both the elder and the young boy look down at the strings, and the boy uses both of his hands to play. Tanner portrays the elder as an essential, steadying figure, who both offers guidance and steps back to empower the boy to discover music by making it with his own hands.[4] The black Episcopal priest Alexander Crummell had a similar bearing in his relationship with W. E. B. Du Bois in his published work. Meeting Crummell at Wilberforce University's commencement ceremony,

Figure 10. Henry Ossawa Tanner, *The Banjo Lesson*, 1893, oil on canvas, 49 × 35.5 inches/ 124.5 × 90.2 centimeters (Courtesy of the Collection of the Hampton University Museum, Hampton, Va.).

Du Bois wrote that he felt "the fineness of [Crummell's] character—his calm courtesy, the sweetness of his strength, and his fair blending of the hope and truth of life." Du Bois continued, "Instinctively I bowed before this man, as one bows before the prophets of the world." Regretting that his era cared little for men of character such as Crummell and his regal stature, Du Bois believed that "In another age he might have sat among the elders of the land in purple-bordered toga."[5] From the vantage point of Du Bois and Tanner, the character of male elders transmitted lessons across generations that promoted the values of courtesy and masculine, racial uplift.

The image of the religious elder makes its way into other twentieth-century black literature, including that of Richard Wright. Wright presents a more complex and at times volatile relationship with his religious grandmother, who stepped in as a surrogate parent. In *Black Boy*, he explores his grandmother's stern discipline and her use of corporal punishment to enforce the rules of her household. He also delves into how her biblical literalism informed her relationships to others and the world. In doing so, he exposed how not only religious insight and values but also trauma got passed down across generations. As he put it, "Granny bore the standard of God, but she was always frightening."[6] In contrast to his autobiography's harsh criticism of his grandmother, Wright provides a more generous analysis in his essay "Memories of My Grandmother," which was published with his novel *The Man Who Lived Underground*. The novel tells the story of a fictional character, Fred Daniels, whom the New York City police falsely accused of murder and who escaped into the city's sewer system after a violent interrogation. What follows are surreal scenes of Daniels catching glimpses of the culture and corruption of the world above ground. Wright explains in "Memories of My Grandmother" that his grandmother's religion provided the grounds for the novel's surrealism. In the essay, Wright wrestles with his grandmother's religion, which he at once rejects as a personal article of faith and at the same time mines for cultural resources that he uses as the basis of his work. He argues that because the world of Mississippi was not built for her, she withdrew from that world and looked upon it from her religious vantage point as an outsider who sought to create meaning out of random events. He incorporated this into his portrayal of Fred Daniels's experience in the sewer, with Wright attempting to "put a man *outside* of life and let him live *within* life, just as my grandmother had done." With his grandmother's surrealistic worldview as his baseline, Wright structured his novel like a jazz musician who improvised on this basic theme.[7] Animating the story of Fred Daniels and his surreal experience underground, the religious worldview of Wright's grandmother drove the narrative from behind the scenes. So, while he gave voice to multigenerational tensions, he also gained value from his grandmother's perspective.

Other African American narratives capture the material, kin, and emotional labor of elders, and Maya Angelou's *I Know Why the Caged Bird Sings* is among this literature. Angelou, like Frederick Douglass, learned to respect elders in her community. She wrote about the obligations of young people to elders such that "All adults had to be addressed as Mister, Missus, Miss, Auntie, Cousin, Unk, Uncle, Buhbah, Sister, Brother and a thousand other appellations indicating familial relationship and the lowliness of the addressor." The language that Angelou uses is also telling—she labels her largely absent biological mother as "Mother," but she calls her grandmother

"Momma" throughout the text. In so doing, she distinguished the intimate, long-term relationship she had with her grandmother. And, like other black figures, Angelou received the wisdom of her elder as a compass to survive the threat of violence in the Jim Crow South. Her grandmother taught her and her brother "to use the paths of life that she and her generation and all the Negroes gone before had found, and had been found to be safe ones."[8] In her work, Angelou exposes fissures and tensions within her community and reveals how black people survived under white supremacy by highlighting the role of her grandmother as a guiding force.

A complex representation of the elders also stood at the heart of the autobiography of Cornelia Walker Bailey of Sapelo Island, Georgia. By the time she wrote *God, Dr. Buzzard, and the Bolito Man*, she had become an elder and drew on the storytelling style she learned from her progenitors to portray black life on the Georgia Sea Islands. From the beginning, the elders put their stamp on her, and it runs throughout her narrative. She wrote, "Growing up over here, the basic thing every child had to do was satisfy the elders. If the elders said a blessing had been put on you, you *had* to fulfill it." Her way of fulfilling her "blessing" was through the gift of being "able to see and hear and *do* things that the ordinary person wouldn't be able to do." Throughout the autobiography, which is as much a recounting of community and the influence of her elders as it is of her individual life, she fulfills this mission by preserving collective knowledge. And in doing so she recollects and embodies eldership and multigenerational relationships—of generations who laid claim to the land, the cultural continuities and differences across generations, and the conflicts between the young and the old. She recalled how elders pulled back the veneer her schoolteachers painted over slavery's cruelties, how elders told her just enough to make her want to make her own discoveries. She also saw conflicts that rippled across the generations. On an occasion when her grandmother Winnie thought she had been disrespected, she predicted about Bailey that "You'll have bad luck the rest of your days." The elders could hurt, sending out words that wounded or suffering from disease, as with her grandmother's arthritis that made her immobile. But they could also heal; as Bailey put it, "The old people knew the secrets of roots and herbs."[9] Elders were not just incidental characters in her narrative—rather, the narrative turned around them. They carried around historical memory in their aged bodies; they were physically limited but filled with wisdom, insightful about the nature of power and power of nature, and conduits of religious values.

A wide range of other black artists and thinkers conceived of their elders as walking on moral high ground. Such was the case with Howard Thurman, who was raised in Jim Crow Florida but rose to such prominence that in 1953 *Life* magazine named him as one of the twelve greatest preachers of the twentieth century, one whom the black public intellectual and journalist Lerone Bennett called a "20th century holy man."[10] Thurman credits his grandmother and other community elders for his social, religious, and moral development. Upon his conversion to Christianity, his elders reminded him that he had become a new person and, by their witness, he had to pay attention to his personal conduct. "Looking back," he writes in his autobiography, "it is clear to me that the watchful attention of my sponsors in the church served to enhance my consciousness that whatever I did with my life *mattered*." Thurman's grandmother reinforced this message, tracing this sensibility to the inspiration of a slave preacher who preached at her plantation when she was young. He ended his sermon about the crucifixion with a message of transcendence. Despite what the world might tell them, he exhorted, "You are not slaves! You are God's children." Whenever the young Thurman's faith waned, his grandmother recounted this story, and at the end he said, "There would be a slight stiffening in her spine as we sucked in our breath. When she had finished, our spirits had been restored."[11] Drawing upon the influence of her slave preacher, she transmitted by the power of her words, memory, and example a sense of dignity, value, and worth to the next generation. Over the course of his life cycle, Thurman built on the foundations of his elders' faith that they were "God's children" and their belief that his life and what he did with it mattered.

The voices of elders echo in the work of other memoirs through their words of wisdom. In *Remnants*, Rosemarie Freeney Harding and her daughter Rachel trace their cultural roots to southwest Georgia, where Harding's great-grandmother Mariah Grant, known by her people as Grandma Rye, cultivated seeds of community care that stretched across multiple generations. Grandma Rye was an herbalist and a seer, a resource for the community. And she also knew about power and how it worked, having lived through slavery and remembering slave patrols, fugitives, and losing her children through the slave trade. As Rosemarie Freeney Harding put it, "What we know about Grandma Rye is that she is the farthest back we can go in the female line of my family. My mother's mother's mother. We know she fished and healed and survived slavery. She cooked over an open hearth and told her grands and great-grands about the people who risked death to be free."

By recounting that history and offering that care, Grandma Rye sought to pass on the wisdom of the enslaved to her descendants; "She prayed this to God: *Bless all the generations that follow me. The generations that come from me. My children and their children and their children's children.*"[12]

The figure of the elder in the modern black artistic imagination resonated with the elder in black memoirs. They represented, said, and saw things in ways that young people had not yet developed the capacity to do. Baby Suggs in Toni Morrison's *Beloved* had to be old to carry the fragments of memory, to preach, and to speak to the condition of her people in the way she did. Being young would have made it impossible for Baby Suggs to contain the psychic and spiritual weight of her character. She was no minor character—rather, Morrison introduces her on the first page of the novel. Lying in her sickbed at home when her grandsons ran away from their haunted house, Baby Suggs remained still: "Suspended between the nastiness of life and the meanness of the dead, she couldn't get interested in leaving life or living it." She had seen enough nastiness and had moments thinking it was impossible to escape the legacy of slavery. When her daughter Sethe suggested that they move, Baby Suggs replied, "What'd be the point? . . . Not a house in the country ain't packed to its rafters with some dead Negro's grief."[13] Her own children had been scattered, with four dying and four taking flight. At the end of her life, her deep faith had been broken, the faith that she spoke of earlier in her sermon in the clearing when she preached, "Here . . . in this here place, we flesh; flesh that weeps, laughs; flesh that dances on bare feet in grass. Love it. Love it hard." "Love your eyes, hands, mouth, neck, liver, and lungs, womb, and private parts," she said, and "More than your life-holding womb and your life-giving parts, hear me now, love your heart. For this is the prize."[14]

Julie Dash builds on this tradition. In her film *Daughters of the Dust* that examines the Great Migration, Dash explores the question "*What if* we had a great-grandmother who could not physically make the journey north but who could send her spirit with them [those who migrated]." She answers it with the character of Nana Peazant, who grounded her Gullah Sea Island community in the wisdom and knowledge of her elders and ancestors. Dash opens the film with Nana's transformation from a young woman to an elder. The 88-year-old great-grandmother of a generation of women who are contemplating a move to the mainland, Nana Peazant draws on the memory of the ancestors and literally commands respect from her descendants. When tending to the family graveyard, she reminds her great-grandson Eli that she visited her grandfather's grave "every day since the day he died." She continued, "It's up to the living to keep in touch with the dead." And in the background, her voice rang out to her descendants: "Respect your elders! Respect your family! Respect your ancestors!" She passed on words of wisdom to Eli, advising him to "Call on those old Africans, Eli. They'll come to you when you least expect them. They'll hug you up quick and soft like the warm sweet wind. Let those old souls come into your heart. . . . Let them feed your head with wisdom that ain't from this day and time." Centering her narrative on the cultural continuities and tensions between generations and pulling on African American oral history and folk traditions, Dash characterizes the elder, particularly the woman elder, as an essential figure in black culture who connected the past, the present, and the future. As Nana Peazant put it, "The ancestors and the womb are one."[15]

The figure of the elder also operates in Colson Whitehead's novel *The Nickel Boys*. The main character Elwood is raised by his grandmother Harriet after being abandoned by a father whose service in World War II made him restless and intolerant of life in the Jim Crow South and by a mother who had no interest in motherhood under Southern segregation. His grandmother had her own experiences of loss. Whitehead writes, "Her father died in jail after a white lady downtown accused him of not getting out of the way on the sidewalk," and her husband Monty died during a barfight at "Miss Simone's" when he "stepped up to protect one of Simone's dishwashers from three white men." But the loss of her grandson Elwood stung the most when he got entangled in the system, was falsely accused of a crime, and ended up in Nickel Academy "reform" school. As Whitehead puts it about the grandmother and grandson relationship, "The day the court officer came for Elwood was the worst goodbye. It had been the two of them for so long."[16] Elwood's youth, treatment in Nickel Academy, and fate show why it was Harriet's worst goodbye.

The cultural production of African Americans has reflected historical and contemporary experiences of navigating multigenerational relationships. This historical moment poses yet another set of problems to those relationships and to black eldership. Family members who were not able to fully grieve elders lost to the pandemic, African American workers who were exposed to the virus while they worked on the frontlines, or grandparents playing a familiar role to grandchildren who lost their parents are recent examples of this history. At the same time, some seek new ways to connect with their elders, such as in the creative relationship between musicians Esperanza Spalding and the elder Wayne Shorter.[17] Multigenerational relationships have stayed alive as black people and communities adapt and continue to improvise. Out of this black wisdom tradition of eldership can come a set of values by which to live—values that can yield depth, insight, and regeneration.

NOTES

The following abbreviations appear in the notes:

AHC	James G. Kenan Research Center at the Atlanta History Center
FOFB	Records of the Field Offices for the State of Virginia, Bureau of Refugees, Freedmen, and Abandoned Lands, 1865-1872, National Archives and Records Administration, Washington, D.C.
GHS	Georgia Historical Society, Savannah
HSP	Historical Society of Pennsylvania, Philadelphia
LOV	Library of Virginia, Richmond
NARA	National Archives and Records Administration, Washington, D.C.
PAS	Pennsylvania Abolition Society
RL	David M. Rubenstein Rare Book & Manuscript Library, Duke University, Durham, N.C.
SCL	South Caroliniana Library, University of South Carolina, Columbia
SHC	Southern Historical Collections, Wilson Library, University of North Carolina, Chapel Hill
UVA	Albert and Shirley Small Special Collections Library, University of Virginia, Charlottesville
VHS	Virginia Historical Society, Richmond

Introduction

1. Thomas Wentworth Higginson, *Army Life in a Black Regiment* (Boston: Fields, Osgood, 1870), 40–41 and 131–34; Louis Masur, *Lincoln's Hundred Days: The Emancipation Proclamation and the War for the Union* (Cambridge, Mass.: Harvard University Press, 2012), 205–210; Steven Hahn, *A Nation Under Our Feet: Black Political Struggles in the Rural South from Slavery to the Great Migration* (Cambridge, Mass.: Harvard University Press, 2003), 91–107; Steven Hahn, *The Political Worlds of Slavery and Freedom* (Cambridge, Mass.: Harvard University Press, 2009), 76; W. E. B. DuBois, *Black Reconstruction: Toward a History of the Part Which Black Folk Played in the Attempt to Reconstruct Democracy in America*, 1860–1880 (Millwood, N.Y.: Krause-Thomson, 1976), 79–80 and 123–26.

2. Ira Berlin, *Generations of Captivity: A History of African-American Slaves* (Cambridge, Mass.: Harvard University Press, 2004), 2–3; Ira Berlin et. al., *Free at Last: A*

Documentary History of Slavery, Freedom, and the Civil War (New York: Free Press, 1992), 310–18; Robin D. G. Kelley, *Freedom Dreams: The Black Radical Imagination* (Boston: Beacon Press, 2002), 110–18.

3. James Walvin, *Crossings: Africa, the Americas and the Atlantic Slave Trade* (London: Reaktion Books, 2013), 124–42; Justin Roberts, *Slavery and the Enlightenment in the British Atlantic, 1750–1807* (New York: Cambridge University Press, 2013); Richard S. Dunn, *A Tale of Two Plantations: Slave Life and Labor in Jamaica and Virginia* (Cambridge, Mass.: Harvard University Press, 2014); Robin Blackburn, *The Making of New World Slavery: From the Baroque to the Modern, 1492–1800* (London: Verso, 1997); Stephanie Smallwood, *Saltwater Slavery: A Middle Passage from Africa to American Diaspora* (Cambridge, Mass.: Harvard University Press, 2007).

4. Jean-Baptiste Labat, *Nouveau Voyage aux Isles D'America* (1724) in Stanley Engerman et al., *Slavery* (New York: Oxford University Press, 2001), 171.

5. Deborah Gray-White, *Ar'n't I a Woman: Female Slaves in the Plantation South* (New York: W. W. Norton, 1985), 114–18.

6. Sharla Fett, *Working Cures: Healing, Health and Power on Southern Slave Plantations* (Chapel Hill: University of North Carolina Press, 2000), 72–76; Steven Hahn, *A Nation Under Our Feet*, 37–39.

7. Sari Edelstein, *Adulthood and Other Fictions: American Literature and the Unmaking of Age* (New York: Oxford University Press, 2019), 62.

8. My work builds on a rich literature that highlights the role of elders in antebellum African American history and culture; in addition to Gray-White, Fett, and Edelstein, see Sterling Stuckey, *Slave Culture: Nationalist Theory and the Foundations of Black America* (New York: Oxford University Press, 1987), 81–92; Sterling Stuckey, *Going through the Storm: The Influence of African American Art in History* (New York: Oxford University Press, 1994); Leslie Pollard, *Complaint to the Lord: Historical Perspectives on the African American Elderly* (Selinsgrove, Pa.: Susquehanna University Press, 1996); Stacey Close, *Elderly Slaves of the Plantation South* (New York: Garland, 1997); Venetria Patton, *The Grasp That Reaches Beyond the Grave* (Albany: SUNY Press, 2013).

9. Frederick Douglass, *Narrative of the Life of Frederick Douglass: An American Slave, Written by Himself*, ed. John W. Blassingame, John R. McKivigan, and Peter P. Hinks (New Haven, Conn.: Yale University Press, 2001), 13 and 39–41; *My Bondage and My Freedom* (New York: Miller, Orton & Mulligan, 1855), 35–50 and 69–70; *Life and Times of Frederick Douglass: His Early Life as a Slave, His Escape from Bondage, and His Complete History* (New York: Gramercy Books, 1993), 1–5 and 17. This book spells Douglass's grandmother's name as "Betsy Bailey" based on William McFeely, *Frederick Douglass* (New York: W. W. Norton, 1991) and David Blight, *Frederick Douglass: Prophet of Freedom* (New York: Simon and Schuster, 2018), which appear to use her owner Aaron Anthony's 1827 slave inventory to derive the spelling of her name. In most cases, when I incorporate direct quotations from manuscript and published materials, I use the spelling and punctuation that appear in the original sources.

10. Harriet Jacobs, *Incidents in the Life of a Slave Girl. Written By Herself*, ed. L. Maria Child (Boston, 1861); Charles Ball, *Slavery in the United States: A Narrative of the Life and Adventures of Charles Ball* (New York: John S. Taylor, 1837), 16–24 and 38–39.

11. George Rawick, ed., Georgia Narratives, vol. 13, part 3 of *The American Slave: A Composite Biography* (Westport., Conn: Greenwood Press, 1972), 200.

12. Sari Edelstein, *Adulthood and Other Fictions*, 44–70.

13. Habiba Ibrahim, *Black Age: Oceanic Lifespans and the Time of Black Life* (New York: New York University Press, 2021), 5–15.

14. Pat Thane, "Social Histories of Old Age and Aging," *Journal of Social History* 37, no. 1 (Autumn, 2003): 93–111; Pat Thane, ed. *A History of Old Age* (Los Angeles: J. Paul Getty Museum, 2005); see also, W. Andrew Achenbaum, *Old Age in the New Land: The American Experience since 1790* (Baltimore: Johns Hopkins University Press, 1978); Carol Haber, *Beyond Sixty-Five: The Dilemma of Old Age in America's Past* (New York: Cambridge University Press, 1983); Howard Chudacoff, *How Old Are You?* (Princeton, N.J.: Princeton University Press, 1989).

15. Jennifer Morgan, *Laboring Women: Reproduction and Gender in New World Slavery* (Philadelphia: University of Pennsylvania Press, 2004); Deborah Gray-White, *Ar'n't I a Woman*; Marie Jenkins Schwartz, *Birthing a Slave: Motherhood and Medicine in the Antebellum South* (Cambridge, Mass.: Harvard University Press, 2010); Libra R. Hilde, *Slavery, Fatherhood, and Paternal Duty in African American History in the Long Nineteenth Century* (Chapel Hill: University of North Carolina Press, 2020); Vincent Brown, *The Reaper's Garden: Death and Power in the World of Atlantic Slavery* (Cambridge, Mass.: Harvard University Press, 2010); David Roediger, "And Die in Dixie: Funerals, Death and Heaven in the Slave Community, 1700–1865," *Massachusetts Review* 22, no. 1 (Spring 1981): 163–83; Corinne T. Field, *The Struggle for Equal Adulthood: Gender, Race, Age, and the Fight for Citizenship in Antebellum America* (Chapel Hill: University of North Carolina Press, 2014); Daina Berry, *The Price for Their Pound of Flesh: The Value of the Enslaved, from Womb to the Grave, in the Building of a Nation* (Boston: Beacon Press, 2017); Erik Seeman, *Speaking with the Dead in Early America* (Philadelphia: University of Pennsylvania Press, 2019).

16. Corinne T. Field and Nicholas L. Syrett, "AHR Roundtable, Chronological Age: A Useful Historical Category of Analysis," *American Historical Review* 125, no. 2 (April 2020): 379.

17. My thinking about the politics of age has been shaped by the concept of "mortuary politics," as spelled out by Vincent Brown in *The Reaper's Garden*, 5–12.

18. Here, I draw upon Kwame Anthony Appiah's theory of identity in *The Lies That Bind: Rethinking Identity* (New York: W. W. Norton, 2018), 8–32.

19. Kimberlé Crenshaw, "Mapping the Margins: Intersectionality, Identity Politics, and Violence Against Women of Color," *Stanford Law Review* 43, no. 6 (July 1991): 1241–99; Sumi Cho, Kimberlé Williams Crenshaw and Leslie McCall, "Toward a Field of Intersectionality Studies: Theory, Applications, and Praxis," *Signs* 38, no. 4 (Summer 2013): 785–810; Wilma King, "'Prematurely Knowing of Evil Things': The Sexual Abuse

of African American Girls and Young Women in Slavery and Freedom," *Journal of African American History* 99, no. 3 (Summer 2014): 173–96.

20. Ibrahim, *Black Age*.

21. Wilma King, *Stolen Childhood: Slave Youth in Nineteenth Century America*, 2nd ed. (Bloomington: Indiana University Press, 2011); Marie Jenkins Schwartz, *Born in Bondage: Growing Up Enslaved in the Antebellum South* (Cambridge, Mass.: Harvard University Press, 2001); on racial capitalism, see Cedric Robinson, *Black Marxism* (Chapel Hill: University of North Carolina Press, 2000).

22. In addition to works cited above, my work builds on studies of slave community formation such as John Blassingame, *The Slave Community: Plantation Life in the Antebellum South* (New York: Oxford University Press, 1979); Margaret Washington-Creel, *"A Peculiar People": Slave Religion and Community Culture Among the Gullahs* (New York: New York University Press, 1988); Charles Joyner, *Down by the Riverside: A South Carolina Slave Community* (Urbana: University of Illinois Press, 1985); Brenda Stevenson, *Life in Black and White: Family and Community in the Slave South* (New York: Oxford University Press, 1996); Dylan Penningroth, *The Claims of Kinfolk: African American Property and Community in the Nineteenth Century South* (Chapel Hill: University of North Carolina Press, 2003); Daina Berry, *"Swing the Sickle for the Harvest Is Ripe": Gender and Slavery in Antebellum Georgia* (Urbana: University of Illinois Press, 2010).

23. Ira Berlin, *Generations of Captivity*; Ira Berlin, *Many Thousands Gone: The First Two Centuries of Slavery in North America* (Cambridge, Mass.: Harvard University Press, 1998); though not to the same extent as Berlin, Philip Morgan uses a crop-centered and time-space approach in *Slave Counterpoint: Black Culture in the Eighteenth Century Chesapeake and Lowcountry* (Chapel Hill: University of North Carolina Press, 1998).

24. Uri McMillan, *Embodied Avatars: Genealogies of Black Feminist Art and Performance* (New York: New York University Press, 2015), 26–63; Benjamin Reiss, *The Showman and the Slave: Race, Death, and Memory in Barnum's America* (Cambridge, Mass.: Harvard University Press, 2010); Hershini Bhana-Young, *Illegible Will: Coercive Spectacles of Labor in South Africa and the Diaspora* (Durham: Duke University Press, 2017), 111–20.

25. George Fitzhugh, *Cannibals All!, or Slaves Without Masters* (Richmond, Va.: A. Morris, 1857), 278.

26. George Fitzhugh, *Sociology of the South, or the Failure of Free Society* (Richmond, Va.: A. Morris, 1854), 68.

27. David Blight, *Race and Reunion: The Civil War in American Memory* (Cambridge, Mass.: Belknap Press of Harvard University Press, 2001).

28. Kenneth Goings, *Mammy and Uncle Mose: Black Collectibles and American Stereotyping* (Bloomington: Indiana University Press, 1994); Deborah Gray-White, *Ar'n't I a Woman*, 27–61; Micki McElya, *Clinging to Mammy: The Faithful Slave in American Memory* (Cambridge, Mass.: Harvard University Press, 2007).

29. Jean Elizabeth Van Dyke, "March's Musical Recitations" (Lebanon, Ohio: March Bros., 1915), 3–5; C. A. White, "The Old Home ain't what it used to be" (Boston: White,

Smith & Perry, 1872); "They Made It Twice As Nice As Paradise: And They Called It Dixieland" (New York: Jerome H. Remick, 1916), Balch Institute for Ethnic Studies Sheet Music Collection, box 4, Historical Society of Pennsylvania (HSP), Philadelphia.

Chapter 1

1. Van Sevenhuysen to Ass. of X, Elmina, 16th November 1701, in *The Dutch and the Guinea Coast: A Collection of Documents from the General State Archive at the Hague*, ed. and trans. Albert Van Dantzig (Accra, Ghana: GAAS Printing, 1978), 75.

2. Stephanie Smallwood, *Saltwater Slavery: A Middle Passage from Africa to American Diaspora* (Cambridge, Mass.: Harvard University Press, 2008); Jennifer Morgan, *Laboring Women*; Alexander Byrd, *Captives and Voyagers: Black Migrants Across the Eighteenth Century British Atlantic World* (Baton Rouge: Louisiana State University Press, 2008); Daniel Littlefield, *Rice and Slaves: Ethnicity and the Slave Trade in Colonial South Carolina* (Urbana: University of Illinois Press, 1991); Michael Gomez, *Exchanging Our Country Marks: The Transformation of African Identities in the Colonial and Antebellum South* (Chapel Hill: University of North Carolina Press, 1998).

3. "Otto Friedrich von der Groeben's Account of His Voyage to Guinea, 1682–83," in *Brandenburg Sources for West African History, 1680–1700*, ed. Adam Jones (Stuttgart: Franz Steiner Verlag Wiesbaden GMBH, 1985), 36.

4. "Samuel Brun's Voyages of 1611–12," in *German Sources for West African History, 1599–1669*, ed. Adam Jones (Wiesbaden: Franz Steiner Verlag GMBH, 1983), 62.

5. "Samuel Brun's Voyages of 1611–12," 53–54.

6. "Wilhelm Johann Müller's Description of the Fetu Country, 1662–9," in *German Sources for West African History, 1599–1669*, 153.

7. "Wilhelm Johann Müller's Description of the Fetu Country, 1662–9," 152–53.

8. "Johann Peter Oettinger's Account of His Voyage to Guinea, 1692–93" in *Brandenburg Sources for West African History, 1680–1700*, 189; my thinking here about European perceptions of African bodies and its implications for the slave trade has been shaped by Morgan, *Laboring Women*.

9. *Pieter van den Broecke's Journal of Voyages to Cape Verde, Guinea and Angola (1605–1612)*, ed. and trans. J. D. La Fleur (London: Hakluyt Society, 2000), 59–60.

10. *Pieter van den Broecke's Journal of Voyages to Cape Verde, Guinea and Angola (1605–1612)*, 59–60.

11. *The Republic of Plato*, Benjamin Jowett, trans. (New York: Willey Book, 1901), 51, retrieved from http://books.google.com; on spiritual exercises, see Pierre Hadot, *What Is Ancient Philosophy?* (Cambridge, Mass.: Harvard University Press, 2002) and *Philosophy as a Way of Life*, ed. and trans. Arnold I. Davidson (Malden, Mass.: Blackwell, 1995); Pat Thane, *Old Age in English History: Past Experiences, Present Issues* (New York: Oxford University Press, 2000), 31–43.

12. "Samuel Brun's Voyages of 1611–12," 82.

13. William Bosman, *A New and Accurate Description of the Coast of Guinea, Divided into the Gold, the Slave, and the Ivory Coasts* (London: Frank Cass, 1967), 360.

14. "Wilhelm Johann Müller's Description of the Fetu Country, 1662–9," 256.

15. "Wilhelm Johann Müller's Description of the Fetu Country, 1662–9," 256.

16. "Wilhelm Johann Müller's Description of the Fetu Country, 1662–9," 255.

17. "Wilhelm Johann Müller's Description of the Fetu Country, 1662–9," 256.

18. "Samuel Brun's Voyages of 1611–12," 68.

19. "Wilhelm Johann Müller's Description of the Fetu Country, 1662–9," 150.

20. "Samuel Brun's Voyages of 1611–12," 91; "Michael Hemmersam's Description of the Gold Coast, 1639–1645," in *German Sources for West African History, 1599–1669*, 121–22; and "Wilhelm Johann Müller's Description of the Fetu Country, 1662–9," 150–52.

21. Bosman, *A New and Accurate Description of the Coast of Guinea*, 110.

22. "Wilhelm Johann Müller's Description of the Fetu Country, 1662–9," 255–56.

23. Bosman, *A New and Accurate Description of the Coast of Guinea*, 142.

24. *Pieter van den Broecke's Journal of Voyages to Cape Verde, Guinea and Angola (1605–1612)*, 96.

25. "Samuel Brun's Voyages of 1611–12," 51.

26. "Samuel Brun's Voyages of 1611–12," 51.

27. *Monumenta Missionaria Africana: Africa Ocidental (1471–1531)*, vol. 1, collected and annotated by Padre Antonio Brasio (Lisbon: Agencia Geral Do Ultramar Divisao de Publicacoes e Biblioteca, 1952), 56–63.

28. *Monumenta Missionaria Africana*, vol. 1, 61–65.

29. *Monumenta Missionaria Africana*, vol. 1, 79.

30. Anne Hilton, *The Kingdom of Kongo* (New York: Clarendon Press of Oxford University Press, 1985), 50–53.

31. Filippo Pigafetta and Duarte Lopes, *A Report of the Kingdom of Kongo, and the Surrounding Countries* (New York: Negro Universities Press, 1969),77.

32. Pigafetta and Lopes, *A Report of the Kingdom of Kongo*, 78.

33. Pigafetta and Lopes, *A Report of the Kingdom of Kongo*, 72.

34. Pigafetta and Lopes, *A Report of the Kingdom of Kongo*, 81.

35. *Pieter van den Broecke's Journal of Voyages to Cape Verde, Guinea and Angola (1605–1612)*, 59–60; see also, *The Portuguese in West Africa, 1415–1670*, ed. Malyn Newitt (New York: Cambridge University Press, 2010), 213; Joseph Miller, *Way of Death: Merchant Capitalism and the Angolan Slave Trade, 1730–1830* (Madison: University of Wisconsin Press, 1988), 81.

36. Kwame Anthony Appiah, *The Honor Code: How Moral Revolutions Happen* (New York: W. W. Norton, 2010).

37. *Pieter van den Broecke's Journal of Voyages to Cape Verde, Guinea and Angola (1605–1612)*, 59.

38. Pigafetta and Lopes, *A Report of the Kingdom of Kongo*, 60.

39. *Monumenta Missionaria Africana*, vol. 1, 56.

40. *Monumenta Missionaria Africana*, vol. 1, 146.

41. *Monumenta Missionaria Africana*, vol. 1, 194–95.

42. "Samuel Brun's Voyages of 1611–12," 61–62.

43. Pigafetta and Lopes, *A Report of the Kingdom of Kongo*, 112.

44. Pigafetta and Lopes, *A Report of the Kingdom of Kongo*, 112–13.

45. Pigafetta and Lopes, *A Report of the Kingdom of Kongo*, 87; Jason Young, *Rituals of Resistance: African Atlantic Religion in Kongo and the Lowcountry South in the Era of Slavery* (Baton Rouge: Louisiana State University Press, 2007), 109–13; Sharla Fett, *Working Cures: Healing, Health and Power on Southern Plantations* (Chapel Hill: University of North Carolina Press, 2002), 40–41.

46. Bosman, *A New and Accurate Description of the Coast of Guinea*, 472.

47. Bosman, *A New and Accurate Description of the Coast of Guinea*, 479–80.

48. Bosman, *A New and Accurate Description of the Coast of Guinea*, 57.

49. "Wilhelm Johann Müller's Description of the Fetu Country, 1662–9," 181.

50. "Samuel Brun's Voyages of 1611–12," 88.

51. "Samuel Brun's Voyages of 1611–12," 88.

52. "Wilhelm Johann Müller's Description of the Fetu Country, 1662–9," 168.

53. "Wilhelm Johann Müller's Description of the Fetu Country, 1662–9," 181–82.

54. "Michael Hemmersam's Description of the Gold Coast, 1639–1645," 123.

55. Igor Kopytoff, "Ancestors as Elders in Africa," *Africa: Journal of the International African Institute* 41, no. 2 (April 1971): 129–42.

56. Bosman, *A New and Accurate Description of the Coast of Guinea*, 481.

57. Bosman, *A New and Accurate Description of the Coast of Guinea*, 481–83 (quotation from 482).

58. Bosman, *A New and Accurate Description of the Coast of Guinea*, 385.

59. "Wilhelm Johann Müller's Description of the Fetu Country, 1662–9," 255–56.

60. "Journal Containing the Most Remarkable Incidents Occurring with This Government Between 16th March and 15th April, Extracted by J. Elzevier," in *The Dutch and the Guinea Coast*, 349.

61. "Wilhelm Johann Müller's Description of the Fetu Country, 1662–9," 256.

62. "Wilhelm Johann Müller's Description of the Fetu Country, 1662–9," 214.

63. "Samuel Brun's Voyages of 1611–12," 91.

64. "Wilhelm Johann Müller's Description of the Fetu Country, 1662–9," 153–54.

65. "Wilhelm Johann Müller's Description of the Fetu Country, 1662–9," 154.

66. Richard Jobson, *The Golden Trade* (New York: Da Capo, 1968), 69.

67. Jobson, *The Golden Trade*, 78.

68. Jobson, *The Golden Trade*, 76–77; for a more precise definition and treatment of marabouts, see Rudolph T. Ware III, *The Walking Qur'an: Islamic Education, Embodied Knowledge, and History in West Africa* (Chapel Hill: University of North Carolina Press, 2014), 78–80.

69. "Samuel Brun's Voyages of 1611–12," 88.

70. Bosman, *A New and Accurate Description of the Coast of Guinea*, 201.

71. Bosman, *A New and Accurate Description of the Coast of Guinea*, 202.

72. *Olfert Dapper's Description of Benin (1668)*, trans. Adam Jones (Madison: University of Wisconsin, 1998), 22; for a broader discussion of the connection between

eldership, gender, and ethnicity, see Sandra E. Greene, "Family Concerns: Gender and Ethnicity in Pre-Colonial West Africa," *International Review of Social History* 44 (1999), supplement, 15–21.

73. Pigafetta and Lopes, *A Report of the Kingdom of Kongo*, 90.

74. "Wilhelm Johann Müller's Description of the Fetu Country, 1662–9," 215.

75. *Pieter van den Broecke's Journal of Voyages to Cape Verde, Guinea and Angola (1605–1612)*, 98.

76. "Samuel Brun's Voyages of 1611–12," 55.

77. "Samuel Brun's Voyages of 1611–12," 54.

78. *Pieter van den Broecke's Journal of Voyages to Cape Verde, Guinea and Angola (1605–1612)*, 39–40.

79. "Samuel Brun's Voyages of 1611–12," 55.

80. *Equiano's Travels: His Autobiography; the Interesting Narrative of the Life of Olaudah Equiano or Gustavus Vassa*, ed. Paul Edwards (London: Heinemann, 1967), 18–19. While Vincent Carretta's study titled *Equiano, the African: Biography of a Self-Made Man* (Athens: University of Georgia Press, 2005) raises questions about the full veracity of Equiano's narrative, it can still be useful as source of either eyewitness or second-hand information.

81. W. de la Palma, to Ass. of X, Elmina, 10th October 1703, in *The Dutch and the Guinea Coast*, 90.

82. "Samuel Brun's Voyages of 1611–12," 69.

83. Resolutions of the Director-General and Council at Elmina, 13th February 1684, in *The Dutch and the Guinea Coast*, 42–43.

84. Pigafetta and Lopes, *A Report of the Kingdom of Kongo*, 58–59 and 63.

85. Bosman, *A New and Accurate Description of the Coast of Guinea*, 472–73.

86. See for example Randy J. Sparks, *The Two Princes of Calabar: An Eighteenth-Century Atlantic Odyssey* (Cambridge, Mass.: Harvard University Press, 2004), 54–56.

87. *Pieter van den Broecke's Journal of Voyages to Cape Verde, Guinea and Angola (1605–1612)*, 59–60 and 96.

88. "Samuel Brun's Voyages of 1611–12," 92.

89. Verschueren to Ass. of X, 24th November 1739, in *The Dutch and the Guinea Coast*, 345.

90. Willem de la Palma to Presidial Chamber, 10th October 1703, in *The Dutch and the Guinea Coast*, 101.

91. Minutes of Elmina Council, 18th July 1731, in *The Dutch and the Guinea Coast*, 261.

92. Johannes Postma, *The Dutch in the Atlantic Slave Trade, 1600–1815* (New York: Cambridge University Press, 1990), 228; Ray Kea, *A Social and Cultural History of Ghana from the Seventeenth to the Nineteenth Century: The Gold Coast in the Age of the Atlantic Slave Trade*, book 1 (Lewiston, N.Y.: Edwin Mellen Press, 2012), 116–20; Jennifer L. Morgan, *Reckoning with Slavery: Gender, Kinship, and Capitalism in the Early Black Atlantic* (Durham: Duke University Press, 2021), 171; Nayan Chanda, *Bound Together:*

How Traders, Preachers, Adventurers, and Warriors Shaped Globalization (New Haven, Conn.: Yale University Press, 2008), 222.

93. Instructions from Isaac Jan Nys to Martin Witte, 3rd July 1687 in *The Dutch and the Guinea Coast*, 24–25; the Brandenburger Johann Peter Oettinger provided a sense of what those values might be. Concerning the trade at Accra in 1692–93 when he landed at the Gold Coast town, Oettinger wrote, "A male slave cost about 25 thaler, a female 20 to 22, a boy 12 to 14 and a girl about 10." Johann Peter Oettinger's account of his voyage to Guinea, 1692–93 in *Brandenburg Sources for West African History*, 189.

94. The South Sea Company: Minutes of the Committee of Correspondence, 22d Octo'r, 1717, in *Documents Illustrative of the History of the Slave Trade to America*, ed. Elizabeth Donnan, vol. 2 (Washington, D.C.: Carnegie Institution of Washington, 1930), 219.

95. John Barbot at Old Calabar, in 1698, in *Documents Illustrative of the Slave Trade*, vol. 1, 419.

96. The Royal African Company: Minutes and Further Report of the Committee of Trade, Mar. 14th 1720[/1], in *Documents Illustrative of the Slave Trade*, vol. 2, 257.

97. Hertogh to Pranger, October 1733, in *The Dutch and the Guinea Coast*, 294.

98. Otto Friedrich von der Groeben's Account of His Voyage to Guinea, in *Brandenburg Sources for West African History, 1680–1700*, 37.

99. The Owners of the *Union* to Captain Richard Prankard, Bristol, January 28th 1732–33, in *Documents Illustrative of the Slave Trade*, vol. 2, 445.

100. Otto Friedrich von der Groeben's Account of His Voyage to Guinea, 36.

101. Voyage of the *Hannibal*, 1693–94, in *Documents Illustrative of the Slave Trade*, vol. 1, 401.

102. Robert W. Harms, *The Diligent: A Voyage Through the Worlds of the Slave Trade* (New York: Basic Books, 2002), 247.

103. Journal of the *Arthur*, Dec. 5, 1677–May 25, 1678, in *Documents Illustrative of the Slave Trade*, vol. 1, 228.

104. Daniel Wescomb to Francis Lynn, February 23, 1721, in *Documents Illustrative of the Slave Trade*, vol. 2, 256.

105. Contract Between the South Sea Company and the Royal African Company (1713), in *Documents Illustrative of the Slave Trade*, vol. 2, 159.

106. Instructions to Captain William Barry, Bristol, Oct 7th, 1725, in *Documents Illustrative of the Slave Trade*, vol. 2, 327.

107. The Royal African Company: Minutes of the Committee of Trade, Febry 16th, 1721, in *Documents Illustrative of the Slave Trade*, vol. 2, 249–50.

108. James Barbot's Voyage to the Congo River, August 28, 1700, in *Documents Illustrative of the Slave Trade*, vol. 1, 459.

109. Voyage of the *Hannibal*, 1693–94, in *Documents Illustrative of the Slave Trade*, vol. 1, 407.

110. Accounts of the *Sarah Bonaventura*, 1676–1677, in *Documents Illustrative of the Slave Trade*, vol. 1, 218–21.

111. Accounts of the *Swallow*, 1679–1681, and Accounts of the *Arminian Merchant*, 1689–91, in *Documents Illustrative of the Slave Trade*, vol. 1, 257 and 372.

112. John Merewether to Peter Burrell, Jamaica, Septem'r 6th 1736, in *Documents Illustrative of the Slave Trade*, vol. 2, 459.

113. Captain John Blake to the Guinea Company, Vintan River in the River Gambae, 15th of February [1651/2], in *Documents Illustrative of the Slave Trade*, vol. 1, 135.

114. Voyage of the *Hannibal*, 1693–94, in *Documents Illustrative of the Slave Trade*, vol. 1, 398.

115. The Guinea Company to James Pope, London, the 17 September 1651, in *Documents Illustrative of the Slave Trade*, vol. 1, 135.

116. The Guinea Company to James Pope, London, the 9 of December 1651, in *Documents Illustrative of the Slave Trade*, vol. 1, 131.

117. Instructions to Captain Samuel Kempthorne, London, the 4th May 1686, in *Documents Illustrative of the Slave Trade*, vol. 1, 354.

118. William Hardringe and Nicholas Prideaux to the Royal African Company, Barbados, the 11th Feb'ry 1692/3, in *Documents Illustrative of the Slave Trade*, vol. 1, 391.

119. Edwyn Stede and Stephen Gascoigne to the Royal African Company, Barbados, the 11th April 1683, in *Documents Illustrative of the Slave Trade*, vol. 1, 306.

120. Hender Molesworth and Rowland Powell to the Royal African Company, Jamaica, Feb. 15, 1679/80, in *Documents Illustrative of the Slave Trade*, vol. 1, 255.

121. Henry Carpenter and Robert Helmes to the Royal African Company, Nevis the 24th Decemb'r, 1681, in *Documents Illustrative of the Slave Trade*, vol. 1, 275.

122. Description of the Coast of Guinea, in *Documents Illustrative of the Slave Trade*, vol. 1, 441–42.

123. Edwyn Stede and Stephen Gascoigne to the Royal African Company, Barbados, Decemb. the 2d: 1678, in *Documents Illustrative of the Slave Trade*, vol. 1, 240.

124. Receipt of Pedro Diez Troxxilla for Slaves, 1660, in *Documents Illustrative of the Slave Trade*, vol. 1, 149.

125. Vice-Director Beck to Director Stuyvesant, Curacao, July 28, 1657, in *Documents Illustrative of the Slave Trade*, vol. 1, 139–40.

126. Journal of the *Arthur*, Dec. 5, 1677–May 25, 1678, in *Documents Illustrative of the Slave Trade*, vol. 1, 232.

127. Edwyn Stede and Stephen Gascoigne to the Royal African Company, Barbados, the 11th April 1683, in *Documents Illustrative of the Slave Trade*, vol. 1, 305.

128. The Case of the Thomas and Francis, in *Documents Illustrative of the Slave Trade*, vol. 1, 214.

129. Vice-Director Beck to Director Stuyvesant, Curacao, August, 1659, in *Documents Illustrative of the Slave Trade*, vol. 1, 140–41.

130. William Byrd I to Sadleir and Thomas, February 10th, 1685, in *The Correspondence of the Three William Byrds of Westover, Virginia, 1684–1776*, vol. 1, ed. Maron Tingling (Charlottesville: University Press of Virginia, 1977), 50.

131. William Byrd I to Sadleir and Thomas, October the 18th, 1686, in *The Correspondence of the Three William Byrds*, vol. 1, 65.

132. Henrietta McBurney, *Illuminating Natural History: The Art and Science of Mark Catesby* (New Haven, Conn.: Yale University Press, 2021), 239 and 242.

133. Henry Laurens to Peter Woodhouse, 18th November 1755, in *The Papers of Henry Laurens, Volume Two: Nov. 1, 1755–Dec. 31, 1758*, ed. Philip M. Hamer and George C. Rogers Jr. (Columbia: University of South Carolina Press, 1970), 16.

134. Henry Laurens to Thomas Hinde, 23d December 1755, in *The Papers of Henry Laurens*, 49.

135. Henry Laurens to Robert and John Thompson & Co., in *The Papers of Henry Laurens*, 77.

136. Henry Laurens to Devonsheir, Reeve & Lloyd, 18th May 1756, in *The Papers of Henry Laurens*, 194.

137. Advertisement, *South Carolina Gazette*, January 15, 1756, in *The Papers of Henry Laurens*, 67; for a broader discussion of the preference for slaves from specific regions in Africa, see Daniel C. Littlefield, *Rice and Slaves*, 74–114; Judith Carney, *Black Rice: The African Origins of Rice Cultivation in the Americas* (Cambridge, Mass.: Harvard University Press, 2001); Michael Gomez, *Exchanging Our Country Marks.*

138. Henry Laurens to Richard Oswald & Co., 13 April 1756, in *The Papers of Henry Laurens*, 169.

139. Henry Laurens to Helme & Fowler, 19th June 1756, in *The Papers of Henry Laurens*, 227.

140. Henry Laurens to John Knight, 28th May 1756, in *The Papers of Henry Laurens*, 204.

141. Henry Laurens to John & William Halliday, 14th February 1757 in *The Papers of Henry Laurens*, 455.

142. Advertisements, *South Carolina Gazette*, October 6 and 13, 1758, in *The Papers of Henry Laurens*, 548–49.

143. Henry Laurens to James Smith, 7th January 1757 in *The Papers of Henry Laurens*, 400.

144. Henry Laurens to John & William Halliday, 14th February 1757 in *The Papers of Henry Laurens*, 455.

145. Henry Laurens to Gidney Clarke, 20th November 1756, in *The Papers of Henry Laurens*, 357.

146. Henry Laurens to Richard Oswald, 19th July 1756, in *The Papers of Henry Laurens*, 266.

147. Henry Laurens to Samuel &William Vernon, 5th July 1756, in *The Papers of Henry Laurens*, 238.

148. Henry Laurens to Robert & John Thompson & Co., 6th August 1756, in *The Papers of Henry Laurens*, 275.

149. Henry Laurens to Richard Oswald & Co. 10th July 1756, in *The Papers of Henry Laurens*, 246.

150. Henry Laurens to John Knight, 28th May 1756, in *The Papers of Henry Laurens*, 204.

151. Peter Manigault to Ralph Izard, Septr. 6th 1771, in Letterbook of Peter Manigault, 22 October 1763–3 May 1772 (typescript by Maurice Crouse in the possession of the author), 156.

152. Peter Manigault to Ralph Izard, 13th April 1765, in Letterbook of Peter Manigault, 18.

153. Peter Manigault to Isaac King, Septr. 6th 1771, in Letterbook of Peter Manigault, 163; Peter Manigault to Ralph Izard, 28th Febry 1772, in Letterbook of Peter Manigault, 174.

154. Peter Manigault to Ralph Izard, 19th Augt. 1765, in Letterbook of Peter Manigault, 26.

155. Peter Manigault to Ralph Izard, 4th July 1771, in Letterbook of Peter Manigault, 156; Peter Manigault to Ralph Izard, 1771, in Letterbook of Peter Manigault, 166.

156. Peter Manigault to Danl Blake, 9th Novr. 1769, in Letterbook of Peter Manigault, 110.

157. Peter Manigault to Ralph Izard, 25th Jany 1772, in Letterbook of Peter Manigault, 170.

158. Robert Jordan Commonplace Book, 1738–1958 (mss5: 5 J 7664:1), Virginia Historical Society (VHS), Richmond.

159. Nathan Talley Slave List, 1770, Jerdone Family Papers, 1749–1873, accession no. 20415, Personal Papers Collection, Library of Virginia (LOV), Richmond.

160. William Waller Hening, *The Statutes at Large; Being a Collection of All the Laws of Virginia, from the First Session of the Legislature in the Year 1619*, vol. 3 (Philadelphia: Thomas Desilver, 1823), 87–88. For an examination of the question of the aged as chargeable, see Alix Lerner, "Aging in Bondage: Slavery, Debility, and the Problem of Dependency in the Antebellum South" (PhD diss., Princeton University, 2016).

161. *Peter Kalm's Travels in North America* (1937) in *A Documentary History of Slavery in North America*, ed. Willie Lee Rose (Athens: University of Georgia Press, 1999), 48–49.

162. Robert Carter to Mikajah Perry, July 13, 1723, in Rose, *A Documentary History of Slavery in North America*, 44.

163. Laws of New Jersey Concerning Negroes and Mulatto Slaves from 1682 to 1788, 29–31, and 56–57, Pennsylvania Abolition Society (PAS) Papers, HSP.

164. *Virginia Gazette*, June 13, 1761, in Lathan A. Windley, *Virginia and North Carolina*, vol. 1 of *Runaway Slave Advertisements: A Documentary History from the 1730s to the 1790s* (Westport, Conn.: Greenwood Press, 1983), 44. For a discussion of Windley, see Gomez, *Exchanging Our Country Marks*.

165. *South-Carolina Gazette and General Advertiser*, December 23 to December 27, 1783, in Lathan A. Windley, *South Carolina*, vol. 3 of *Runaway Slave Advertisements: A Documentary History from the 1730s to the 1790s* (Westport, Conn.: Greenwood Press, 1983), 24.

166. *Virginia Gazette*, May 21, 1767, in Windley, *Virginia and North Carolina*, 53.

167. *Virginia Gazette*, April 29, 1773, in Windley, *Virginia and North Carolina*, 321.

168. *Maryland Journal and Baltimore Advertiser*, January 26, 1779, in Lathan A. Windley, *Maryland*, vol. 2 of *Runaway Slave Advertisements: A Documentary History from the 1730s to the 1790s* (Westport, Conn.: Greenwood Press, 1983), 218.

169. *Maryland Gazette*, March 1, 1787, in Windley, *Maryland*, 166.

170. *Virginia Gazette*, August 4, 1768, in Windley, *Virginia and North Carolina*, 288.

171. *South-Carolina and American General Gazette*, September 11, 1777, in Windley, *South Carolina*, 510.

172. *Maryland Gazette*, October 16, 1766, in Windley, *Maryland*, 67.

173. *Cape-Fear Mercury*, December 29, 1773, in Windley, *Virginia and North Carolina*, 462.

174. *South-Carolina Gazette and Country Journal*, December 24, 1771, in Windley, *South Carolina*, 670–71.

175. *Gazette of the State of Georgia*, January 19, 1786, in Lathan A. Windley, Georgia, vol. 4 of *Runaway Slave Advertisements: A Documentary History from the 1730s to the 1790s* (Westport, Conn.: Greenwood Press, 1983), 136.

176. *Maryland Gazette*, March 22, 1770, in Windley, *Maryland*, 80.

177. *Georgia Gazette*, July 23, 1766, in Windley, *Georgia*, 18.

178. *North-Carolina Gazette*, August 1, 1777, in Windley, *Virginia and North Carolina*, 446.

179. *Maryland Gazette*, November 10, 1768 in Windley, *Maryland*, 75; *South Carolina Gazette*, February 22 to February 29, 1748, in Windley, *South Carolina*, 81; and *South-Carolina Gazette*, November 14 to November 21, 1761, in Windley, *South Carolina*, 206.

180. *Virginia Gazette*, August 10, 1769, in Windley, *Virginia and North Carolina*, 72; *Georgia Gazette*, July 27, 1768, in Windley, *Georgia*, 31.

181. *Gazette of the State of Georgia*, April 26, 1787, in Windley, *Georgia*, 148; *Maryland Journal and Baltimore Advertiser*, June 29, 1787, in Windley, *Maryland*, 364.

182. *Maryland Journal and Baltimore Advertiser*, March 31, 1786, in Windley, *Maryland*, 344.

183. *Georgia Gazette*, April 25, 1765, in Windley, *Georgia*, 11.

184. *Virginia Gazette*, February 28, 1755, in Windley, *Virginia and North Carolina*, 32.

185. *Virginia Gazette*, March 10, 1774, in Windley, *Virginia and North Carolina*, 334.

186. *South Carolina Gazette*, October 4, 1773, in Windley, *South Carolina*, 330; *Virginia Gazette*, April 29, 1773, in Windley, *Virginia and North Carolina*, 131; *South Carolina Gazette and Country Journal*, May 22, 1770, in Windley, *South Carolina*, 655.

187. *South Carolina Gazette*, January 9 to January 16, 1762, in Windley, *South Carolina*, 210; *South Carolina and American General Gazette*, November 4, 1780, in Windley, *South Carolina*, 571; and *Royal Gazette* [Charleston, S.C.], September 8 to September 12, 1781, in Windley, *South Carolina*, 587.

188. *Royal Georgia Gazette*, January 4, 1781, in Windley, *Georgia*, 81.

189. *South Carolina Gazette*, July 1, 1745, in Windley, *South Carolina*, 63; *South Carolina Gazette*, October 22, 1753, in Windley, *South Carolina*, 124; and *South-Carolina Gazette*, March 15 to March 22, 1760, in Windley, *South Carolina*, 182.

190. *Maryland Journal and Baltimore Advertiser*, October 5, 1784, in Windley, *Maryland*, 319.

Chapter 2

1. Isaac Jefferson, Memoirs of This Slave of Thomas Jefferson's as Told to Charles Campbell, This Being Part of a Reconstruction by Campbell After the Loss of the Original, 16 May 1845, accession no. 3440, Albert and Shirley Small Special Collections Library (UVA), University of Virginia, Charlottesville.

2. Betts and Gregory, Circular, 1861 March (?), issued to "Dear Sir" (Mss4 B4666 a 1), VHS, Richmond.

3. Charles Friend, Diary, June 14 and 15, 1841, Charles Friend Diary, 1841–1846, Friend Family Papers, 1792–1871 (Mss1 F9156 a 1), VHS; Edward Baptist elaborates on the meaning of the term "hands" as a synonym for slaves in *The Half Has Never Been Told: Slavery and the Making of American Capitalism* (New York: Basic Books, 2016).

4. Berry, *The Price for Their Pound of Flesh.*

5. Account Book, 1851–1883, 23, section 4, Haxall Family Papers, 1835–1920 (Mss1 H3203 c), VHS.

6. Typescript of 1850 and 1858 Slave List, GHS 1290, Manigault Family Plantation Records, 1845–1876, Georgia Historical Society (GHS), Savannah.

7. Valuation of Property Recd, by C. H. Binns, ca. 1854, Binns Family Estate Papers, 1814, ca. 1854, accession no. 20543, Personal Papers collection, LOV.

8. "Age of Negroes," Account Book, 1831–1863, Scott Family Papers, 1783–1881 (Mss1 Sco866 d), VHS.

9. "List of James A. Scotts Negroes and Their Ages in 1860," John Fitzgerald Papers, 1805–1878 (Mss1 F5764 c), VHS.

10. "Number and Ages of Negroes in Our Possession," March 1839, and List of Slaves, n.d., Gooch Family Papers, 1812–1961 (Mss1 G5906 a), VHS.

11. County Court Free Negro Register, 1794–1832, Southampton County Circuit Court Records, microfilm, reel 90, LOV.

12. Blair Bolling, Account Book, 1826–1855, Bolling Family Papers, 1749–1956 (Mss1 B6386 a), VHS.

13. John Fayette Dickinson, Diary, 1st February 1855, John Fayette Dickinson Diary, 1850–1890, 82, Dickinson Family Papers, 1805–1988 (Mss1 D5607 a), VHS.

14. Richard Eppes, Diary, October 3, 1859, 37, Richard Eppes Diary, August 12, 1859–July 1, 1862, section 46, Eppes Family Papers, 1722–1948 (Mss1 Ep734 d), VHS.

15. For an insightful reflection on mourning and black women's history, see Jessica Millward, "Black Women's History and the Labor of Mourning," *Souls* 18, no. 1 (2016): 161–65.

16. Douglass, *Narrative of the Life of Frederick Douglass*, 13; Sari Edelstein, *Adulthood and Other Fictions*, 45–49.

17. Berry, *Price for Their Pound of Flesh*; Walter Johnson, *Soul by Soul: Life Inside the Slave Market* (Cambridge, Mass.: Harvard University Press, 1999).

18. Slave List, May 31, 1815, Pollard Family Papers, 1723–1936 (Mss1 P7637 b), VHS.

19. Slave List, January 11, 1837, section 7, Ambler Family Papers, 1638–1809 (Mss1 Am167 c), VHS.

20. Slave list, n.d., list folder, Burwell Family Papers, 1813–1928 (Mss1 B9585 a), VHS.

21. Account Book of John Fayette Dickinson, 1st February 1855, 1850–1890, 82, Dickinson Family Papers, 1805–1988, VHS; this inventory was updated to include 1859 valuations.

22. Pre-1865 Slave List, series 2.1.1, folder 66, Branch Family Papers, accession no. 2718, Southern Historical Collections (SHC), Wilson Library, University of North Carolina, Chapel Hill.

23. St. Simons Slave List, 1806, box 1; Richard Corbin, Slave List, March 28, 1859; Madame La Viscountess De Dampierre, Slave List, 1859; Descriptive Slave List, 1860; and Hopeton Plantation Slave List, March 22, 1861, Francis Porteus Corbin Papers, 1662–1885, box 2, David M. Rubenstein Rare Book & Manuscript Library (RL), Duke University, Durham, N.C.

24. Slave List, May 31, 1815, Pollard Family Papers, VHS.

25. Pre-1865 Slave List, series 2.1.1, folder 66, Branch Family Papers, SHC.

26. Benjamin Toler, Slave List, November 1783 (Mss2 T5757 a), VHS; Slave List, n.d., Burwell Family Papers, VHS.

27. Slave List, January 11, 1837, Ambler Family Papers, VHS; Register of Jos Dupuy's Negroes, Commonplace Book of Joseph Dupuy, section 4, Dupuy Family Papers, 1781–1896 (Mss1 D9295 c), VHS; Slave List, November 28, 1858, Richard Eppes Diary, November 20, 1858–August 11, 1859, section 45, Eppes Family Papers, VHS.

28. "Number and Ages of Negroes in Our Possession," March 1839, and List of Slaves, n.d., Gooch Family Papers, VHS.

29. Laura Krogan Kamoie, "Three Generations of Planter-Businessmen: The Tayloes, Slave Labor, and Entrepreneurialism in Virginia, 1710–1830" (PhD diss., College of William and Mary, 1999), 192–93; Inventories, 1837 and 1838, Tayloe Family Papers, 1708–1861 (Mss1 T2118 d), VHS.

30. St. Simons Slave List, 1806, Francis Porteus Corbin Papers, box 1, RL.

31. Slave List, 1859, Madame La Viscountess De Dampierre, and Descriptive Slave List, 1860, Francis Porteus Corbin Papers, box 2, RL.

32. For studies of the scale and structure of the domestic slave trade, see Johnson, *Soul by Soul*; Berry, *Price for Their Pound of Flesh*; Baptist, *The Half Has Never Been Told*; Steven Deyle, *Carry Me Back: The Domestic Slave Trade in American Life* (New York: Oxford University Press, 2005); Sharla Fett, *Working Cures: Healing, Health and Power on Southern Plantations* (Chapel Hill: University of North Carolina Press, 2000);

Michael Tadman, *Speculators and Slaves: Masters, Traders, and Slaves in the Old South* (Madison: University of Wisconsin Press, 1989).

33. Slave List, 1860, Clinch-Waldburger Family Papers, 1790–1864, accession no. 41638, LOV.

34. Slave List, [1830?], and Deed of Gift, April 20, 1833, box 2, series 2.1.1, 1830–1838, Peter Evans Smith Papers, 1738–1944, accession no. 677, SHC.

35. Letter, April 14, 1848, box 1, series 1.1.2 (1847–1850), Francis Asbury Dickens Papers, 1729–1934, accession no. 218, SHC.

36. Ella Gertrude Thomas Journal, Feb. 17, 1856 (Typed Copy), 113–14, Ella Gertrude Clanton Thomas Papers, 1848–1978, RL.

37. Letter, James Smith to John Swann, July 22, 1812, series 1, 1784–1816, Swann Family Papers, 1784–1983, accession no. 2827, SHC.

38. Letter, James Smith to John Swann, July 26, 1812, series 1, 1784–1816, Swann Family Papers, SHC.

39. William Jones Dell to James Patterson, May 8, 1811, Francis Porteus Corbin Papers, box 1, Correspondence and Papers, RL.

40. Bill of Sale, Bibb County, Georgia, January 3, 1860, Henry Slaughter Collection, box 38, folder 79, Archives Research Center, Atlanta University Center Robert Woodruff Library, Atlanta; Jacobs, *Incidents in the Life of a Slave Girl*, 26–27.

41. Copy of List of Negroes Allotted Martha Wales in the 1st of January 1837, List of Negroes Belonging to Martha Wales and in Possession of Saunders in the Year 1849, and Statement of Sales Made at New London, Nov 29th 1849 of Negroes Belonging to the Estate of Martha Wales by Her Committee, Saunders Family Papers, 1829–1908 (Mss1 Sa878 a), VHS.

42. For slave hires, see Jonathan D. Martin, *Divided Mastery: Slave Hiring in the American South* (Cambridge, Mass.: Harvard University Press, 2004), 57–65.

43. Hires for the Year 1837 and 1838; List of Deaths of Servants, George Family, Papers, 1733–1920, accession no. 24642, City of Richmond Circuit Court Records, Local Government Records Collection, LOV.

44. List of Hires, 1824, 1825, 1826, section 1, Eggleston Family Papers, 1777–1899 (Mss1 Eg396 b), VHS.

45. Slave List, folder 1, Glenn Family Papers, 1792–1846, accession no. 277-z, SHC.

46. Plantation Journal, 1851–1862, 1866–1873, 8 and 22 in the Edmund Ruffin Jr. Journal, accession no. 639-z, SHC.

47. Sick List, 1st June 1841, Section 1, Charles Friend Diary, Friend Family Papers, VHS.

48. Richard Eppes, Diary, November 30, 1859, 79, Richard Eppes Diary, August 12, 1859–July 1, 1862, section 46, Eppes Family Papers, VHS.

49. Account Book of John Fayette Dickinson, 39, Dickinson Family Papers, VHS.

50. Plantation Journal, 1851–1862, 1866–1873, 6, 7, 178, and 179 in the Edmund Ruffin Jr. Journal, SHC.

51. Account Book, 1851–1883, 23, section 4, Haxall Papers, VHS.

52. Overton Harris Letter, 17 September 1825, accession no. 23388, Personal Papers Collection, LOV.

53. Richard Eppes, Diary, November 30, 1859, 79, Richard Eppes Diary, August 12, 1859–July 1, 1862, section 46, Eppes Family Papers, VHS.

54. Thomas Maguire, Farm Diary, July 14, 15, and 17, 1859; June 1 and 4, 1860; June 23, 25, 28, 29, and 30, 1861; May 18 and 28, 1861; January 6 and 13, 1862; February 14, 1862; December 29, 1863; and January 19 and 25, 1864, Thomas Maguire Papers, 1834–1949, James G. Kenan Research Center at the Atlanta History Center (AHC).

55. Manager's Journal, 20 and 27, series 2.2.1, section 4, 1854–65, Branch Family Papers, SHC.

56. Michael Johnson, "Work, Culture, and the Slave Community: Slave Occupations in the Cotton Belt in 1860," *Labor History* 27, no. 3 (1986): 325; for an in-depth discussion of the labor performed by aged slaves, see Stacey Close, *Elderly Slaves in the Plantation South* (New York: Garland, 1997).

57. Manager's Journal, 20, vol. 4, 1854–1865, series 2.2.1, Branch Family Papers, SHC.

58. Edward Rawle to Francis Corbin, December 39, 1833, Francis Porteus Corbin Papers, box 1, Correspondence and Papers, 1830–1839, RL.

59. Hamilton Couper to Francis Corbin, June 19, 1859, Francis Porteus Corbin Papers, box 2, Correspondence and Papers, 1850–1859, RL.

60. Richard Eppes, Diary, August 29, 1859, and April 1, 1860, 15 and 147, Richard Eppes Diary, August 12, 1859–July 1, 1862, section 46, Eppes Family Papers, VHS.

61. GHS0012, James Martin Gibbons Letter, 1784, GHS.

62. A list of the "Bryan" House and Yard Servants at Eagle Point, Gloucester County, Virginia, from 1845 to 1865, Papers Concerning the Bryan Family Servants, n.d., accession no. 9822-d, UVA.

63. Alexander Dick Journal, 1806–1809, 85 and 229, accession no. 4528, UVA.

64. Letter from Martha Dabney to Her Sister Fanny, March 1st (no year), section 7, Montague Family Papers, 1808–1939 (Mss1 M7607 a), VHS; for a comprehensive examination of white women slaveholders, see Stephanie Jones-Rogers, *They Were Her Property: White Women as Slaveholders in the American South* (New Haven, Conn.: Yale University Press, 2019).

65. Richard Eppes, Diary, March 2, 1860, 134, Richard Eppes Diary, August 12, 1859–July 1, 1862, section 46, Eppes Family Papers, VHS.

66. Vincent Brown, *The Reaper's Garden*, 93–102; for a study of old age and property relationships, see Hendrik Hartog, *Someday All This Will Be Yours: A History of Inheritance and Old Age* (Cambridge, Mass.: Harvard University Press 2012).

67. Smith Shepherd 1795 Will, section 4, Shepherd Family Papers, 1790–1862 (Mss1 Sh485 a), VHS.

68. Sally Fain Will, series 1.2, Financial and Legal Papers, 1834–1861, 1883, Bullock and Hamilton Papers, 1757–1971, accession no. 101, SHC.

69. Petition, William and Elizabeth Pickens, November 7, 1808, Petitions (Emancipation), Nov.–Dec. 1808, General Assembly Session Records, State Archives of North Carolina, Raleigh.

70. Petition, John Crenshaw, Virginia Superior Court of Law and Chancery (Richmond) Papers, 1817–1820 (Mss4 V8 a), VHS.

71. John Warwick Will, 1848 March 20, probated in Amherst County, Va. (Mss2 W26787 a), VHS.

72. Account Book, Fife Family Papers, box 1, accession no. 5943, UVA.

73. Caroline Sharman Petition, Lancaster County Free and Negro Slave Record, 1751–1861, misc. papers, box 1, LOV.

74. Petition, Elizabeth Ruckle and Samuel Ruckle, January 14, 1847, Jefferson County Records, box 126, folder 77, microfilm, LOV.

75. Petition, Nathaniel Tatum on Behalf of Isham Tatum (Deceased), December 10, 1857, Madison County Records, box 152, folder 72, microfilm, LOV.

76. Petition, Thomas Brooks, August 12, 1855, Louisa County Negro and Slave Records, 1770–1864, box 1, misc. folder, 1850, 1853, 1855–1856, 1864–1865, LOV.

77. "List of James A. Scotts Negroes and their Ages in 1860," John Fitzgerald Papers, 1805–1878, VHS.

78. Account Book of Garrett Scott, Scott Family Papers, 1783–1881, VHS.

79. "A List of Deaths of Servants and List of Negro Hires and Divisions of Negroes, 1836–1842," George Family Papers, box 4, folder 23, LOV.

80. Slave Birth Record, Accession no. 672-z, SHC.

81. "A List of Negroes Belonging to Francis Jerdone Taken 1st of January 1770," Slave Record Book, Jerdone Family Papers, 1749–1873, accession no. 20415, Personal Papers Collection, LOV.

82. Christ Episcopal Church, Charlottesville, Va., Records, 1836–1970, accession no. 9682, 54–56, UVA.

83. Minute Book of Richmond [Va.] Board of Health, 21 and 28, section 16, Gooch Family Papers, VHS.

84. Edward Rawles to Francis Corbin, July 27, 1833, Francis Porteus Corbin Papers, box 1, Corbin Correspondence and Papers, 1820–1839, RL.

85. Edward Rawles to Francis Corbin, August 11, 1833, Francis Porteus Corbin Papers, box 1, Correspondence and Papers, 1820–1839, RL.

86. Manager's Journal, 86,vol. 4, 1854–1865, series 2.2.1, folder, 105, Branch Family Papers, SHC.

87. Plantation Journal, 1851–1862, 1866–1873, 185 in the Edmund Ruffin Jr. Journal, SHC.

88. Plantation Journal, 1851–1862, 1866–1873, 178, in the Edmund Ruffin Jr. Journal, SHC.

89. Everard Green Baker, Diary, June 30, 1854, Everard Green Baker Diary, vol. 2, Everard Green Baker Papers, 1848–1876, SHC.

Chapter 3

1. Frederick Douglass, *Life and Times of Frederick Douglass* (New York: Gramercy Books, 1993), 1–3; David Blight, *Frederick Douglass: Prophet of Freedom*, 9–13; Sterling Stuckey, *Going Through the Storm: The Influence of African American Art in History* (New York: Oxford University Press, 1994), 33–36.

2. The idea of the ledgers of racial capitalism is derived from Cedric Robinson's work on racial capitalism and the ledgers of a world system in *Black Marxism: The Making of the Black Radical Tradition* (Chapel Hill: University of North Carolina Press, 2005 [orig. 1983]), 111–16.

3. "Register of Jos Dupuy's Negroes," section 4, Dupuy Family Papers, VHS.

4. John Billups Ledger, 1774–1856, accession no. 20998, Business Records Collection, LOV.

5. Section on Slavery, in Jennie F. Stephenson, "My Father and His Household Before, During, and After the War," April 22, 1897, Early Family Papers, VHS.

6. Slave List, n.d., in Note to C. W. Gooch, Richmond Virginia, Gooch Family Papers, VHS.

7. Slave List, March 1839, Gooch Family Papers, VHS,

8. "A List of Deaths of Servants and List of Negro Hires and Divisions of Negroes, 1836–1842," George Family Papers, box 4, folder 23, LOV.

9. "List of My Negroes on My Plantations in Albemarle County Taken January 1, 1770," Jerdone Family Papers, LOV.

10. Plantation Manager's Journal, 83 and 87; "A List of Negroes at Live Oak, 1862," series 2.2.1, Branch Family Papers, SHC.

11. Ella Gertrude Clanton Thomas Journal, July 31, 1863, 121, Ella Gertrude Clanton Thomas Papers, RL.

12. "Negroes of Blanfield with Their Ages, November 17, 1834," Account Book of Robert Beverley, 1769–1843 and William Bradshaw Beverley, 1791–1866, Beverley Family Papers, 1654–1901 (Mss1 B4678 a), VHS.

13. Names and Ages of Negroes at Blanfield Belonging to William B. Beverley in the Year 1850, Account Book of Robert Beverley, 1769–1843, and William Bradshaw Beverley, 1791–1866, Beverly Family Papers, VHS.

14. Robert Henderson Allen, Diary, July 1, 1861, Robert Henderson Allen Diary, 1858–1863, 305, Allen Family Papers, 1850–1910 (Mss1 AL546 a), VHS.

15. *John C. Cohoon Account Book, 1810–1860, Nansemond County Virginia*, University Publications of America, Records of Ante-bellum Southern Plantations (series E, pt. 1, microfilm, reel 39).

16. Minutes of the Richmond Board of Health, June 18, 1849, 8 and 21, section 16, Gooch Family Papers, VHS.

17. Minutes of the Richmond Board of Health, July 19, 1849, 50, section 16, Gooch Family Papers, VHS; Polly Scott's age is estimated in the 1850 census mortality records in the National Archives and Records Administration (NARA), Washington, D.C.;

Non-Population Census Schedules for Virginia, 1850–1880, Archive Collection T1132, Archive Roll no. 1, Census year 1849, West District, Henrico, Va., 296 in Ancestry.com. *U.S. Federal Census Mortality Schedules, 1850–1885* [https://www.ancestrylibrary.com/discoveryui-content/view/2216109:8756], Provo, Utah.

18. "A List of Ye Negroes at Warrhall, 8 February 1771," Taylor Family Papers, 1709–1829, South Caroliniana Library (SCL), University of South Carolina, Columbia.

19. Thomas Smith to Peter Taylor, July 14, 1773, Taylor Family Papers, SCL.

20. Fett, *Working Cures*, 72–76.

21. Jacobs, *Incidents in the Life of a Slave Girl*, 17.

22. Jacobs, *Incidents in the Life of a Slave Girl*, 14, 16, and 82.

23. Ball, *Slavery in the United States*, 38–39.

24. Journal of Alexander Dick, 12 July 1807, 85, UVA.

25. Douglass, *My Bondage and My Freedom*, 69.

26. Douglass, *My Bondage and My Freedom*, 70.

27. Douglass, *My Bondage and My Freedom*, 69–70.

28. Douglass, *My Bondage and My Freedom*, 71–72.

29. Douglass, *My Bondage and My Freedom*, 55–56.

30. Richard Eppes, "Names and Ages of Negroes Belonging to the Estate of Richard Eppes, Appomattox, November 20, 1858," Richard Eppes Diary, November 20, 1858–August 11, 1859, section 45, Eppes Family Papers, VHS.

31. Richard Eppes, Diary, March 25, 1861, 291, Richard Eppes Diary, August 12, 1859–July 1, 1862, section 46, Eppes Family Papers, VHS.

32. Letter to Paul to Lucy Marks, April 6, 1778, Lewis, Anderson, and Marks Families Papers, 1771–1908, accession no. 9041, UVA.

33. Letter, Charles (Stephen Greenhill) to William Greenhill, July 31, 1825, Bland Family Papers, 1713–1825 (Mss1 B6108 a), VHS.

34. Ira Berlin, *Slaves Without Masters: The Free Negro in the Antebellum South* (New York: Pantheon, 1974), 146–48.

35. Loren Schweninger, *Appealing for Liberty: Freedom Suits in the South* (New York: Oxford University Press, 2018); Kimberly Welch, *Black Litigants in the Antebellum American South* (Chapel Hill: University of North Carolina Press, 2018), 66–67; Samantha Seeley, *Race, Removal, and the Right to Remain: Migration and the Making of the United States* (Chapel Hill: University of North Carolina Press, 2021); my thinking about the use of petitions has also been shaped by Rebecca J. Scott, *Slave Emancipation in Cuba: The Transition to Free Labor, 1860–1899* (Princeton, N.J.: Princeton University Press, 1985).

36. Walter Johnson argues that time was the grounds for political conflict in New World Slavery in "Possible Pasts: Some Speculations on Time, Temporality, and the History of Atlantic Slavery," in "Time and the African American Experience," special issue, *Amerikastudien/American Studies* 45, no. 4 (2000), 485–99.

37. Alix Lerner, "Aging in Bondage: Slavery, Debility, and the Problem of Dependency in the Antebellum South" (PhD diss., Princeton University, 2016).

38. William Waller Hening, ed., *The Statutes at Large: Being a Collection of All the Laws of Virginia, from the First Session of the Legislature I the Year 1619, 13 vols.* (Richmond, 1809–23) in Willie Lee Rose, *A Documentary History of Slavery in North America* (Athens: University of Georgia Press, 1976), 63.

39. Petition for Ned, November 28, 1836, General Assembly Session Records, Petitions November 1836–January 1837, State Archives of North Carolina.

40. Petition of Frederick James, November 12, 1816, General Assembly Session Records, Nov.–Dec. 1816, Petitions folder (Revolutionary War), State Archives of North Carolina.

41. Supporting Statement to Petition of Frederick James, November 12, 1816, General Assembly Session Records, Nov.–Dec. 1816, Petitions folder (Revolutionary War), State Archives of North Carolina.

42. Petition of Wheeling, Virginia, Residents Regarding Richard Morris, February 26, 1848, Ohio County, Virginia, Legislative Petitions of the General Assembly, 1776–1865, box 190, folder 60, microfilm, LOV.

43. Petition of David Kendall Regarding Slave Daniel, November 1850, General Assembly Session Records, Miscellaneous Reports and Petitions, November 1850–January 1851, State Archives of North Carolina.

44. Petition of James Dunn, November 2, 1854, General Assembly Session Records, November 1854–February 1855, State Archives of North Carolina.

45. Petition of Osborn Jeffreys, December 17, 1798, General Assembly Session Records, Petitions, November–December 1798, State Archives of North Carolina.

46. Petition of Caroline Winslow and Malinda Carmon Regarding Slave Betty, General Assembly Records, Petitions, November 1854–February 1855, State Archives of North Carolina.

47. Petition Regarding Dolly, March 7, 1847, General Assembly Session Records, Petitions, November 1854–February 1855, State Archives of North Carolina.

48. Petition of Citizens of Cumberland County, Petitions, November 1850–January 1851, General Assembly Session Records, State Archives of North Carolina.

49. GHS 1760, Act of Manumission to Fanny Hickman and Her Children, 1834–1840, GHS.

50. Petition of Blackwell McAlester, November 22, 1808, General Assembly Session Records, Joint Committee Reports (Claims & Others, Divorce and Alimony, Emancipation, Finance, and Propositions & Grievances), November–December 1808, State Archives of North Carolina.

51. Report of the Committee on Emancipation on the Petition of Blackwell McAlester of the County of Brunswick, General Assembly Session Records, Joint Committee Reports (Claims & Others, Divorce and Alimony, Emancipation, Finance, and Propositions & Grievances), November–December 1808, State Archives of North Carolina.

52. Petition Regarding Lucy, December 21, 1833, Lunenberg County, Legislative Petitions of the General Assembly, 1776–1865, box 150, folder 74, microfilm, LOV.

53. Statement of Richard May in Petition Regarding Lucy, Lunenberg County, box 150, folder 74, microfilm, LOV.

54. Petition Regarding Lucy, December 21, 1833, Lunenberg County, Legislative Petitions of the General Assembly, 1776–1865, box 150, folder 74, microfilm, LOV.

55. Petition of Lucy Boaman, December 16, 1835, Lunenberg County, Legislative Petitions of the General Assembly, 1776–1865, box 150, folder 79, microfilm, LOV.

56. Petition Regarding Lucy, January 6, 1835, Lunenberg County, Legislative Petitions of the General Assembly, 1776–1865, box 150, folder 77, microfilm, LOV.

57. Affidavit of Charlotte Winn, Lunenberg County, Legislative Petitions of the General Assembly, 1776–1865, box 150, folder 76, microfilm, LOV.

58. Petition of Lucy Boaman, December 23, 1835, Lunenberg County, Legislative Petitions of the General Assembly, 1776–1865, box 150, folder 79, microfilm, LOV.

59. Petition of Amy Grason, February 10, 1831, Loudoun County, Legislative Petitions of the General Assembly, 1776–1865, box 144, folder 7, microfilm, LOV.

60. Martha Jones, *Birthright Citizens: A History of Race and Human Rights in Antebellum America* (New York: Cambridge University Press, 2018).

61. Petition for Nathan Dunlap, December 2, 1834, Rockingham County, Legislative Petitions of the General Assembly, 1776–1865, box 225, folder 34, microfilm, LOV.

62. Statement of Martha S. Parks in Ackey White Petition, Norfolk (Borough) Records, Legislative Petitions of the General Assembly, 1776–1865, box 269, folder 85, microfilm, LOV.

63. Petition of Ackey White, December 28, 1836, Norfolk (Borough) Records, Legislative Petitions of the General Assembly, 1776–1865, box 269, folder 85, microfilm, LOV.

64. Simon Abrahams Will, February 5, 1838, in Petition of Gabriel Jones, Richmond City Records, box 283, folder 25, microfilm, LOV.

65. Petition of Gabriel Jones, February 26, 1851, Richmond City Records, Legislative Petitions of the General Assembly, 1776–1865, box 283, folder 25, microfilm, LOV.

66. Petition of Jenny Parker, November 23, 1813, Surry County Records, Legislative Petitions of the General Assembly, 1776–1865, box 240, folder 23, microfilm, LOV.

67. Petition of Sam Johnson and affidavit of William Phillips, January 19, 1835, Fauquier County Records, Legislative Petitions of the General Assembly, 1776–1865, box 74, folder 3, microfilm, LOV.

68. Petition Regarding Sam and Sookey, n.d., General Assembly Session Records, Petitions, November 1856–February 1857, State Archives of North Carolina.

69. Petition of John Caruthers Stanly, November 19, 1798, General Assembly Session Records, Petitions, November–December 1798, State Archives of North Carolina.

70. Petition of Molly Horniblow, November 30, 1842, General Assembly Session Records, Petitions, November 1842–January 1843, State Archives of North Carolina.

71. Rachel Collins Petition, December 9, 1836, Norfolk (Borough), Legislative Petitions of the General Assembly, 1776–1865, box 269, folder 31, microfilm, LOV.

72. Petition of John Elson, Free Black, January 10, 1837, Richmond City, Legislative Petitions of the General Assembly, 1776–1865, box 280, folder 38, microfilm, LOV.

73. Deposition of Joseph Mays, January 4, 1837, Richmond City, Legislative Petitions of the General Assembly, 1776–1865, box 280, folder 38, microfilm, LOV.

74. Petition of Phillis and Hannah, December 3, 1828, Montgomery County Records, Legislative Petitions of the General Assembly, 1776–1865, box 172, folder 14, microfilm, LOV.

75. Petition of David Ward, July 19, 1827, Pittsylvania County Records, Legislative Petitions of the General Assembly, 1776–1865, box 199, folder 22, microfilm, LOV.

76. Statement of John Rutledge, November 27, 1837, Pittsylvania County Records, Legislative Petitions of the General Assembly, 1776–1865, box 199, folder 22, microfilm, LOV.

77. Petition of David Ward, July 19, 1827, Pittsylvania County Records, Legislative Petitions of the General Assembly, 1776–1865, box 199, folder 22, microfilm, LOV.

78. Petition of Titus Brown, December 5, 1834, Loudon County Records, Legislative Petitions of the General Assembly, 1776–1865, box 144, folder 38, microfilm, LOV; for a more general discussion of the problem of attributing a precise age to the enslaved, see Edelstein, *Adulthood and Other Fictions*, 44–49.

79. Petition of Isaac Harris, December 18, 1815, Frederick County Records, Legislative Petitions of the General Assembly, 1776–1865, box 82, folder 21, microfilm, LOV.

80. Petition of Jacob Smith (on Behalf of Abraam Smith), General Assembly Session Records, Petitions, November 1854–February 1855, State Archives of North Carolina.

81. Will, Slave, Petition, Campbell County, December 18, 1815, Legislative Petitions of the General Assembly, 1776–1865, box 46, folder 78, microfilm, LOV.

82. Bowling Clark Statement Attached to Will, Slave, Petition, Campbell County, December 18, 1815, Legislative Petitions of the General Assembly, 1776–1865, box 46, folder 78, microfilm, LOV.

83. Petition of Amy, February 15, 1848, Chesterfield County Records, Legislative Petitions of the General Assembly, 1776–1865, box 56, folder 67, microfilm, LOV.

84. Jennifer Morgan, *Laboring Women*, 81–99.

85. Petition of Dolly Woodson, January 9, 1834, Richmond City Records, Legislative Petitions of the General Assembly, 1776–1865, box 279, folder 77, microfilm, LOV.

86. Statement of J. N. Chamberlyne, c. 1834, Richmond City Records, Legislative Petitions of the General Assembly, 1776–1865, box 279, folder 77, microfilm, LOV.

87. Petition of Fountaine Wells and Others on Behalf of Yarico, January 31, 1835, Albemarle County, Legislative Petitions of the General Assembly, 1776–1865, box 4, folder 50, microfilm, LOV.

88. Petition of John Dunn Scott, December 8, 1832, General Assembly Session Records, Petitions (Concerning Slaves), November 1832–January 1833, State Archives of North Carolina.

89. Denis Comer Petition, Fairfax County, January 12, 1837, Legislative Petitions of the General Assembly, 1776–1865, box 70, folder 68, microfilm, LOV.

90. Petition of Sterling, October 22, 1814, Chesterfield County, Legislative Petitions of the General Assembly, 1776–1865, box 55, folder 22, microfilm, LOV.

91. Petition of Robin, Free Black, January 26, 1836, Culpepper County, Legislative Petitions of the General Assembly, 1776–1865, box 60, folder 15, microfilm, LOV.

92. Petition of Edmund Briggs, January 12, 1850, Monroe County Records, Legislative Petitions of the General Assembly, 1776–1865, box 170, folder 12, microfilm, LOV.

93. Hill Ballard Petition, December 10, 1812, Nansemond County, Legislative Petitions of the General Assembly, 1776–1865, box 175, folder 66, microfilm, LOV.

94. Statement of John Smith, December 4, 1829, Rockingham County, Legislative Petitions of the General Assembly, 1776–1865, box 225, folder 15, microfilm, LOV.

95. Supporting Statement, December 2, 1829, Rockingham County Records, Legislative Petitions of the General Assembly, 1776–1865, box 225, folder 15, microfilm, LOV.

96. Petition of William Strother, December 23, 1829, Rockingham County, Legislative Petitions of the General Assembly, 1776–1865, box 225, folder 15, microfilm, LOV.

97. Petition of Bolling Vaugh Regarding Slave Ben; Affidavit Regarding Slave Ben, December 13, 1815, Legislative Petitions of the General Assembly, 1776–1865, box 179, folder 44, microfilm, LOV; this case reflected the phenomenon of mixed-status marriage between slaves and free blacks, as explored in Tera Hunter, *Bound in Wedlock: Slave and Free Black Marriage in the Nineteenth Century* (Cambridge, Mass.: Harvard University Press, 2017), 91–101.

98. Petition of Arthur, February 18, 1848, Chesterfield County Records, Legislative Petitions of the General Assembly, 1776–1865, box 56, folder 66, microfilm, LOV.

99. Petition of Lucy Crawford and Delila, December 21, 1835, Washington County Records, Legislative Petitions of the General Assembly, 1776–1865, microfilm, LOV.

Chapter 4

1. Roy E. Finkenbine, "Belinda's Petition: Reparations for Slavery in Revolutionary Massachusetts," *William and Mary Quarterly*, 3rd series, 64, no. 1 (January 2007): 97–98; https://royallhouse.org/belinda-suttons-1783-petition-full-text/; Belinda and her petition were popularized by Ta-Nehisi Coates in "The Case for Reparations," *Atlantic*, June 2014.

2. James Oliver Horton and Lois E. Horton, *In Hope of Liberty: Culture, Community, and Protest Among Northern Free Blacks, 1700–1860* (New York: Oxford University Press, 1997), 71.

3. Gary B. Nash and Jean R. Soderlund, *Freedom by Degrees: Emancipation in Pennsylvania and Its Aftermath* (New York: Oxford University Press, 1991), 111.

4. David Gellman, *Emancipating New York: The Politics of Slavery and Freedom, 1777–1827* (Baton Rouge: Louisiana State University Press, 2006), 153.

5. Graham Russell Hodges, *Black New Jersey: 1664 to the Present Day* (New Brunswick, NJ: Rutgers University Press, 2018), 57.

6. James Gigantino, *The Ragged Road to Abolition: Slavery and Freedom in New Jersey, 1775–1865* (Philadelphia: University of Pennsylvania Press, 2016), 27.

7. Gigantino, *Ragged Road to Abolition*, 7; Joanne Pope Melish, *Disowning Slavery: Gradual Emancipation and "Race" in New England, 1780–1860* (Ithaca, NY: Cornell University Press, 1998), 88.

8. Nash and Soderlund, *Freedom by Degrees*, 111; Hodges, *Black New Jersey*, 76–79; Graham Russell Hodges, *Root and Branch: African Americans in New York and East Jersey, 1613–1863* (Chapel Hill: University of North Carolina Press, 1999), 173; Gigantino, *Ragged Road to Abolition*, 149–73.

9. Nash and Soderlund, *Freedom by Degrees*, 195.

10. Gigantino, *Ragged Road to Abolition*; Nash and Soderlund, *Freedom by Degrees*, 187–92.

11. Hodges, *Root and Branch*, 173 and 179.

12. See Paul J. Polgar, *Standard Bearers of Equality: America's First Abolitionist Movement* (Chapel Hill: University of North Carolina Press, 2019).

13. Richard Waln to Son, May 5, 1790, Committee of Correspondence Letterbook, vol. 1, 1789–1794, PAS Papers, microfilm, series 2, reel 11, HSP.

14. Sarah Prior to Hannah Walter, May 23, 1803, PAS Papers, microfilm, series 2, reel 12, HSP.

15. Polgar, *Standard Bearers*, 101–2.

16. Neill Slubey?, December? 1819, PAS Papers, microfilm, series 2, reel 12, HSP.

17. James Gibson to Elisha Tyson, November 1, 1820, PAS Papers, microfilm, series 2, reel 13, HSP.

18. Their plight resembled that of other poor people in the early modern world. Olwen H. Hufton defines the term "economy of makeshifts" as the ways the poor used migration, charity, kinship relations, begging, petty crime, and other informal means for material support. See *The Poor of Eighteenth-Century France, 1750–1789* (New York: Oxford University Press, 1974).

19. Leslie Harris, *In the Shadow of Slavery: African Americans in New York City, 1626–1863* (Chicago: University of Chicago Press, 2003), 72–79; Nash and Soderlund, *Degrees of Freedom*, 170–93.

20. Richard Allen, *The Life, Experience, and Gospel Labours of the Rt. Rev. Richard Allen* (Philadelphia, 1833), 5–8.

21. Allen, *The Life, Experience, and Gospel Labours of the Rt. Rev. Richard Allen*, 11.

22. Richard Newman, *Freedom's Prophet: Bishop Richard Allen, the AME Church, and the Black Founding Fathers* (New York: New York University Press, 2008).

23. Jarena Lee, *Religious Experience of Jarena Lee, Giving Her Account of Her Call to Preach the Gospel* (Philadelphia, 1849).

24. Report on March 31, 1864, Board of Education Minute Book, 1840–1865, vol. 5, 469, PAS Papers, microfilm, series 2, reel 8, HSP.

25. Jarene Lee in the United States Federal Census, Archive Roll no. M653_1158, Census year 1860, Philadelphia Ward 8, Philadelphia, Pa., 63, image: 67; Family History Library Film no. 805158 in Ancestry.com. *1860 United States Federal Census* [https://www.ancestrylibrary.com/discoveryui-content/view/4460458:7667], Provo, Utah; Frederick

Knight, "The Many Names for Jarena Lee: A Note on Historical Sources," *Pennsylvania Magazine of History and Biography* 141, no. 1 (January 2017): 59–68.

26. Letter from Benjamin Banneker, May 6, Committee of Correspondence Letterbook, vol. 1, 1789–1794, PAS Papers, microfilm, series 2, reel 11, HSP.

27. Elias Elicot to James Pemberton, June 10, 1791, Committee of Correspondence Letterbook, vol. 1, 1789–1794, PAS Papers, microfilm, series 2, reel 11, HSP.

28. Benjamin Banneker to James Pemberton, September 3, 1791, Leon Gardiner Papers, box 5G, folder 1, HSP.

29. Benjamin Banneker Letter, September (?) 1791, Committee of Correspondence Letterbook, vol. 1, 1789–1794, PAS Papers, microfilm, series 2, reel 11, HSP.

30. William Goddard to James Pemberton, September 13, 1791, Committee of Correspondence Letterbook, vol. 1, 1789–1794, PAS Papers, microfilm, series 2, reel 11, HSP.

31. Jos. Townsend Letter, 1793, Committee of Correspondence Letterbook, vol. 1, 1789–1794, PAS Papers, microfilm, series 2, reel 11, HSP.

32. *The Eccentric Biography; or, Memoirs of Remarkable Female Characters, Ancient and Modern. . . .* (Worcester: Isaiah Thomas, 1804), 9.

33. *The Eccentric Biography*, 11.

34. PAS Committee of Guardians, Minute Book, 1790–1796, vol. 1, 67–68, PAS Papers, microfilm, series 1, reel 6, HSP.

35. Board of Education Minute Book, 1797–1803, vol. 1, 43–48, PAS Papers, microfilm, series 1, reel 7, HSP.

36. *Biographical Sketches and Interesting Anecdotes of Persons of Colour*, compiled by A. Mott (New York: W. Alexander and Son, 1826), 78.

37. *Biographical Sketches and Interesting Anecdotes of Persons of Colour*, 76–77.

38. *Biographical Sketches and Interesting Anecdotes of Persons of Colour*, 75–76.

39. *Biographical Sketches and Interesting Anecdotes of Persons of Colour*, 76.

40. *Biographical Sketches and Interesting Anecdotes of Persons of Colour*, 77.

41. *Biographical Sketches and Interesting Anecdotes of Persons of Colour*, 109–14.

42. Frederick Knight, "Black Women, Eldership, and Communities of Care in the Nineteenth Century North," *Early American Studies* 17, no. 4 (Fall 2019): 545–61; Report on March 31, 1864, Board of Education Minute Book, 1840–1865, vol. 5, 469–71, PAS Papers, microfilm, series 1, reel 8, HSP. Many black women in Philadelphia were from the South, which had longstanding African American quilting traditions. John Michael Vlach, *The Afro-American Tradition in Decorative Arts* (Athens: University of Georgia Press, 1990 [repr. 1978]), 44–75; Gladys Marie Fry, *Stitched from the Soul: Slave Quilts from the Antebellum South* (New York: Dutton Studio Books, 1990).

43. See for example Meeting Minutes, March 4, 1863; June 3, 1863; and February 3, 1864, Minutes of the Board of Trustees and Cash Books, Records of Mother Bethel AME Church, 1760–1972 (AME Church Records), microfilm, reel 2, HSP. See also Erica Armstrong Dunbar, *A Fragile Freedom: African American Women and Emancipation in the Antebellum City* (New Haven: Yale University Press, 2008).

44. Church Minutes, February 4, 1835, Minute and Trial Book of the AME Church, AME Church Records, microfilm, reel 8, HSP.

45. Church Minutes, November 5, 1834, Minute and Trial Book of the AME Church, AME Church Records, microfilm, reel 8, HSP.

46. Report on March 31, 1864, Board of Education Minute Book, 1840–1865, vol. 5, 470–71, PAS Papers, microfilm, series 1, reel 8, HSP.

47. Report on March 31, 1864, Board of Education Minute Book, 1840–1865, vol. 5, 469, PAS Papers, microfilm, series 1, reel 8, HSP.

48. Allen, *The Life, Experience, and Gospel Labours of the Rt. Rev. Richard Allen*, 9.

49. Lee, *Religious Experience*, 28 and 42.

50. Newman, *Freedom's Prophet*, 81.

51. Knight, "Many Names for Jarena Lee," 66; Terania Lee in the 1840 Federal Census, Archive Roll no. 483, Census year 1840, Philadelphia Walnut Ward, Philadelphia, Pa., 44, image 683, Family History Library Film no. 0020554, Ancestry.com. *1840 United States Federal Census* [https://www.ancestrylibrary.com/discoveryui-content/view/2876257:8057], Provo, Utah.

52. Geranna Lee in the 1850 United States Federal Census, Archive Roll no. M432_821, Census year 1850, Southwark Ward 3, Philadelphia, Pa., 214A, image 433, Ancestry.com. *1850 United States Federal Census* [https://www.ancestrylibrary.com/discoveryui-content/view/5190824:8054], Provo, Utah.

53. Jarene Lee in the United States Federal Census, Archive Roll no. M653_1158, Census year 1860, Philadelphia Ward 8, Philadelphia, Pa., 63, image 67, Family History Library Film no. 805158, Ancestry.com. *1860 United States Federal Census* [https://www.ancestrylibrary.com/discoveryui-content/view/4460458:7667], Provo, Utah.

54. *McElroy's City Directory for 1863. . . .*, 26th ed. (E. C. and J. Biddle: Philadelphia, 1863), 438; Knight, "Many Names for Jarena Lee," 67.

55. Report on March 31, 1864, Board of Education Minute Book, 1840–1865, vol. 5, 470–71, PAS Papers, microfilm, series 1, reel 8, HSP.

56. Report on March 31, 1864, Board of Education Minute Book, 1840–1865, vol. 5, 469–71, PAS Papers, microfilm, series 1, reel 8, HSP.

57. *Aunt Beckie and Aunt Betsy, Aged Coloured Women* (Philadelphia, 1863), 2–3.

58. Almshouse (Philadelphia, Pa.) Records, 1767–1837, vol. 1, HSP; "Statistics of the Almshouse," 1837, HSP.

59. *Sketches of the History, Character, and Dying Testimony of Beneficieries of the Colored Home, in the City of New York*, prepared by Mary W. Thompson (New York: John F. Trow, 1851), 67–71.

60. *Sketches of the History, Character, and Dying Testimony*, 17.

61. *Sketches of the History, Character, and Dying Testimony*, 22.

62. *Sketches of the History, Character, and Dying Testimony*, 23.

63. *Sketches of the History, Character, and Dying Testimony*, 33.

64. *Sketches of the History, Character, and Dying Testimony*, 71–72.

65. Sarah Prior to Hannah Walter, May 23, 1803, PAS Papers, microfilm, series 2, reel 12, HSP.

66. *The Eccentric Biography*, 11.

67. Report on March 31, 1864, Board of Education Minute Book, 1840–1865, vol. 5, 469–71, PAS Papers, microfilm, series 1, reel 8, HSP.

68. *Constitution and Rules to Be Observed by the Friendly Society of St. Thomas's African Church of Philadelphia* (Philadelphia: W. W. Woodward, 1797).

69. Member List, Order Book, Daughters of Africa Records, Leon Gardiner Papers, HSP.

70. Minute Book, August 6, 1822, Daughters of Africa Records, Leon Gardiner Papers, HSP.

71. Order Book, June 18, 1823, Daughters of Africa Records, Leon Gardiner Papers, HSP.

72. Order Book, July 15 and 18, 1823, Daughters of Africa Records, Leon Gardiner Papers, HSP.

73. Order Book, July 8, 1822, Daughters of Africa Records, Leon Gardiner Papers, HSP.

74. Order Book, November 23, 1822, and January 2, 1823, Daughters of Africa Records, Leon Gardiner Papers, HSP.

75. *Address Delivered Before the African Female Benevolent Society of Troy, on Wednesday, February 12, 1834. . . .* (Troy: R. Buckley, 1834), 6–7.

76. *Address Delivered Before the African Female Benevolent Society of Troy*, 7.

77. Annual Report in *Address Delivered Before the African Female Benevolent Society of Troy.*

78. Gouverneur Emerson, M.D., "Medical Statistics: Being a Series of Tables, showing the Mortality in Philadelphia, and Its Immediate Causes, During a Period of Twenty Years," *American Journal of the Medical Sciences* 1 (Philadelphia: Carey, Lea and Carey, 1827), 120–21.

79. Gouverneur Emerson, M.D., "Medical Statistics; Consisting of Estimates Relating to the Population of Philadelphia, and Its Changes as Influenced by the Deaths and Births During a Period of Ten Years, Viz. from 1821 to 1830 Inclusive," *American Journal of the Medical Sciences* 9 (Philadelphia: Carey and Lea, 1831), 20.

80. Emerson, "Medical Statistics: Being a Series of Tables," 138.

81. Emerson, "Medical Statistics: Being a Series of Tables," table 2; the structure of the data can be explained in part by the US Census that used more broad categories for whites than for blacks.

82. Emerson, "Medical Statistics; Consisting of Estimates Relating to the Population of Philadelphia," 19–20.

83. Emerson, "Medical Statistics; Consisting of Estimates Relating to the Population of Philadelphia," 20.

84. Emerson, "Medical Statistics; Consisting of Estimates Relating to the Population of Philadelphia," 35.

85. Minutes, 1826, Minutes of the Union Benevolent Sons of Bethel AME Church (a Burial Society), 1826–1844, AME Church Records, microfilm, reel 8, HSP.

86. Minutes, June 12, 1833, Minutes of the Union Benevolent Sons of Bethel AME Church (a Burial Society), 1826–1844, AME Church Records, microfilm, reel 8, HSP.

87. Minutes, April 1843, Minutes of the Union Benevolent Sons of Bethel AME Church (a Burial Society), 1826–1844, AME Church Records, microfilm, reel 8, HSP.

88. Minutes, March 24, 1831, Minutes of the Union Benevolent Sons of Bethel AME Church (a Burial Society), 1826–1844, AME Church Records, microfilm reel 8, HSP.

89. Receipt Book by the Secretary of Bethel AME Church, 1832–1847, AME Church Records, microfilm, reel 3, HSP.

90. Drew Gilpin Faust, *This Republic of Suffering: Death and the American Civil War* (New York: Vintage, 2008), 6–7.

91. *Sketches of the History, Character, and Dying Testimony*, 20–21.

92. *Sketches of the History, Character, and Dying Testimony*, 25.

93. *Sketches of the History, Character, and Dying Testimony*, 41.

94. *Sketches of the History, Character, and Dying Testimony*, 72.

95. *The Eccentric Biography*, 10.

96. Leslie Harris, *In the Shadow: African Americans in New York City, 1626–1863* (Chicago: University of Chicago Press, 2003), 93.

97. *Biographical Sketches and Interesting Anecdotes of Persons of Colour*, 72.

98. *Biographical Sketches and Interesting Anecdotes of Persons of Colour*, 73.

99. *Biographical Sketches and Interesting Anecdotes of Persons of Colour*, 74.

100. *Aunt Beckie and Aunt Betsy, Aged Coloured Women*, 2–3.

101. *Aunt Beckie and Aunt Betsy, Aged Coloured Women*, 4.

102. *Aunt Beckie and Aunt Betsy, Aged Coloured Women*, 5–6.

103. *Aunt Beckie and Aunt Betsy, Aged Coloured Women*, 7.

104. *Narrative of Phebe Ann Jacobs* (New York: American Tract Society, c. 1850).

105. *Biographical Sketches and Interesting Anecdotes of Persons of Colour*, 152–62 (quotation from 162).

106. *Sketches of the History, Character, and Dying Testimony*, 18.

107. Sarah Prior to Hannah Walter, May 23, 1803, PAS Papers, microfilm, series 2, reel 12, HSP.

108. Letter from Henry Sipkins, April 6, 1834, Leon Gardiner Papers, box 1G, folder 6, HSP.

109. "Our Children," *Christian Recorder*, microfilm, October 2, 1854, 11.

110. *Biographical Sketches and Interesting Anecdotes of Persons of Colour*, 141–42.

111. Hannah Van Buskerk (Grover) to Cato Way, June 3, 1805, PAS Papers, microfilm, series 2, reel 12, HSP.

112. *Biographical Sketches and Interesting Anecdotes of Persons of Colour*, 113–14.

113. Moses Gillingham to Thomas Shipley, March? 24, 1824, PAS Papers, microfilm, series 2, reel 13, HSP.

114. *Biographical Sketches and Interesting Anecdotes of Persons of Colour*, 182.

115. Minutes, May 23, 1794, PAS Committee of Guardians, Minute Book, vol. 1, 1790–1796, 72–73, PAS Papers, microfilm, series 1, reel 6, HSP.

116. Frisby Henderson to Isaac Barton, March 20, 1834, PAS Papers, microfilm, series 2, reel 13, HSP.

117. Lee, *Religious Experience*, 31–33, 61–62, and 80 (quotation from 80).

118. Rebecca Cox Jackson, *Gifts of Power: The Writings of Rebecca Jackson, Black Visionary, Shaker Eldress*, ed. Jean McMahon Humez (Amherst: University of Massachusetts Press, 1981), 11–42 (quotations from 262–63).

119. *Articles of Association of the African Methodist Episcopal Church, of the City of Philadelphia, in the Commonwealth of Pennsylvania* (Philadelphia: John Ormrod, 1799), 3–7, 10 and 11.

120. *Articles of Association of the African Methodist Episcopal Church*, 8–11.

121. Allen, *The Life, Experience, and Gospel Labours of the Rt. Rev. Richard Allen*, 19–21.

122. *The Doctrines and Discipline of the African Methodist Episcopal Church*, 10th rev. ed. (Philadelphia: Printed by James H. Bryson, 1860), 128.

123. *The Doctrines and Discipline of the African Methodist Episcopal Church*, 69.

124. *The Doctrines and Discipline of the African Methodist Episcopal Church*, 155.

125. *The Doctrines and Discipline of the African Methodist Episcopal Church*, 126–28 (quotation from 128).

126. "Presiding Elder Question Not Settled," *Christian Recorder*, microfilm, March 4, 1856.

127. *AME Magazine* 1, no. 2, October 1841, 51.

128. Minutes, September 2, 1823, Minute Book, 89, AME Church Records, microfilm, reel 8, HSP.

129. Minutes, September 8, 1825, Minute Book, AME Church Records, microfilm, reel 8, HSP.

130. Minutes, April 9, 1829, Minute Book, 107, AME Church Records, microfilm, reel 8, HSP.

131. Minutes, April 8, 1829, Minute Book, 105–7, AME Church Records, microfilm, reel 8, HSP.

132. Minutes, October 13, 1830, Minute Book, AME Church Records, microfilm, reel 8, HSP.

133. Minutes, September 29, 1859, Minute Book of Bethel AME Church, 1859–1865, AME Church Records, microfilm, reel 8, HSP.

134. Minutes, October 27, 1859, Minute Book of Bethel A. M. E. Church, 1859–1865, AME Church Records, microfilm, reel 8, HSP.

135. Minutes, July 22, 1829, Minute Book, AME Church Papers, microfilm, reel 8, HSP.

136. Minutes, April 12, 1859, Minute Book of Bethel A. M. E. Church, 1859–1865, AME Church Records, microfilm, reel 8, HSP.

137. Minutes, February 27, 1862, Minute Book of Bethel A. M. E. Church, 1859–1865, AME Church Records, microfilm, reel 8, HSP.

138. Minutes, April 12, 1859, Minute Book of Bethel A. M. E. Church, 1859–1865, AME Church Records, microfilm, reel 8, HSP.

139. Minutes, March 28, 1859, Minute Book of Bethel A. M. E. Church, 1859–1865, AME Church Records, microfilm, reel 8, HSP.

140. Minutes of the Union Benevolent Sons of Bethel A. M. E. Church, May 14, 1828, AME Church Records, microfilm, reel 8, HSP.

141. Minute Book, 6–9 (quote from 9), Daughters of Africa Records, Leon Gardiner Papers, HSP.

142. Minute Book, 16, Daughters of Africa Records, Leon Gardiner Papers, HSP.

143. Minute Book, 27, Daughters of Africa Records, Leon Gardiner Papers, HSP.

144. Minute Book, 5, Daughters of Africa Records, Leon Gardiner Papers, HSP.

145. Minute Book, 9, Daughters of Africa Records, Leon Gardiner Papers, HSP.

146. Letter to the Moderator of the Session of the First African Presbyterian Church, September 12, 1854, Leon Gardiner Papers, box 4G, folder 1, HSP.

147. Minutes of the AME Church, August 5, 1822, AME Church Records, microfilm reel 8, HSP.

148. Minutes of the AME Church, August 11, 1822, AME Church Records, microfilm reel 8, HSP.

149. Minutes, November 18, 1863, Minute Book of Bethel A. M. E. Church, 1859–1865, AME Church Records, microfilm reel 8, HSP.

150. Minutes, February 1, 1859, Minute Book of Bethel A. M. E. Church, 1859–1865, AME Church Records, microfilm reel 8, HSP.

151. Minutes of the Official Board, Leaders and Stewards, 1848–1849, AME Church Records, microfilm reel 5A, HSP; Bishop Daniel Alexander Payne, *History of the African Methodist Episcopal Church* (Nashville, Tenn.: Publishing House of the A. M. E. Sunday-School Union, 1891), 223–27.

152. Minutes, April 22, 1863, Minute Book of Bethel A. M. E. Church, 1859–1865, AME Church Records, microfilm, reel 8, HSP.

153. Minutes, April 20, 1863, Minute Book of Bethel A. M. E. Church, 1859–1865, AME Church Records, microfilm, reel 8, HSP.

154. Minutes, April 30, 1863, Minute Book of Bethel A. M. E. Church, 1859–1865, microfilm reel 8, AME Church Records, HSP.

155. Minutes of the AME Church (c. 1829), AME Church Records, microfilm reel 8, HSP.

156. February 22, 1841, Minute Book of the United Daughters of Tapsico, 1837–1847, AME Church Records, microfilm reel 8, HSP.

157. *An Appeal to the Females of the African Methodist Episcopal Church by Mary Still. And Published by the Request of the Publication Society of the A.M.E. Church of Philadelphia* (Philadelphia: Peter McKenna and Son, 1867), 4.

158. *An Appeal to the Females of the African Methodist Episcopal Church*, 4.

159. *An Appeal to the Females of the African Methodist Episcopal Church*, 4.

160. *Memoir of Old Elizabeth, a Colored Woman; with a Short Account of Her Last Sickness and Death* (Philadelphia: David Heston, 1866), 6.

161. *Memoir of Old Elizabeth*, 12.

162. *Memoir of Old Elizabeth*, 13.

163. *Memoir of Old Elizabeth*, 16.

164. *Sketches of the History, Character, and Dying Testimony*, 42–46.

165. Jacob White et al. to the Session of the 1st Presbyterian Church, April 6, 1859, Leon Gardiner Papers, box 4G, folder 1, HSP.

166. Minutes, April 13, 1854, Banneker Institute Minute Book, 1853–1855, 16, Leon Gardiner Papers, HSP.

167. Minutes, October 12, 1859, Banneker Institute Minute Book, 1855–1859, 211–14, Leon Gardiner Papers, HSP.

168. Minutes, n.d., Banneker Institute Minute Book, 1855–1859, 64, Leon Gardiner Papers, HSP.

169. Minutes, n.d., Banneker Institute Minute Book, 1855–1859, 67–68, Leon Gardiner Papers, HSP.

170. This refers to Enels J. Adams of Philadelphia, *McElroy's City Directory for 1854 McElroy's City Directory for 1854* (https://archive.org/details/mcelroysphiladel1854amce), 3.

171. Minutes, August 23, 1854, Banneker Institute Minute Book, 1853–1855, 32–33, Leon Gardiner Papers, HSP.

Chapter 5

1. Lucy Russel, Letter, April 24, 1864, William C. Russel Papers, 1856–1865, section A, RL.

2. Lucy Russel, Letter, May 25, 1864, William C. Russel Papers, 1856–1865, section A, RL.

3. "Negroes Taken from a Mount Airy Dec 16th and Delivered to Wm. Tayloe Dec. 24th 1861—for safe keeping," Account Book, Tayloe Family Papers, VHS.

4. Plantation and Farm Instruction, Regulation, Record, Inventory, and Account Book, Mount Airy Inventory, January 1861, Tayloe Family Papers, VHS.

5. Thomas Maguire, Farm Diary, September 2, 1864, Thomas Maguire Papers, MSS 145, AHC.

6. Thomas Maguire, Farm Diary, September 29, 1864, Thomas Maguire Papers, MSS 145, AHC.

7. Thomas Maguire, Farm Diary, October 4, 1864, Thomas Maguire Papers, MSS 145, AHC.

8. Thomas Maguire, Farm Diary, October 20, 1864, Thomas Maguire Papers, MSS 145, AHC.

9. Thomas Maguire, Farm Diary, October 28, 1864, Thomas Maguire Papers, MSS 145, AHC; for scholarship on escapes from slavery during the Civil War, see for example Thavolia Glymph, *The Women's Fight: The Civil War's Battles for Home, Freedom, and Nation* (Chapel Hill: University of North Carolina Press, 2020), chapter 3; Steven Hahn, *The Political Worlds of Slavery and Freedom* (Cambridge, Mass.: Harvard University Press, 2009), chapter 2; Stephanie Camp, *Closer to Freedom: Enslaved*

Women and Everyday Resistance in the Plantation South (Chapel Hill: University of North Carolina Press, 2004), chapter 5.

10. Letter to Maxwell T. Clarke, May 5, 1863, box 1, folder 1, Maxwell Troax Clarke Papers, 1854–1890, accession no. 2592, SHC.

11. List of Runaways in "Negroes Taken from a Mount Airy Dec 16th and Delivered to Wm. Tayloe Dec. 24th 1861—for Safe Keeping," Account Book, Tayloe Family Papers, VHS.

12. Copy of a List of Negroes Taken off by the Yankees 1862, Richard Eppes Diary, August 12, 1859, July 1, 1862, section 46, Richard Eppes Papers, VHS.

13. Overton Bernard, Diary, December 25, 1862, Overton Bernard Diary, 1858–1863, Overton and Jesse Bernard Diaries, 1824-91, accession no. 62-z, SHC.

14. Letter to Maxwell T. Clarke, May 10, 1862, box 1, folder 1, Maxwell Troax Clarke Papers, 1854–1890, SHC.

15. Letter, August 10, 1862, box 1, folder 2, Maxwell T. Clark Papers, 1854–1890 (June–August 1862), SHC.

16. Richard Eppes, Diary, January 31, 1861, 274, Richard Eppes Diary, August 12, 1859–July 1, 1862, section 46, Richard Eppes Papers, VHS.

17. Overton Bernard, Diary, January 1, 1863, Overton Bernard Diaries, accession no. 62-z , SHC.

18. John Emory Bryant Letter No. 3, January 1, 1864, John Emory Bryant Papers, box 2, letters 1864–1865 folder, RL.

19. Ella Gertrude (Clanton) Thomas Journal (September 22, 1864–November 13, 1870) May 8, 1865, 66, RL.

20. Edward Wasmuth Diary, 21, accession no. 3571-z. SHC.

21. Edward Wasmuth Diary, 53–54, SHC.

22. Margaret Ann Grimball, Diary, 1 of 2, September 7, 1862, Grimball Family Papers,1683-1930, accession no. 980, SHC.

23. Rev. Horace James, *Annual Report of the Superintendent of Negro Affairs in North Carolina, 1864. With an Appendix, Containing the History and Management of the Freedmen in this Department up to June 1st, 1865* (Boston: W. W. Brown, 1865), 22.

24. James, *Annual Report of the Superintendent of Negro Affairs in North Carolina, 1864*, 27.

25. James, *Annual Report of the Superintendent of Negro Affairs in North Carolina, 1864*, 24.

26. James, *Annual Report of the Superintendent of Negro Affairs in North Carolina, 1864*, 25.

27. James, *Annual Report of the Superintendent of Negro Affairs in North Carolina, 1864*, 26.

28. Board of Education, Minute Book, c. 1863, vol. 5 (1840–1865), PAS Papers, microfilm, series 1, Reel 8, HSP.

29. Meeting Minutes, September 15, 1864, Board of Education, Minute Book, vol. 5 (1840–1865), 477–79, PAS Papers, microfilm, series 1, reel 8, HSP.

30. Board of Education, Minute Book, vol. 5 (1840–1865), 433–34, PAS Papers, microfilm, series 1, reel 8, HSP.

31. Union Civil War Soldier's Letter, MS 893, GHS.

32. "The Georgia Educational Movement," January 1866, 4, John Emory Bryant Papers, Official Papers and Writings, Political 1865–1869, RL.

33. Letter to J. E. Bryant, April 15, 1867, John Emory Bryant Papers, Georgia Letters: 1866–67, RL.

34. Thomas Maguire, Farm Diary, June 4 and 5, 1865, box 1, folder 4, Thomas Maguire Papers, MSS 145, AHC; for groundbreaking work on African American efforts at family reunification, see Leon Litwack, *Been in the Storm So Long: The Aftermath of Slavery* (New York: Alfred A. Knopf, 1979), chapter 6; and Heather Andrea Williams, *Help Me to Find My People: The African American Search for Family Lost in Slavery* (Chapel Hill: University of North Carolina Press, 2012), chapter 4.

35. Letter, Peter Davis to Bettie Amis, March 25, 1867, series 3, Elizabeth Amis Cameron Blanchard Family Papers, accession no. 3357, SHC.

36. Agreement Between Green H. Brewer and Sam, Hannah and Children, Telfair County, Georgia, August 14, 1865, Henry Slaughter Collection, box 38, folder 95, Atlanta University Center Robert Woodruff Library, Archives Research Center, Atlanta.

37. John Emory Bryant, Diary, July 1, 1866, John Emory Bryant Papers, RL.

38. Slave List, November 20, 1858, Richard Eppes Diary, November 20, 1858–August 11, 1859, section 45, Richard Eppes Papers, VHS.

39. Richard Eppes, Diary, April 5, 1866, 81, Richard Eppes Diary, September 1, 1865–July 4, 1867, section 47, Richard Eppes Papers, VHS.

40. Letter from Frank Martin to Joe Perkins, Esq., 1874, Fluvanna County Collection, M-1725, MSS8386, UVA.

41. Preston Hedrick to General O. O Howard, June 20, 1867, Subordinate Field Offices—Cumberland Court House, Danville, Records of the Field Offices for the State of Virginia, Bureau of Refugees, Freedmen, and Abandoned Lands, 1865-1872 (FOFB), M1913, NARA, microfilm, roll 71.

42. Ella Gertrude Clanton Thomas Journal, October 22, 1868–November 30, 1870, December 3, 1868, 22–23, Ella Gertrude Thomas Clanton Papers, RL.

43. Richard Eppes, Diary, September 13, 1865, 7, Richard Eppes Diary, September 1, 1865–July 4, 1867, section 47, Richard Eppes Papers, VHS.

44. Richard Eppes, Diary, May 31, 1866, 130, Richard Eppes Diary, September 1, 1865–July 4, 1867, section 47, Richard Eppes Papers, VHS.

45. Richard Eppes, Diary, "Madison Ruffin in Account with Richard Eppes," 382, Richard Eppes Diary, September 1, 1865–July 4, 1867, section 47, Richard Eppes Papers, VHS; Slave List, November 28 1858, Richard Eppes Diary, November 20, 1858–August 11 1859, Section 45, Richard Eppes Papers, VHS.

46. Marcus Sterling Hopkins, Diary, January 13, 1868, MSS 4656, UVA; see also, Catherine A. Jones, *Intimate Reconstructions: Children in Postemancipation Virginia* (Charlottesville: University of Virginia Press, 2015), 54.

47. Thomas Maguire, Farm Diary, October 11, 1865, and January 2, 1866, Thomas Maguire Papers, MSS 145, AHC.

48. William George Matton, Memoirs, chapters 1–7, 2 and 3, William George Matton Papers, 1859-1887, RL.

49. Marcus Sterling Hopkins, Diary, February 10, 1868, MSS 4656, UVA.

50. Ella Gertrude Clanton Thomas Journal, September 22, 1864- October 1866, May 29, 1865, 82, Ella Gertrude Thomas Clanton Papers, RL.

51. Memoirs of Robert Philip Howell, Volume 1, 24, accession no. 1959-z, SHC. Emphasis in the original.

52. Richard Eppes, Diary, September 13, 1865, 7–8, Richard Eppes Diary, Section 47, Richard Eppes Papers, VHS.

53. Richard Eppes, Diary, August 1866, 186–87, Richard Eppes Diary, September 1, 1865–July 4, 1867, section 47, Richard Eppes Papers, VHS.

54. Claim of York Stevens, June 12, 1876, Office of the Commissioners of Claims, memorandum no. 21423, William Wiseham Paine Papers, folder 23, GHS; for an in-depth treatment of slave property ownership, see Dylan Penningroth, *Claims of Kinfolk: African-American Property and Community in the Nineteenth-Century South* (Chapel Hill: University of North Carolina Press, 2003).

55. Annual Report of the Overseers of the Poor for the County of King George County, Statement on People at the Poor House, 1855 and 1857. . . . , box 16, accession no. 41899, LOV.

56. Annual Report of the Overseers of the Poor for the County of King George County, Stetement on People at the Poor House, 1866. . . . , box 16, accession no. 41899, LOV.

57. King George Co., 1868 Tax and Fiscal Petition to Exempt Certain Negroes from Taxes. . . . , box 16, accession No. 41899, LOV.

58. George H. French to A. S. Flagg, April 5, 1866, Drummundtown (Subassistant Commissioner), Letters Sent, Endorsements, Letters Received, and Orders Issued, vol. 149, 1865–67, FOFB, microfilm, roll 73.

59. Office of the Superintendent, Freedmen's Bureau, Norfolk, Virginia, Order No. 2, March 6, 1866, Drummundtown (Subassistant Commissioner), Letters Sent, Endorsements, Letters Received, and Orders Issued, vol. 149, 1865–67, FOFB, microfilm, roll 73; Jim Downs, *Sick from Freedom: African-American Illness and Suffering During the Civil War and Reconstruction* (New York: Oxford University Press, 2012), 120–36.

60. Gen. H. W. Halleck to Gen. Levy, June 22, 1865, Dinwiddie Courthouse (Dinwiddie County, Assistant Superintendent), Letters and Orders Received May–Oct 1865, March 1866, and Feb. 1867–Jan. 1868, FOFB, microfilm, roll 72.

61. Captain Asa Gregory to Brig. General McKibbin, July 11, 1865, Dinwiddie Courthouse (Dinwiddie County, Assistant Superintendent), Letters and Orders Received May–Oct 1865, March 1866, and Feb. 1867–Jan. 1868, FOFB, microfilm, roll 72.

62. Memo, August 11, 1865, James Chaplin Beecher Memorandum Book, 1865–1866, James Chaplin Beecher Papers, RL.

63. Memo, August 15, 1865, James Chaplin Beecher Memorandum Book, 1865–1866, James Chaplin Beecher Papers, RL.

64. Memo, October 10, 1865, James Chaplin Beecher Memorandum Book, 1865–1866, James Chaplin Beecher Papers, RL.

65. Register of Complaints and List of Persons Receiving Rations, 23–30, Subordinate Field Offices—Charlotte Court House, Charlottesville, FOFB, microfilm, roll 65.

66. Register of Complaints and List of Persons Receiving Rations, 39, Subordinate Field Offices—Charlotte Court House, Charlottesville, FOFB, microfilm, roll 65.

67. Letter from Wm E. Ganaway to Col. Jordan, n.d., Subordinate Field Offices—Farmville County, Records Relating to Complaints and Court Cases and Indentures, and Reports and Estimates, 1865–66, FOFB, microfilm, roll 82.

68. Malvia Robinson, July 31, 1867, Subordinate Field Offices—Alexandria, Complaints and Decisions from January 11, 1867, to December 15, 1868, FOFB microfilm, roll 51.

69. Lucy Williams vs. James Henry Edmunds, May 13, 1868, Subordinate Field Offices—Alexandria, Complaints and Decisions from January 11, 1867 to December 15, 1868, FOFB, microfilm, roll 51.

70. Geo. W. Graham to John H. Taylor, November 24, 1868, Subordinate Field Offices—Boydton, FOFB, microfilm, roll 60.

71. Memo, September 23, 1865, James Chaplin Beecher Memorandum Book, 1865–1866, James Chaplin Beecher Papers, RL.

72. Memo, September 9, 1865, James Chaplin Beecher Memorandum Book, 1865–1866, James Chaplin Beecher Papers, RL.

73. Memo, October 11, 1865, James Chaplin Beecher Memorandum Book, 1865–1866, James Chaplin Beecher Papers, RL.

74. Edward Wasmuth Diary, 20, April 22, 1865, SHC.

75. William Russel to Aunt Ellen, June 12, 1864, William C. Russel Papers, section A, RL.

76. Ella Gertrude Clanton Thomas, Journal, October 22, 1868–Nov. 13, 1870, 153, Ella Gertrude Clanton Thomas Papers, RL.

77. Sarah Carter Diary, 5, VHS.

78. Letter, January 25, 1863, David Franklin Thorpe Papers, 1854-1944, accession no. 4262, SHC; for interpretations of slave baptisms in the lowcountry, see Jason Young, *Rituals of Resistance Slavery*, 81–102; Sterling Stuckey, *Slave Culture*, 36–40; Creel, *"A Peculiar People": Slave Religion and Community-Culture Among the Gullahs*, 283–95.

79. Report on March 31, 1864, Board of Education Minute Book, vol. 5, 1840–1865, 469–72, PAS Papers, microfilm, Series 1, reel 8, HSP.

80. For the literature on black mortuary practices, see David Roediger, "And Die in Dixie: Funerals, Death, and Heaven in the Slave Community, 1700–1865," *Massachusetts Review* 22, no. 1 (Spring 1981): 163–83; Vincent Brown, *The Reaper's Garden: Death and Power in the World of Atlantic Slavery* (Cambridge, Mass.: Harvard University Press,

2010); Erik Seeman, *Death in the New World: Cross-Cultural Encounters, 1492–1800* (Philadelphia: University of Pennsylvania Press, 2010), Chapter 6.

81. Thomas H. Keels, *Philadelphia Graveyards and Cemeteries* (Charleston: Arcadia, 2003), 79–80; Bethel Burying Grounds Project, https://bethelburyinggroundproject.com/

82. W. B. Cooper to Jacob White, December 29, 1879, American Negro Historical Society Papers, 1875–79, Leon Gardiner Papers, box 11G, folder 3, HSP.

83. Eliza Baker Receipt, September 15, 1877, American Negro Historical Society Papers, 1875–79, Leon Gardiner Papers, box 11G, folder 3, HSP.

84. Note from Henrietta DuTertre, July 9, 1883, American Negro Historical Society, 1880–83, Leon Gardiner Papers, box 11G, folder 4, HSP; my thinking here is influenced by Penningroth, *Claims of Kinfolk.*

85. Minutes of the Trustees and Cash Books, April 25, 1867, and November 30, 1868, AME Church Records, microfilm, reel 2, HSP.

86. *Proceedings of the Eighth Annual Meeting of the Home for the Aged and Infirm Colored People* (Philadelphia: Merrihew and Sons, 1872), 9 and 15–16.

87. Dunbar, *Fragile Freedom*, 5. This was the case in other places like New York as well.

88. *Proceedings of the First Annual Meeting* (1865), 12.

89. *Proceedings of the Third Annual Meeting* (1867), 7.

90. *Proceedings of the Third Annual Meeting* (1867), 8.

91. *Proceedings of the Fourth Annual Meeting* (1868), 7.

92. *Proceedings of the Fourth Annual Meeting* (1868), 2; *Proceedings of the Fifth Annual Meeting* (1869), 3.

93. *Proceedings of the Nineteenth Annual Meeting* (1883), 7.

94. *Proceedings of the Twenty-Third Annual Meeting* (1887), 5.

95. *Proceedings of the Twenty-First Annual Meeting* (1885), 6.

96. *Proceedings of the Twentieth Annual Meeting* (1884), 39.

97. *Proceedings of the Twenty-Ninth Annual Meeting* (1893), 9.

98. *Proceedings of the Sixth Annual Meeting* (1870), 8.

99. *Proceedings of the Twentieth Annual Meeting* (1884), 11.

100. *Proceedings of the Nineteenth Annual Meeting* (1883), 10.

101. *Proceedings of the Twenty-Sixth Annual Meeting* (1890), 8.

102. *Proceedings of the First Annual Meeting* (1865), 9.

103. *Proceedings of the Seventeenth Annual Meeting* (1881), 8.

104. *Proceedings of the Eighteenth Annual Meeting* (1882), 7.

105. *Proceedings of the Eighteenth Annual Meeting* (1882), 5.

106. *Proceedings of the Nineteenth Annual Meeting* (1883), 8.

107. *Proceedings of the Eighth Annual Meeting* (1872), 7; *Proceedings of the Eighteenth Annual Meeting* (1882), 7; *Proceedings of the Twenty-Eighth Annual Meeting* (1892), 10.

108. *Proceedings of the First Annual Meeting* (1865), 3.

109. *Proceedings of the Twenty-Third Annual Meeting* (1887), 12; *Proceedings of the Twenty-Fifth Annual Meeting* (1889), 13–14.

110. *Proceedings of the Eighth Annual Meeting* (1872), 27–28; *Proceedings of the Twentieth Annual Meeting* (1884), 5; *Proceedings of the Twenty-Third Annual Meeting* (1887), 12; *Proceedings of the Twenty-Fifth Annual Meeting* (1889), 13–14.

111. *Proceedings of the Sixth Annual Meeting* (1870), 5–6; *Proceedings of the Seventh Annual Meeting* (1871), 5–6; *Proceedings of the Eighth Annual Meeting* (1872), 5–6 and 9–11; *Proceedings of the Seventeenth Annual Meeting* (1881), 11.

112. *Proceedings of the Eighteenth Annual Meeting* (1882), 8.

113. *Proceedings of the Nineteenth Annual Meeting* (1883), 7; *Proceedings of the Twentieth Annual Meeting* (1884), 9–10.

114. *Proceedings of the Seventh Annual Meeting* (1871), 7–8; *Proceedings of the Seventeenth Annual Meeting* (1881), 7; *Proceedings of the Nineteenth Annual Meeting* (1883), 6–7.

115. *Proceedings of the Twenty-Third Annual Meeting* (1887), 6.

116. *Proceedings of the Twenty-First Annual Meeting* (1885), 10.

117. *Proceedings of the Twenty-Third Annual Meeting* (1887), 6.

118. *Proceedings of the Twenty-Ninth Annual Meeting* (1893), 7.

119. *Proceedings of the Twenty-First Annual Meeting* (1885), 9–10.

120. *Proceedings of the Twenty-Ninth Annual Meeting* (1893), 35.

121. *Proceedings of the Twenty-First Annual Meeting* (1885), 8.

122. *Proceedings of the Eighth Annual Meeting* (1872), 15–16; *Proceedings of the Ninth Annual Meeting* (1873), 10; *Proceedings of the Seventeenth Annual Meeting* (1881), 15.

123. *Proceedings of the Eighth Annual Meeting* (1872), 15; *Proceedings of the Eighth Annual Meeting* (1872), 16; *Proceedings of the Ninth Annual Meeting* (1873), 10.

124. *Proceedings of the First Annual Meeting* (1865), 11.

125. *Proceedings of the Third Annual Meeting* (1867), 6–7.

126. *Proceedings of the Third Annual Meeting* (1867), 8.

127. *Proceedings of the Fifth Annual Meeting* (1869), 7.

128. *Proceedings of the Seventeenth Annual Meeting* (1881), 9.

129. *Proceedings of the Thirty-Third Annual Meeting* (1897).

130. *Proceedings of the Sixth Annual Meeting* (1870), 7–8; *Proceedings of the Eighth Annual Meeting* (1872), 15.

131. *Proceedings of the Thirtieth Annual Meeting* (1894), 53–54.

Epilogue

1. Pollard, *Complaint to the Lord*, 68–86; *Second Annual Report of the "Shelter" for Aged and Infirm Colored People of Baltimore City* (Baltimore: William J. Carter, 1884), 7.

2. Catherine Clinton, *Harriet Tubman: The Road to Freedom* (New York: Little, Brown, 2004), 206–14.

3. Mary Frances Berry, *My Face Is Black Is True: Callie House and the Struggle for Ex-Slave Reparations* (New York: Vintage Books, 2005).

4. Albert Boime, "Henry Ossawa Tanner's Subversion of Genre," *Art Bulletin* 75, no. 3 (September 1993): 419–27; Naurice Frank Woods, "Henry Ossawa Tanner's Negotiation of Race and Art: Challenging 'The Unknown Tanner,'" *Journal of Black Studies* 42, no. 6 (September 2011): 894–95.

5. W. E. B. Du Bois, *The Souls of Black Folk*, ed. David W. Blight and Robert Gooding Williams (Boston: Bedford/St. Martin's, 1997), 164 and 170.

6. Richard Wright, *Black Boy: A Record of Childhood and Youth* (New York: Harper and Row, 1966 [orig. 1937), 150.

7. Richard Wright, *The Man Who Lived Underground* (New York: Library of America, 2021), 199 and 210–11.

8. Maya Angelou, *I Know Why the Caged Bird Sings* (New York: Ballantine Books, 1997), 28 and 46–47.

9. Cornelia Walker Bailey, *God, Dr. Buzzard, and the Bolito Man: A Saltwater Geechee Talks about Life on Sapelo Island, Georgia* (New York: Anchor Books, 2000), 16–17, 48, 170, and 201.

10. Lerone Bennett, "Howard Thurman: 20th Century Holy Man," *Ebony* (February 1978): 70.

11. Howard Thurman, *With Head and Heart: The Autobiography of Howard Thurman* (New York: Harcourt Brace, 1979), 20–21.

12. Rachel Elizabeth Harding and Rosemarie Freeney Harding, *Remnants: A Memoir of Spirit, Activism, and Mothering* (Durham: Duke University Press, 2015), 7–14.

13. Toni Morrison, *Beloved* (New York: Plume, 1987), 3–5.

14. Morrison, *Beloved*, 88–89.

15. Julie Dash, *Daughters of the Dust: The Making of an African American Women's Film* (New York: New Press, 1992), 29, 75–76, 93–95, and 97.

16. Colson Whitehead, *The Nickel Boys* (New York: Doubleday, 2019), 69–72.

17. Giovanni Russonello, "How Esperanza Spalding and Wayne Shorter Realized His Dream: An Opera," *New York* Times, Nov. 2, 2021, https://www.nytimes.com/2021/11/02/arts/music/wayne-shorter-esperanza-spalding-iphigenia.html.

INDEX

Page numbers in italics refer to illustrations.

ACKNOWLEDGMENTS

In writing about communities of care and elders, I have been fortunate to have been supported by my own. The insightful, patient, and empathic intellectual and emotional labor of friends, family, colleagues, and professionals has made this book possible. I hope that this book is worthy of the generosity and support I have received from others for reasons that are beyond my ability to fully understand.

I began this project while I was working in the history department at Colorado State University. Dialogues with faculty and students prompted me to pursue this topic, and the university and department generously supported research travel to Southern archives that were essential to this book's development. Department colleagues Ruth Alexander, Nathan Citino, Mark Fiege, Elizabeth Jones, Kelly Long, Diane Margolf, and Jared Orsi provided various forms of encouragement, and Ann Little's friendship and support have been critical to this book's conception, development, and publication. Students in my undergraduate and graduate courses challenged me to think harder about black history, and their questions about the presence of elders in American slavery germinated this project. Work with Stephan Greenway and Ashley Rogers were particularly engaging. And I also benefitted from the support of friends from the broader university community including Jim and Wendy Franzen, Mohammad Hirchi, Kurt Kraiger, Erica Suchman, Maura Velazquez-Castillo, and Mary Vogl.

As a faculty member at Morehouse College, colleagues from across campus and in the Atlanta University Center (AUC) have helped bring this book to life. The Morehouse Faculty Research Committee provided a summer research grant that allowed me to make considerable progress on the manuscript. My thinking has been enhanced by current and former Morehouse colleagues including Jann Adams, Oumar Ba, Garikai Campbell, Vicki Crawford, Andrew Douglas, Stephane Dunn, Gregory Hall, Duane Jackson, Kipton Jensen, Adrienne Jones, Sam Livingston, and Linda Zatlin. In the broader AUC community, Beverly Guy-Sheftall and Cynthia Neal Spence have served as professional exemplars, and I am also deeply appreciative of Gloria Wade-Gayles, a preeminent scholar of black elders and of age as a category of analysis. She told me I have to write—in time I have come to understand what she meant.

The Program in African American History Short-term Fellowship at the Library Company of Philadelphia underwrote my research at the Library Company (LCP) and Historical Society of Pennsylvania (HSP). My cohort of fellows, including Laura Edwards, Nathan Jérémie-Brink, Selena Sanderfer, Jordan Stein, and Dominique Zino offered feedback, presented work, and shared source material that enriched this study. Program director Erica Armstrong Dunbar and library director Richard Newman also offered their time and their expertise on Northern black communities that pointed me down key paths. While in Philadelphia, I also relied heavily on the staff at the LCP, HSP, and Philadelphia City Archives. Krystal Appiah's knowledge of the archives led me to a significant body of source material.

The staff at Southern archives also helped me unearth the people and stories at the heart of this book. I could not have completed this work without the work of librarians and archivists at the Albert and Shirley Small Special Collections Library at the University of Virginia, Archives Research Center at the Atlanta University Center Robert W. Woodruff Library, David M. Rubinstein Rare Book & Manuscript Library at Duke University, Georgia Historical Society, James G. Kenan Research Center at the Atlanta History Center, Library of Virginia, North Carolina State Archives, Southern Historical Collection at the University of North Carolina, and Virginia Historical Society.

I have tested the ideas in this book at several scholarly forums. The LCP, the history department at the University of California at Riverside, Shanghai University, the history department and Institute for Global Studies at the University of Minnesota, and the Omohundro Institute offered spaces for creative and critical engagements with this project. Adimede Adelusi-Adeluyi, Ron Aminzade, Jody Benjamin, Rebecca Brannon, Thomas Cogswell, Jason Eden, Katharine Gerbner, Will Jones, Howard Lavine, Malinda Lindquist, Elaine Tyler May, Gloria Whiting, and John Wright have contributed to this book's development.

The generosity of a wide range of other friends and colleagues have offered various forms of support. My mentor, the late Sterling Stuckey, as well as Ray Kea set the intellectual foundations of this work. Words of encouragement and acts of support from Rosanne Adderley, Marlon Bailey, Cheryl Blankenship, Ralph Bouquet, Douglas and Kyrah Daniels, Jelani Favors, the late Adrian Gaskins, Michael Gomez, Rachel Harding and the late Vincent Harding, Dennis and Rebecca Laumann, Arthur McFarlane III, Claudine Michel, Dylan Penningroth, Ruby Sales, Jesse Shipley, Harriet Stuckey, Robert Vinson, and Peter Wood have helped me sustain the work. Rob Crawford, Duane Densler, Adrienne Drolet, Louis and Ron Hodnett, Keithley Pierce, Linda Potter, Colette Slade, and Sid Snyder have also been sources of friendship, encouragement, and hospitality on the journey of completing this work.

Robert Lockhart at University of Pennsylvania Press has worked with me from this book's midpoint to its completion. Providing incisive feedback on multiple drafts, trusting me to follow my instincts, and creating the space for me to discover my voice, Bob's editorial advice has been critical to the transformation of my idea about black elders into book form. I also thank the press's readers for their thorough peer-review reports. An anonymous reader helped clarify the argument and deepen my thinking about age and the process of Northern emancipation, and Cori Field offered recommendations that helped with my conceptual framework, engagement with the literature, scholarly voice, and treatment of historical time and space.

My family has been a steady source of support from the beginning of this project to its conclusion. Each of my siblings—Alicia, Angela, Chris, Herman, Michael, Sheila, and William—along with my extended family members, including Andre, Cassandra, Erica, Gloria, Linda, and Nelson, have enriched my life with your unique gifts. And to Mariya, my peach—words have had their way with us. More than anything, you have given me sunshine and reminded me of the joy of discovery. Lastly, I thank my late father, Herman, late mother, Frances, and late sister, Adrienne. Though they are not able to read this book, it would not have been written without them. May they rest in peace.